THIS BOOK BELONGS TO
The Library of
....
....

©COPYRIGHT2024
ALL RIGHTS RESERVED

The content contained within this book may not be reproduced, duplicated, or transmitted without direct written permission from the author or the publisher. Under no circumstances will any blame or legal responsibility be held against the publisher, or author, for any damages, reparation, or monetary loss due to the information contained within this book. Either directly or indirectly.

Legal Notice:
This book is copyright protected. This book is only for personal use. You cannot amend, distribute, sell, use, quote, or paraphrase any part, or the content within this book, without the consent of the author or publisher.

Disclaimer Notice:
Please note the information contained within this document is for educational and entertainment purposes only. All effort has been executed to present accurate, up-to-date, and reliable, complete information. No warranties of any kind are declared or implied. Readers acknowledge that the author is not engaging in the rendering of legal, financial, medical, or professional advice. The content within this book has been derived from various sources. Please consult a licensed professional before attempting any techniques outlined in this book. By reading this document, the reader agrees that under no circumstances is the author responsible for any losses, direct or indirect, which are incurred as a result of the use of the information contained within this document, including, but not limited to — errors, omissions, or inaccuracies.

I can't tell you how grateful I am that you decided to read my book. My most heartfelt thanks that you took time out of your life to choose my work and I hope you find benefit within these pages. There are so many books available today that offer similar content so that makes it even more humbling that you decided to buying mine.

Tell me what you thought! I am eager to hear your opinion and ideas on what you read as are others who are looking for a good book to buy. Leave a review on Amazon.com so others can benefit from your wisdom!

With much thanks.

Table of Contents

Northern Dreams Pullover	27
Beyond the Basics: Foundation Stitches	39
Rosemary Sweater	53
Beyond the Basics: Linked Crochet	65
Infinity Wrap	70
Alpine Frost Scarf	80
Beyond the Basics: Learn to Love Laceweight	84
Dragonfly Shawl	90
Beyond the Basics: Symbolcraft	108
Boteh Scarf	113
Moorish Mosaic Afghan	120
Big Bow Cardigan	132
Luna Sweater	140
Back to Basics: Weaving in Ends	157
Tunisian Vest	160
Beyond the Basics: Tunisian Crochet Primer	168
Come-and-Play Cardigan	173
Beyond the Basics: Finding Closure	183
Stone Path Hat	194
Back to Basics: Post Stitches	203
Sólás Caomh	206
Kathryn in Beauly Dress and Hat	214
Back to Basics: Changing Color	224
Sir Stephen, the Bunny	226
Beyond the Basics: The Adjustable Ring	236
Babette Blanket	239
Beyond the Basics: Sewing Stitches	249
Boho Blocks Cardigan	252
Ocean Pearls Cardigan	260
Beyond the Basics: Garment Construction: Seaming	276
Sera Lace Top	287

Beyond the Basics: Shoring up on Shells	297
Seafoam Vest	305
Larger Than Life Bag	313
Diamonds Silk Scarf	323
Lace Dress	331
Abbreviations	354
Glossary	358

SUMMARY

The Art of Crochet is a comprehensive guide that delves into the intricate and beautiful world of crochet. This book is a must-have for both beginners and experienced crocheters alike, as it covers everything from the basics to advanced techniques.

The book begins with an introduction to the history and origins of crochet, providing readers with a deeper understanding of this ancient craft. It then moves on to explain the different types of crochet hooks, yarns, and other essential tools needed to get started. The author takes great care in explaining the importance of choosing the right materials, as they can greatly impact the outcome of your crochet projects.

One of the highlights of this book is the detailed step-by-step instructions provided for various crochet stitches. From the basic chain stitch to more complex stitches like the double crochet and treble crochet, each stitch is explained in a clear and concise manner. The author also includes helpful diagrams and illustrations to further assist readers in mastering these techniques.

In addition to teaching the fundamental stitches, The Art of Crochet also explores various crochet patterns and projects. Whether you're interested in creating cozy blankets, stylish scarves, or adorable amigurumi toys, this book has something for everyone. Each pattern is accompanied by detailed instructions, including yarn recommendations, gauge measurements, and finishing techniques.

Furthermore, this book goes beyond just teaching crochet techniques and patterns. It also delves into the creative aspects of crochet, providing tips and inspiration for designing your own unique projects. The author encourages readers to experiment with different colors, textures, and stitch combinations, allowing them to unleash their creativity and create truly one-of-a-kind pieces.

The Art of Crochet also includes a section on troubleshooting common crochet problems. From unraveling stitches to fixing mistakes, the author offers practical solutions to help readers overcome any obstacles they may encounter during their crochet journey.

Overall, The Art of Crochet is a comprehensive and invaluable resource for anyone interested in learning or improving their crochet skills. With its detailed instructions, inspiring patterns, and helpful tips, this book is sure to become a beloved companion for crocheters of all levels. Whether you're a beginner looking to master the basics or an experienced crocheter seeking new challenges, this book is a must-have addition to your crafting library.

The Joy of Creating is a book that explores the immense satisfaction and fulfillment that comes from engaging in the creative process. It delves into the various forms of creativity, such as art, music, writing, and even cooking, and highlights the transformative power that these activities can have on our lives.

The book begins by discussing the inherent human desire to create and how it is deeply ingrained in our nature. It explores the idea that creativity is not limited to a select few individuals, but rather, it is a universal trait that can be nurtured and developed by anyone willing to tap into their innate potential.

Throughout the pages of The Joy of Creating, the author shares personal anecdotes and stories of individuals who have experienced the profound joy and sense of purpose that comes from engaging in creative pursuits. These stories serve as inspiration and encouragement for readers to embark on their own creative journeys, no matter their age or background.

The book also delves into the various obstacles and challenges that can hinder our creative expression, such as self-doubt, fear of failure, and societal pressures. It provides practical strategies and techniques for overcoming these barriers and unlocking our creative potential.

Furthermore, The Joy of Creating explores the therapeutic benefits of engaging in creative activities. It delves into the concept of art therapy and how it can be used as a powerful tool for self-expression, healing, and personal growth. The author emphasizes the importance of creating for oneself, rather than for external validation, and how this mindset can lead to a deeper sense of fulfillment and satisfaction.

In addition to discussing the individual benefits of creativity, The Joy of Creating also explores the societal impact of creative expression. It highlights the role of art and culture in shaping communities and fostering social change. The book showcases examples of artists and creators who have used their work to challenge societal norms, raise awareness about important issues, and inspire positive change.

Overall, The Joy of Creating is a comprehensive exploration of the transformative power of creativity. It serves as a guidebook for individuals seeking to tap into their creative potential, overcome obstacles, and experience the immense joy and fulfillment that comes from engaging in the creative process. Whether you are an aspiring artist, writer, musician, or simply someone looking to infuse more creativity into your life, this book offers valuable insights and practical advice to help you embark on your own creative journey.

To successfully complete a task or project, it is crucial to have the necessary tools and materials at hand. These essential items not only facilitate the process but also ensure the quality and efficiency of the end result. Whether you are a professional or a DIY enthusiast, having the right tools and materials can make all the difference.

When it comes to tools, there are a few basic ones that should be a part of every toolbox. These include a hammer, screwdrivers (both flathead and Phillips), pliers, a tape measure, a level, and an adjustable wrench. These tools are versatile and can be used for a wide range of tasks, from simple repairs to more complex projects. Additionally, having a set of different-sized drill bits and a power drill can greatly speed up the process of drilling holes or driving screws.

In addition to these basic tools, there are also specialized tools that may be required for specific tasks. For example, if you are working with electrical wiring, you will need wire cutters, wire strippers, and a voltage tester. If you are working with plumbing, you will need pipe wrenches, a pipe cutter, and a plunger. These specialized tools are designed to make specific tasks easier and safer.

Apart from tools, having the right materials is equally important. This includes things like nails, screws, and bolts of various sizes, as well as different types of adhesives such as glue or epoxy. Depending on the project, you may also need specific materials like wood, metal, or plastic. It is important to choose materials that are suitable for the task at hand, as using the wrong materials can compromise the integrity and durability of the end result.

Furthermore, safety should always be a top priority when working with tools and materials. It is essential to wear appropriate protective gear, such as safety goggles, gloves, and a dust mask, to prevent injuries or exposure to harmful substances. Additionally, it is important to follow proper safety guidelines and instructions when using tools and materials, as misuse can lead to accidents or damage.

In conclusion, having the essential tools and materials is crucial for successfully completing any task or project. These items not only facilitate the process but also ensure the quality and efficiency of the end result. From basic tools like hammers and screwdrivers to specialized tools for specific tasks, having the right tools can make a significant difference. Similarly, choosing the right materials and following proper safety guidelines are equally important.

Basic crochet stitches are the foundation of any crochet project. These stitches are simple to learn and can be used to create a wide variety of patterns and designs. Whether you are a beginner or an experienced crocheter, it is important to have a solid understanding of these basic stitches.

One of the most commonly used crochet stitches is the chain stitch. This stitch is used to create the foundation row of a crochet project. It is made by pulling the yarn through a loop on the hook, creating a new loop. The chain stitch is often used as a starting point for other stitches and can also be used to create decorative elements in a project.

Another basic crochet stitch is the single crochet stitch. This stitch is made by inserting the hook into a stitch, yarn over, and pull through both loops on the hook. The single crochet stitch creates a dense and sturdy fabric, making it ideal for projects that require durability, such as blankets or bags.

The half double crochet stitch is another commonly used stitch. It is made by yarn over, inserting the hook into a stitch, yarn over again, and pull through all three loops on the hook. The half double crochet stitch creates a slightly taller stitch than the single crochet stitch, making it a great option for projects that require a bit more height, such as scarves or hats.

The double crochet stitch is a taller stitch that is made by yarn over, inserting the hook into a stitch, yarn over again, and pull through the first two loops on the hook, yarn over again, and pull through the remaining two loops on the hook. The double crochet stitch creates a looser and more open fabric, making it ideal for projects that require drape, such as shawls or garments.

Lastly, the treble crochet stitch is the tallest of the basic crochet stitches. It is made by yarn over twice, inserting the hook into a stitch, yarn over again, and pull through the first two loops on the hook, yarn over again, and pull through the next two loops on the hook, yarn over again, and pull through the remaining two loops on the hook. The treble crochet stitch creates a very open and lacy fabric, making it perfect for projects that require a delicate and airy look, such as doilies or lace shawls.

These basic crochet stitches are the building blocks of any crochet project. By mastering these stitches, you will have the skills necessary to create a wide variety of patterns and designs. Whether you are a beginner or

The output for the input A. Advanced Stitches and Techniques would be a comprehensive and in-depth guide on advanced stitching methods and techniques. This guide would cover a wide range of advanced stitches, including but not limited to intricate embroidery stitches, complex knitting patterns, and elaborate crochet techniques.

The guide would begin by providing a brief introduction to the importance and benefits of learning advanced stitches and techniques. It would emphasize how these skills can elevate one's craftsmanship and enable them to create more intricate and visually appealing projects. The guide would also highlight the potential for personal satisfaction and creative expression that comes with mastering advanced stitching techniques.

Next, the guide would delve into the various categories of advanced stitches and techniques. It would provide step-by-step instructions, accompanied by detailed illustrations or photographs, for each stitch or technique. The guide would cover a wide range of stitches, such as cable stitches, lace stitches, smocking stitches, and decorative stitches like French knots and bullion stitches. It would also explore advanced techniques like colorwork, intarsia, and entrelac knitting.

In addition to the instructions, the guide would offer tips and tricks to help readers master each stitch or technique. It would provide guidance on tension control, stitch placement, and troubleshooting common issues that may arise during the learning process. The guide would also include suggestions for suitable projects to practice and showcase the newly acquired skills.

Furthermore, the guide would feature inspirational examples of advanced stitching projects created by skilled artisans. These examples would serve as a source of motivation and encouragement for readers, showcasing the endless possibilities that can be achieved through advanced stitching techniques.

To ensure a comprehensive understanding of the subject matter, the guide would also include explanations of the underlying principles and concepts behind each stitch or technique. This would enable readers to not only replicate the stitches but also adapt and create their own unique variations.

Finally, the guide would conclude with a section on further resources and references for readers who wish to continue exploring advanced stitches and techniques. This section would include recommendations for books, online tutorials, and workshops that can provide additional guidance and support in honing one's skills.

Overall, the output for the input A. Advanced Stitches and Techniques would be a detailed and comprehensive guide that equips readers with the knowledge and skills needed to master a wide range of advanced stitching methods. It would serve as a valuable resource for both experienced crafters looking to expand their repertoire and beginners eager to challenge themselves and take their stitching to the next level.

B. Crochet Tips and Tricks is a comprehensive guide that provides valuable insights and techniques for individuals interested in the art of crochet. Whether you are a beginner or an experienced crocheter, this resource is designed to enhance your skills and take your crochet projects to the next level.

The guide begins by introducing the basics of crochet, including an overview of the necessary tools and materials. It explains the different types of crochet hooks, yarns, and other accessories that are commonly used in this craft. This section also covers the importance of selecting the right materials for your projects, as well as tips for choosing the appropriate hook size and yarn weight.

Moving on, the guide delves into the fundamental stitches and techniques used in crochet. It provides step-by-step instructions and detailed illustrations for each stitch, ensuring that even beginners can easily follow along. From the basic chain stitch to more complex stitches like the double crochet and treble crochet, this guide covers it all. It also includes tips for maintaining consistent tension and achieving even stitches, which are crucial for creating professional-looking crochet pieces.

One of the highlights of B. Crochet Tips and Tricks is its extensive collection of patterns and project ideas. Whether you are interested in making garments, accessories, or home decor items, this guide offers a wide range of patterns to suit your preferences. Each pattern is accompanied by clear instructions, stitch diagrams, and helpful tips to ensure successful completion of the project. Additionally, the guide provides suggestions for customizing and modifying patterns to add your own personal touch.

In addition to the technical aspects of crochet, this guide also addresses common challenges and troubleshooting techniques. It offers solutions for common mistakes, such as dropped stitches or uneven edges, and provides tips for fixing them without having to unravel your entire project. It also covers techniques for joining yarn, changing colors, and weaving in ends, which are essential skills for creating seamless and polished crochet pieces.

Furthermore, B. Crochet Tips and Tricks includes valuable advice for organizing your crochet supplies and maintaining your projects. It offers tips for storing your yarn, hooks, and other accessories to keep them in good condition and easily accessible. The guide also provides suggestions for keeping track of your projects, such as using a crochet journal or digital apps, to stay organized and motivated.

Overall, B. Crochet Tips and Tricks is a comprehensive and user-friendly guide that covers all aspects of crochet. Whether you are a beginner looking to learn the basics or an experienced crocheter seeking to expand your skills.

A. Beginner-Friendly Projects

When it comes to starting a new project, especially for beginners, it is important to choose something that is manageable and not too overwhelming. Beginner-friendly projects are designed to provide a gentle introduction to a particular skill or hobby, allowing individuals to learn and grow at their own pace.

One popular beginner-friendly project is knitting. Knitting is a versatile craft that can be enjoyed by people of all ages and skill levels. Starting with simple patterns and basic stitches, beginners can create scarves, hats, or even small blankets. As they gain confidence and experience, they can move on to more complex patterns and techniques.

Another beginner-friendly project is gardening. Whether it's a small container garden on a balcony or a larger plot in the backyard, gardening offers a hands-on experience that can be both rewarding and educational. Beginners can start with easy-to-grow plants such as herbs or flowers, learning about soil preparation, watering, and basic plant care. As they become more comfortable, they can experiment with different types of plants and even try their hand at growing vegetables.

For those interested in electronics and technology, building a simple circuit can be a great beginner-friendly project. With the help of a beginner's kit, individuals can learn the basics of circuitry and soldering, creating small electronic devices such as a light-up LED badge or a simple alarm system. This project not only introduces beginners to the world of electronics but also helps develop problem-solving and critical thinking skills.

If you're looking for a beginner-friendly project that combines creativity and relaxation, painting or drawing might be the perfect choice. With a variety of mediums to choose from, such as watercolors, acrylics, or colored pencils, beginners can explore different techniques and styles. Starting with simple subjects and basic shapes, they can gradually progress to more complex compositions and detailed artwork.

In conclusion, beginner-friendly projects provide a great opportunity for individuals to explore new skills and hobbies. Whether it's knitting, gardening, electronics, or art, these projects offer a gentle introduction to various activities, allowing beginners to learn and grow at their own pace. So, if you're looking to start a new project, consider choosing one that is beginner-friendly and enjoy the journey of learning and creating.

Seasonal and Holiday Crochet is a popular and versatile category within the world of crochet. It encompasses a wide range of patterns and designs that are specifically created to celebrate various seasons and holidays throughout the year. From cozy winter accessories to vibrant spring decorations, this type of crochet offers endless possibilities for both beginners and experienced crocheters.

One of the main advantages of Seasonal and Holiday Crochet is the opportunity to create unique and personalized items that can be used to decorate your home or give as thoughtful gifts. Whether you're looking to add a festive touch to your living room during Christmas or create a charming Easter basket for your loved ones, there are countless patterns available to suit every occasion.

For those who enjoy the changing seasons, crocheting seasonal items allows you to embrace the beauty and spirit of each time of year. You can create warm and cozy scarves, hats, and blankets for the winter months, using soft and chunky yarns to keep you snug during the colder weather. As spring arrives, you can switch to lighter yarns and create delicate flower motifs or colorful bunting to bring a touch of freshness and renewal to your home.

Holiday crochet is another exciting aspect of this category, as it allows you to celebrate special occasions in a creative and handmade way. From Halloween costumes and decorations to Thanksgiving table settings and Christmas ornaments, there are endless possibilities to explore. You can crochet adorable pumpkins, spooky ghosts, or even a full-fledged turkey centerpiece for your holiday gatherings.

In addition to the joy of creating beautiful and meaningful items, Seasonal and Holiday Crochet also offers a great opportunity to learn and practice new techniques. Each pattern presents its own set of challenges and stitches, allowing you to expand your crochet skills and knowledge. You can experiment with different yarn weights, colors, and stitch combinations to achieve the desired effect and bring your creations to life.

Furthermore, Seasonal and Holiday Crochet is a great way to connect with others who share the same passion. There are numerous online communities, forums, and social media groups dedicated to this specific niche, where you can find inspiration, share your projects, and seek advice from fellow crocheters. It's a wonderful way to be part of a supportive and creative community that appreciates the beauty and artistry of crochet.

In conclusion, Seasonal and Holiday Crochet is a delightful and rewarding category that allows you to infuse your crochet projects with the spirit and joy of different seasons and holidays.

The featured crochet designers are a group of exceptionally talented individuals who have made a significant impact in the world of crochet. These designers have not only mastered the art of crochet but have also created unique and innovative designs that have captured the attention of crochet enthusiasts worldwide.

Each featured crochet designer brings their own distinct style and creativity to the craft. Their designs range from intricate and delicate lacework to bold and vibrant patterns. They have a keen eye for color combinations and a deep understanding of different crochet techniques, allowing them to create stunning and visually appealing pieces.

These designers have also contributed to the crochet community by sharing their knowledge and expertise through tutorials, workshops, and online platforms. They have inspired and empowered aspiring crocheters to explore their creativity and push the boundaries of what can be achieved with crochet.

The featured crochet designers have gained recognition and acclaim for their work, with their designs being featured in prestigious crochet publications and showcased in exhibitions and fashion shows. Their creations have been worn by celebrities and have become highly sought-after pieces in the crochet world.

What sets these designers apart is their ability to constantly innovate and evolve their craft. They are not afraid to experiment with new materials, techniques, and styles, pushing the boundaries of traditional crochet and creating designs that are truly one-of-a-kind. Their passion for crochet is evident in every stitch, and their dedication to their craft is truly inspiring.

In conclusion, the featured crochet designers are a group of exceptionally talented individuals who have made a significant impact in the world of crochet. Their unique designs, creativity, and dedication to their craft have earned them recognition and admiration from the crochet community. They continue to inspire and empower aspiring crocheters to explore their creativity and push the boundaries of what can be achieved with crochet.

The output of the input B. Galleries of Top Crochet Patterns refers to a collection or compilation of the most popular and highly regarded crochet patterns. These patterns are typically showcased in galleries, which can be physical spaces within a crochet store or online platforms dedicated to displaying and sharing crochet designs.

Crochet, a craft that involves creating fabric by interlocking loops of yarn or thread using a crochet hook, has gained immense popularity over the years. As a result, there is a vast array of crochet patterns available, ranging from simple and beginner-friendly designs to intricate and advanced creations. The galleries of top crochet patterns serve as a curated selection of the best and most sought-after patterns within the crochet community.

These galleries often feature a diverse range of crochet projects, including but not limited to garments, accessories, home decor items, and amigurumi (crocheted stuffed toys). Each pattern within the gallery is carefully chosen based on its uniqueness, creativity, and overall appeal. They may be selected by a team of experts, experienced crocheters, or even through community voting systems.

The purpose of these galleries is to provide inspiration and guidance to crochet enthusiasts of all skill levels. They offer a visual representation of the finished projects, allowing individuals to envision how the pattern will look once completed. Additionally, the galleries may include detailed descriptions, materials lists, and step-by-step instructions to assist crocheters in recreating the showcased designs.

For beginners, these galleries can be an excellent starting point, as they often feature patterns that are labeled as easy or beginner-friendly. These patterns typically utilize basic stitches and techniques, making them accessible to those who are new to crochet. Intermediate and advanced crocheters can also benefit from these galleries, as they can discover more complex and challenging patterns to further enhance their skills.

In the digital age, online galleries have become increasingly popular, allowing crocheters from all around the world to access and explore a vast collection of top crochet patterns. These online platforms may be dedicated websites, social media accounts, or even mobile applications. They often provide a user-friendly interface, allowing individuals to browse through different categories, search for specific patterns, and even interact with other members of the crochet community.

In conclusion, the output of the input B. Galleries of Top Crochet Patterns refers to a curated collection of the most popular and highly regarded crochet patterns.

The Journey of Crochet Mastery is a captivating and enriching experience that takes individuals on a transformative path towards becoming skilled and accomplished in the art of crochet. This journey is not just about learning the technical aspects of crochet, but also about exploring one's creativity, honing their craftsmanship, and discovering the joy and satisfaction that comes from creating beautiful and intricate crochet pieces.

The journey begins with the basics of crochet, where participants are introduced to the different types of crochet hooks, yarns, and stitches. They learn how to hold the hook, make a slip knot, and create the foundation chain. As they progress, they delve into the various crochet stitches, such as single crochet, double crochet, and treble crochet, and learn how to combine them to create different patterns and textures.

But the journey of crochet mastery goes beyond just learning the stitches. It is about understanding the principles of design and composition, and how to apply them to crochet projects. Participants learn about color theory, yarn selection, and pattern interpretation, enabling them to make informed choices when it comes to creating their own unique crochet pieces.

Throughout the journey, participants are encouraged to experiment and push their boundaries. They are given opportunities to explore different crochet techniques, such as Tunisian crochet, filet crochet, and amigurumi, allowing them to expand their repertoire and develop their own personal style. They also learn how to read and understand crochet patterns, and gain the confidence to modify and adapt them to suit their own creative vision.

The journey of crochet mastery is not without its challenges. Participants may encounter difficulties in achieving consistent tension, understanding complex patterns, or executing intricate stitch combinations. However, with the guidance and support of experienced instructors and fellow crochet enthusiasts, they are able to overcome these obstacles and grow in their skills and confidence.

As the journey progresses, participants have the opportunity to showcase their crochet mastery through various projects and exhibitions. They can create stunning garments, intricate doilies, cozy blankets, or even whimsical amigurumi creatures. These creations not only serve as a testament to their skill and dedication, but also bring joy and beauty to those who admire and appreciate the art of crochet.

Ultimately, the journey of crochet mastery is a lifelong pursuit. Even after completing the program, participants continue to refine their skills, explore new techniques, and challenge themselves with more complex projects. They become part of a vibrant and supportive community of crochet enthusiasts, where they can share their knowledge, seek inspiration, and celebrate their love for this

Northern Dreams Pullover

Designer Julia Vaconsin's inspiration for this casual pullover was traditional Icelandic sweaters. The lower body and sleeves are worked in the round to the armholes, then are joined together to form the yoke, just as a traditional knitted Lopi would be. Simple stitch patterns form the colorwork yoke, showing off a unique effect that only crochet can achieve. Worked in sportweight alpaca, this sweater is lightweight, close-fitting, and very warm.

Pamela Bethel

Finished Size

32 (36¼, 40, 44¼, 48, 52¼)" (81.5 [92, 101.5, 112.5, 122, 133] cm) bust circumference. Garment shown measures 32" (81.5 cm) and is modeled with 2" (5 cm) negative ease. Fit is snug, sweater will stretch when worn; choose size with 0–2" (0–5 cm) negative ease.

Yarn

DK weight (#3 Light)

shown here: Misti Alpaca Sport (100% baby alpaca; 146 yd [134 m]/1¾ oz [50 g]; ②): #NT-505 natural grey (MC), 9 (11,

13, 15, 16, 18) skeins; #9402 grape (A), #NT100 natural white (B), #VL9100 lavender (C), #2302 petal pink (D), 1 skein each.

note: This yarn has been discontinued. Suggested substitution: Blue Sky Alpaca sportweight.

Hook

Size G/7 (4.5 mm). *Adjust hook size if necessary to obtain correct gauge.*

Notions

Yarn needle; removable markers (m) or waste yarn.

Gauge

23 sts and 21 rows = 4" (10 cm) in sc blo.

Notes

+ Body and sleeves are worked separately in the rnd, then are joined tog at underarms before working yoke all in one piece.
+ Wash, block, and try on body to determine length needed and see how yarn behaves (100% alpaca will stretch) before continuing to yoke.

- Apart from indicated rnds in yoke, sweater is worked in a spiral without joining rnds. When changing colors, work last st of previous color until 2 lps rem on hook, yo with new color and draw through both lps to complete st.
- All sts are worked through the back lp only (blo) unless otherwise stated.

Stitch Guide

Shell (sh): 5 dc in same st.

Body

FOUNDATION RND: With MC, fsc (see page 13) 184 (208, 230, 254, 276, 300), join with sl st in bottom of first fsc, being careful not to twist sts.

RND 1: Sc back lp only (blo) in each st around—184 (208, 230, 254, 276, 300) sc.

Rep Rnd 1, working in a spiral without joining at end of each rnd, until piece measures 15" (38 cm) or desired length to underarm. Lay body flat and, using tail from fsc edge as a guide, place marker (pm) in st to mark first st of rnd; cont rnd to last st before marker, work 92 (104, 115, 127, 138, 150) sts for front, pm in next st, work 88 (99, 110, 121, 131, 143) sts for back leaving rem 4 (5, 5, 6, 7, 7) sts of rnd unworked. Do not fasten off. Remove hook and set body aside (see Notes).

Sleeves

FOUNDATION RND: With MC, fsc 43 (46, 49, 52, 55, 58), join with sl st in bottom of first fsc, being careful not to twist sts.

RND 1: Sc blo in each st around—43 (46, 49, 52, 55, 58) sc.

Pm in first st to mark center of sleeve; move m up as you work. The first st won't stay exactly in the middle of sleeve—it will slant to the left. To keep first st in center of sleeve move m to the right 1 st every 12th rnd or use foundation tail as a guide as in body.

RNDS 2–5: Sc blo around.

RND 6: Sc blo to last st, 2 sc blo in last st—1 st inc'd.

RND 7: Sc blo in first st, 2 sc blo in next st, sc blo to end—1 st inc'd.

Work 8 (7, 6, 5, 4, 3) rnds even. Rep Rnds 6–7. Rep last 10 (9, 8, 7, 6, 5) rnds 9 (10, 13, 15, 18, 19) times—63 (68, 77, 84, 93, 98) sc. Work even until sleeve measures 19 (20, 20½, 21, 21½, 22)" (48 [51, 52, 53, 55, 56] cm) or desired length to underarm. Sl st in marked st. Fasten off. Rep for 2nd sleeve.

Yoke

Join sleeves to body as foll: Reinsert hook in working lp of body. Place sleeve next to body, RS facing, so that marked center of sleeve lines up with marked side of body. Mark off 9 (10, 11, 13, 14, 15) sts over center of each sleeve (original m is in center st)—sk these sts for underarm.

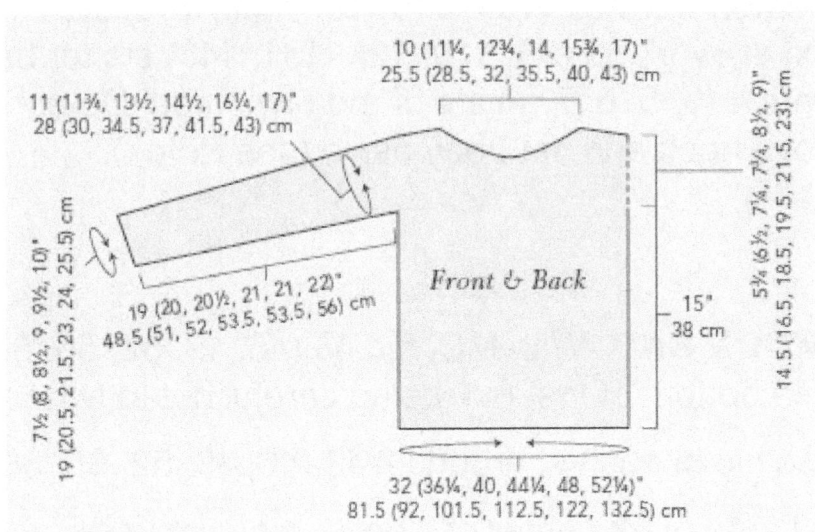

RND 1: Beg with left sleeve, sc in rem 54 (58, 66, 71, 79, 83) sts of left sleeve, sk next 9 (10, 11, 13, 14, 15) sts of body, sc in next 83 (94, 104, 114, 124, 135) sts of front, sc in rem 54 (58, 66, 71, 79, 83) sts of right sleeve, sk next 9 (10, 11, 13, 14, 15) sts of body, sc in next 83 (94, 104, 114, 124, 135) sts of back—274 (304, 340, 370, 406, 436) sc.

Pm in next st to mark new beg of rnd at back-left shoulder. Work 4 (9, 12, 15, 18, 21) rnds even.

NEXT RND: Sc blo to last 4 (0, 0, 4, 4, 0) sts, sc2tog blo (see Glossary) 2 (0, 0, 2, 2, 0) times—272 (304, 340, 368, 404, 436) sts.

Beg colorwork

see Notes on changing colors; work all sts through blo.

RND 1: Sc in next st, *ch 1, sk next st, sc in next 3 sts; rep from * to last 3 sts, ch 1, sk next st, sc in next 2 sts.

RND 2: With A, *sc in next st, working in front of next ch-1 sp, dc in skipped sc 2 rows below, sc in next st of working row, ch 1, sk next st; rep from * around.

RND 3: With B, *sc in next st, ch 1, sk next st, sc in next st, working in front of next ch-1 sp dc in skipped sc 2 rows below; rep from * around.

YOKE RNDS 1–5

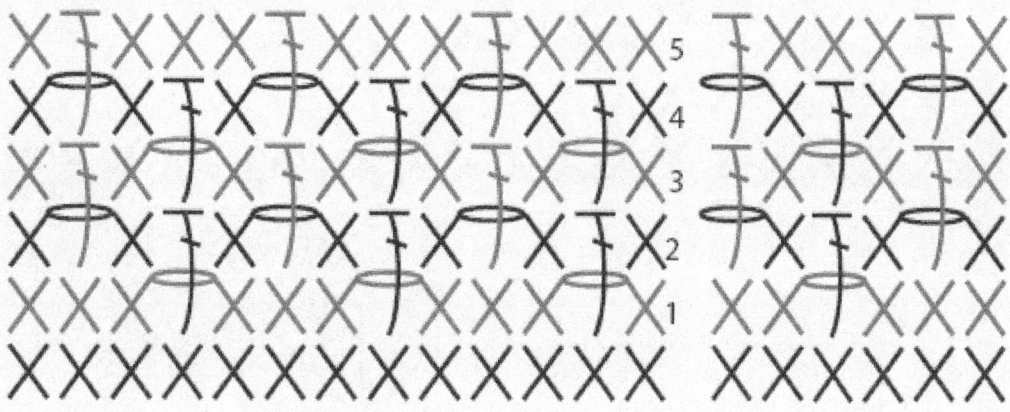

◯ = chain (ch)
• = slip st (sl st)
X = single crochet (sc)

YOKE RNDS 6–12

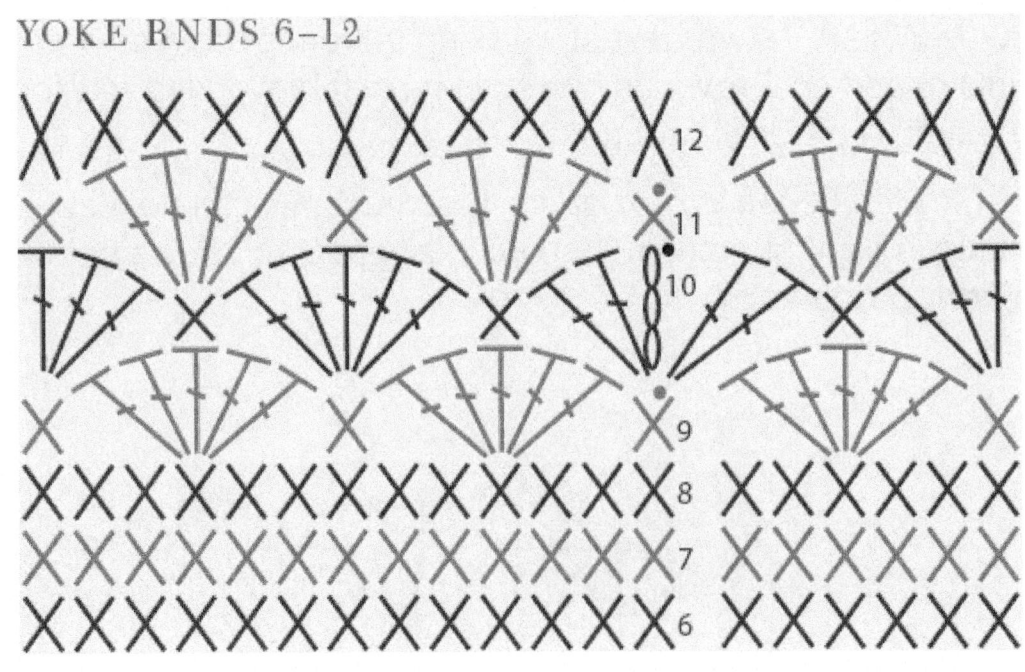

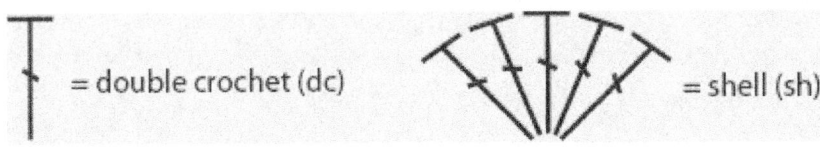

RND 4: With A, Rep Rnd 2.

RND 5: With MC, *sc in next 3 sts, working in front of next ch-1 sp dc in skipped sc 2 rows below, rep from * around.

RND 6 (DEC RND): Sc in next 8 (28, 18, 16, 8, 22) sts, *sc-2tog, sc in next 4 (4, 5, 6, 7, 7) sts; rep from * around—228 (258, 294, 324, 360, 390) sts.

RND 7: With C, sc blo around.

RND 8: With B, sc blo around.

NOTE: *Work all sts through both lps for Rnds 9–12.*

RND 9: With D, *sc in next st, sk 2 sts, sh in next st (see Stitch Guide), sk 2 sts; rep from * around, ending with sl st in first sc of rnd.

RND 10: With A, ch 3 (counts as 3rd dc of sh), 2 dc in same st as sl st, *sc in 3rd dc of next sh, sh in next sc; rep from * to last sh, sc in 3rd dc of sh, 2 dc in bottom ch of beg ch-3, sl st in top of beg ch-3 to join.

RND 11: With D, sc in same ch as join, *4 dc in next sc, sc in 3rd dc of next sh; rep from * around, ending with sl st in first sc to join—190 (215, 245, 270, 300, 325) sts.

RND 12: With B, sc around, do not join.

NOTE: *Resume working all sts through blo.*

RND 13: With C, sc blo around.

RND 14: With MC, sc blo around.

RND 15: *Sc blo in next 3 sts, sc2tog blo; rep from * around—152 (172, 196, 216, 240, 260) sts.

RND 16: Rep Rnd 1.

RND 17: With B, rep Rnd 2.

RND 18: With A, rep Rnd 3.

RND 19: With B, rep Rnd 2.

RND 20: With MC, rep Rnd 5.

RND 21: *Sc blo in next 2 sts, sc2tog blo; rep from * around—114 (129, 147, 162, 180, 195) sts.

RND 22: Sc blo around.

RND 23: With A, sc blo around, ending with sl st in last st. Fasten off.

Finishing

Join A in any st at bottom edge of body, ch 1, working through both lps, sc in each st around bottom edge of sweater. Rep edge for both sleeves at wrist. Handwash in cool water and block to measurements.

Julia Vaconsin designs, crochets, knits, and sews in France. See more of her work at juliavaconsin.com.

Beyond the Basics

Foundation *Stitches*
by MARTY MILLER

One of the first things a beginning crocheter discovers, and something an experienced crocheter knows for sure, is that making the foundation chain and the first row of pattern stitches is one of the most taxing parts of working a crochet pattern. It's often difficult to see the individual chain stitches due to the texture or color of the yarn, or you have to work so many pattern stitches into one chain that the following chains become distorted and you lose them, or you miscount the total number of foundation chains so that you end up running out of chains before you finish working the first row.

Thankfully, there is a little-known family of stitches—called the *foundation stitches*—that more and more crochet designers are using in their patterns to avoid the above problems.

Foundation stitches can be used whenever you have to work a foundation chain and a first row of one type of stitch. Just like the basic crochet stitches (sc, hdc, dc, tr), foundation stitches come in a wide variety of shapes and sizes. There are no standard names for these stitches—some designers call them "foundation single crochet" and "foundation double crochet," some base ch/sc or base ch/dc, and some call the combination a "chainless foundation." We think the first is the clearest and will refer to the stitches accordingly throughout this issue and into the future.

Creating Foundation Single Crochet

STEP 1: Start with a slipknot, ch 2 **(Figure 1)**.

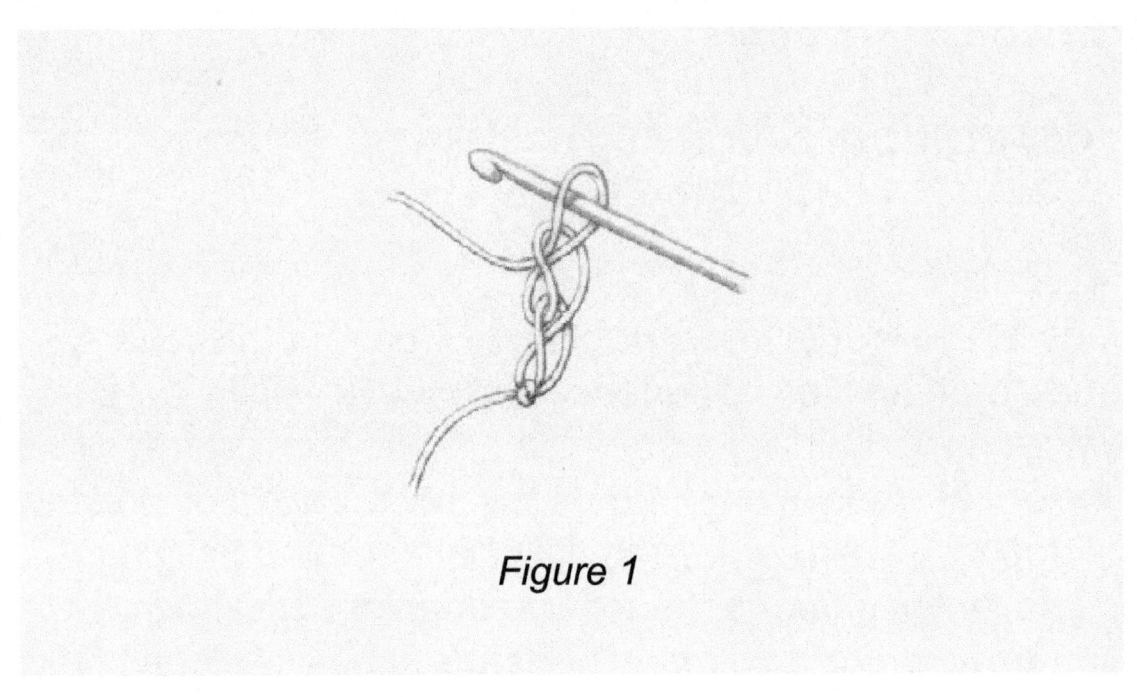

Figure 1

STEP 2: Insert hook in 2nd ch from hook, draw up a loop **(Figure 2)**.

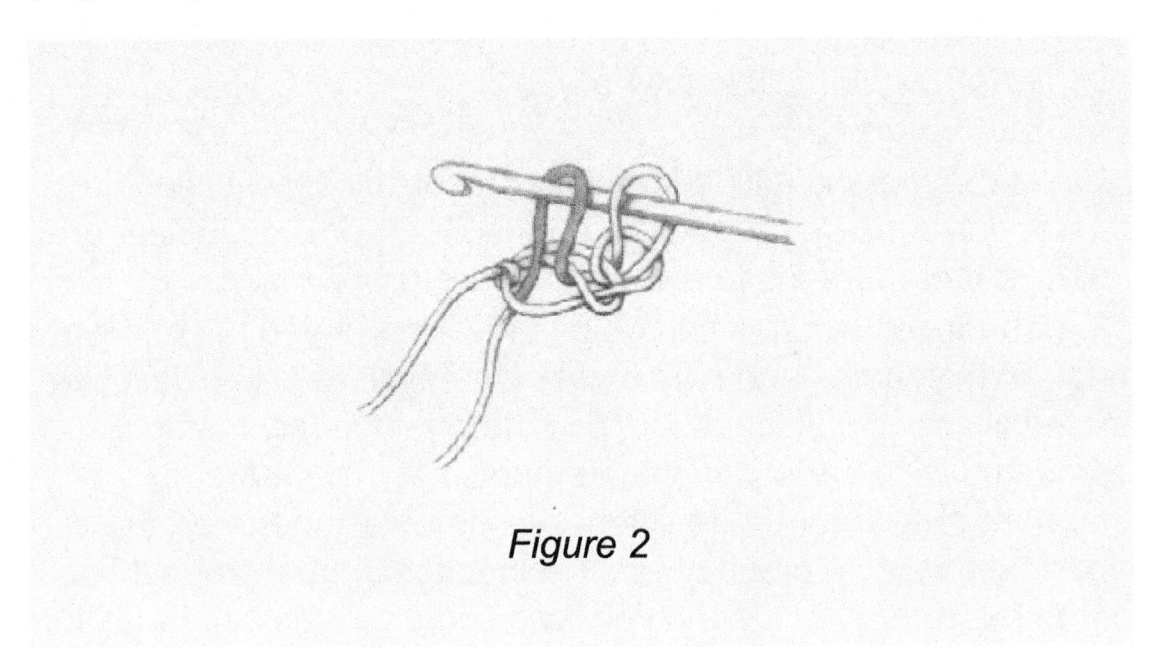

Figure 2

STEP 3: Yo, draw through 1 loop (the "chain") **(Figure 3)**.

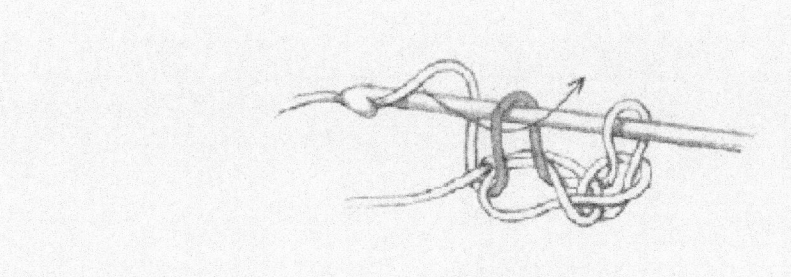

Figure 3

STEP 4: Yo, draw through 2 loops (the "sc") **(Figure 4)**.

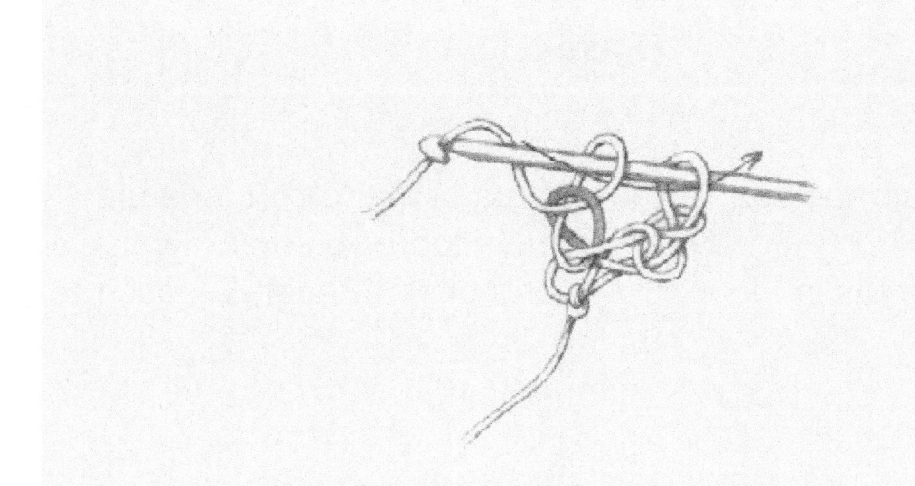

Figure 4

STEP 5: 1 sc with its own ch st (shaded) at the bottom **(Figure 5)**.

Figure 5

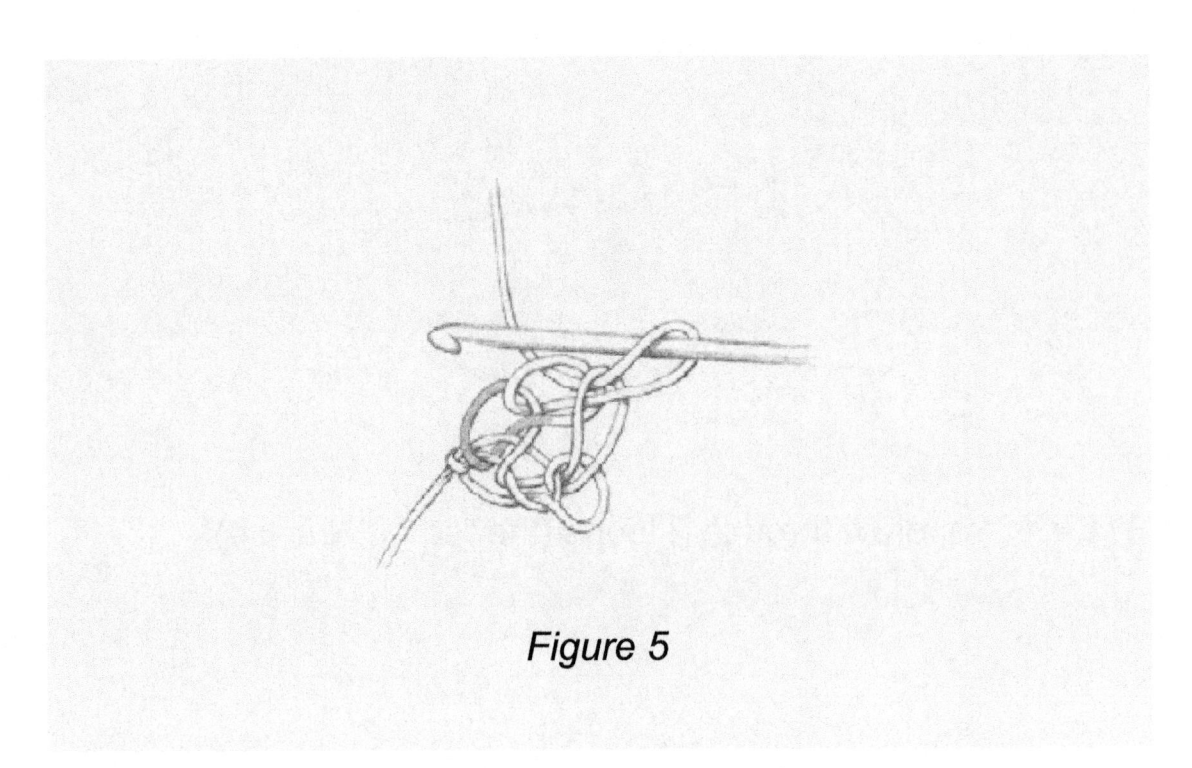

STEP 6: *Insert hook under the 2 loops of the "ch" st (shaded) of the previous st **(Figure 6)**, draw up a loop, yo and draw through 1 loop (as in Figure 3), yo and draw through 2 loops (as in Figure 4).

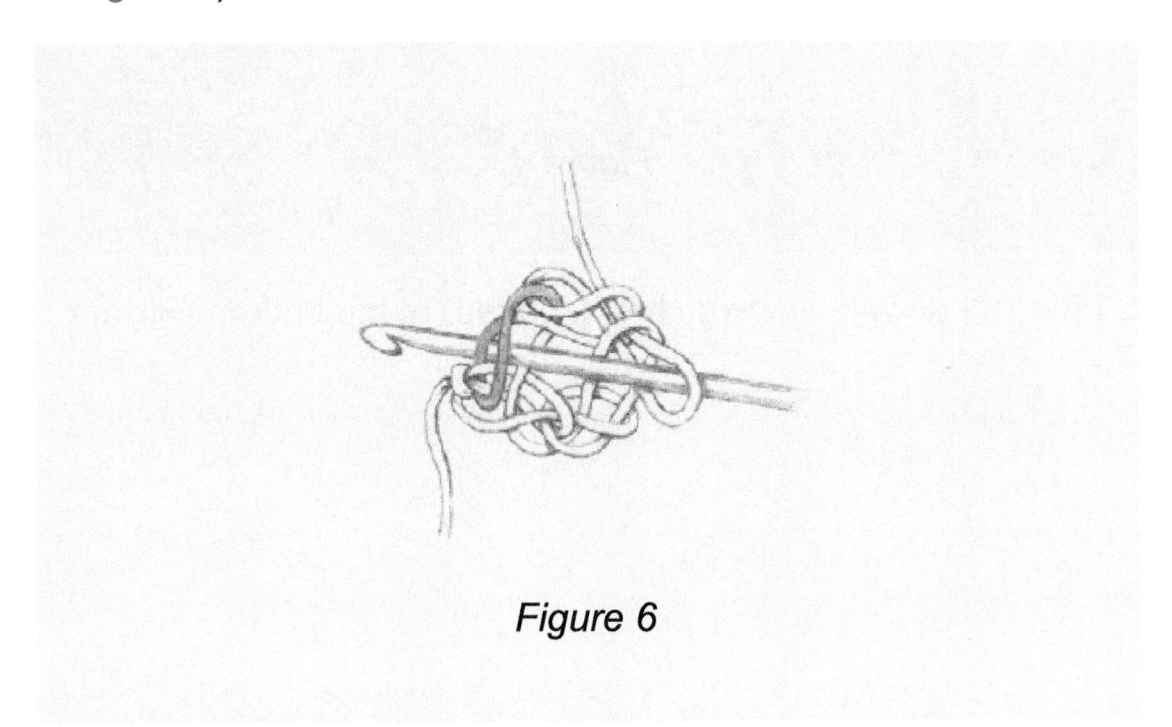

Figure 6

STEP 7: Rep from * for length of foundation **(Figure 7).**

Figure 7

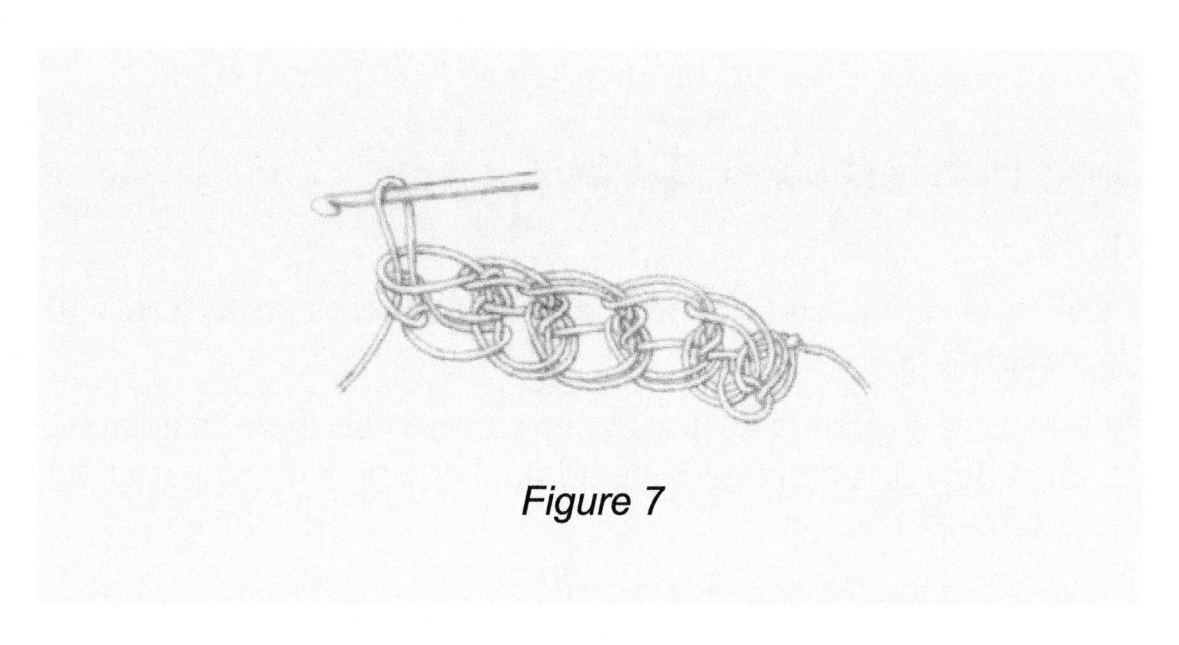

For simplicity's sake, we introduce the foundation double crochet (fdc) and foundation single crochet (fsc) stitches in this article. However, any stitch can be used, and the result is always the same: Foundation stitches replace the traditional foundation chain plus the first row of stitches, improving dramatically upon both.

Foundation stitches are closely related to extended stitches, and understanding the latter will enable you to more easily tackle the former. Made popular by Bill Elmore (and occasionally referred to as "Elmore stitches," accordingly), an extended stitch is made by pulling the yarn through only one loop on the hook before completing a stitch as usual. This extends the height of the stitch, but not as much as working the next-tallest stitch does. For example, an extended single crochet (esc) is taller than a single crochet, but not as tall as a double crochet. In simple terms, making an extended stitch involves working an extra chain into the base of the stitch. It is this extra chain that is exploited to make foundation stitches. After you have made the foundation stitches, you cease working extended stitches and continue by working the second row in normal pattern stitches as directed.

Crochet the following swatches to practice working extended stitches into a traditional foundation chain. Use a smooth, light-colored, worsted-weight yarn and a size H/8 (5 mm) hook.

Basic Double Crochet: Swatch 1

Ch 12.

ROW 1: Dc in 4th ch from hook and in each ch across, turn—10 dc including first ch-3.

ROW 2: Ch 3 (counts as first dc here and throughout) skip first st, dc in next dc and in each dc across, ending with dc in top of ch-3, turn—10 dc.

ROW 3: Repeat Row 2. Fasten off.

Extended Double Crochet: Swatch 2

Ch 13.

ROW 1: Edc (see page 17) in 5th ch from hook and in each ch across, turn—10 edc including first ch-4.

ROW 2: Ch 4 (counts as first edc here and throughout), skip first st, edc in next edc and in each st across, ending with edc in top of ch-4, turn—10 edc.

ROW 3: Repeat Row 2. Fasten off.

Look at these two swatches side by side. The one made of extended double crochet stitches is taller than the one of double crochet stitches. Each stitch is taller by about one chain; that's why you chain four to turn each row instead of the usual three. Make sure you can identify the chain you made at the bottom of each stitch.

Basic Single Crochet: Swatch 3

Ch 11.

ROW 1: Sc in 2nd ch from hook and in each ch across, turn—10 sc.

ROW 2: Ch 1, sc in each sc across, turn.

ROW 3: Repeat Row 2. Fasten off.

Extended Single Crochet: Swatch 4

Ch 12.

ROW 1: Esc (see page 17) in 3rd ch from hook and each ch across, turn—10 esc.

ROW 2: Ch 2 (does not count as the first sc), esc in each esc across, turn.

ROW 3: Repeat Row 2. Fasten off.

Look at these two swatches side by side. The one made with extended single crochet stitches is taller, by about one chain for each row. That's why you chained two to turn each row, instead of the usual one. Make sure you can identify the chain you made at the bottom of each stitch.

Once you have mastered extended stitches and can identify the extra chain, you are ready to make foundation stitches. We'll work with the foundation double crochet first.

NOTE: *To begin a row of foundation stitches, your first stitch is extended; it is counted as a foundation stitch.*

Working Foundation Stitches

Foundation Double Crochet: Swatch 5

NOTE: *I prefer the look of making three chains instead of five when setting up my first foundation double crochet; this turning chain counts as a stitch.*

Ch 3.

STEP 1: Yarn over, insert hook in 3rd chain from hook, yarn over and draw up a loop (3 loops on hook), yarn over and pull through 1 loop (1 chain made), [yarn over and pull through 2 loops] 2 times—1 edc.

STEP 2: Yarn over, insert hook under 2 loops of the chain you made in the first edc in Step 1 (see illustration for indicated loops), yarn over and draw up a loop (3 loops on hook), yarn over and pull through 1 loop (1 chain made), [yarn over and pull through 2 loops] 2 times—1 fdc and 1 edc.

STEP 3: Yarn over, insert hook under 2 loops of the chain you made in the fdc st in Step 2, yarn over and draw up a loop (3 loops on hook), yarn over and pull through 1 loop (1 chain made), [yarn over and pull through 2 loops] 2 times—2 fdc and 1 edc.

Repeat Step 3 eight more times to complete Row 1—12 foundation dc sts, including the turning chain (ch-3) and the first edc. Ch 3, turn.

ROW 2: Skip first st, dc in each st to end—12 dc. Fasten off.

Foundation Single Crochet: Swatch 6

NOTE: *I prefer the look of making two chains instead of three when setting up my first fsc; this turning chain does not count as a stitch.*

Ch 2.

STEP 1: Insert hook into 2nd chain from hook, yarn over and draw up a loop (2 loops on hook), yarn over and pull through 1 loop (1 chain made), yarn over and pull through 2 loops—1 esc.

STEP 2: Insert hook under the 2 loops of the chain you made in the esc made in Step 1, yarn over and draw up a loop (2 loops on hook), yarn over and pull through 1 loop (1 chain made), yarn over and pull through 2 loops—1 fsc and 1 esc.

STEP 3: Insert hook under the 2 loops of the chain made in the foundation sc in Step 2, yarn over and draw up a loop (2 loops on hook), yarn over and pull through 1 loop (1 chain made), yarn over and pull through 2 loops—2 fsc and 1 esc.

Repeat Step 3 seven more times to complete Row 1—10 fsc sts, including the first esc. Ch 1, turn.

ROW 2: Sc in each st across—10 sc. Fasten off.

Notice how relaxed and stretchy the first row of each swatch is; it's not tight like a row worked into a traditional foundation chain. Also, look at the bottom of the first row of foundation stitches. You should see a finished edge that looks like a row of chain stitches or like the top of a row of stitches (if your edge looks different, you probably worked into a different pair of loops in the chain from the previous foundation stitch. See the illustration on page 17 for clarification).

When is it appropriate to use foundation stitches?

As stated earlier, foundation stitches can be used whenever you have to work a foundation chain plus a first row of one type of stitch. Try using foundation stitches in any of these instances:

- When you start a project at the neck or waistband, and if you begin a sleeve at the cuff; foundation stitches are very elastic.

- When you need to add several stitches at the end of a row (see "Increases" below)

- When you are working with dark colored yarns or textured yarns like bouclé, eyelash, ribbon, mohair, or chenille and need to see the stitches more clearly

- When you will work an edging; foundation stitches are easier to crochet into than the bottom of a traditional starting chain.

- When you are not going to add an edging; foundation stitches give you a finished edge.

Increases: *Adding Foundation Stitches to the End of a Row*

When you get to the end of the row and you want to increase by more than one stitch, work an extended stitch in the same place as your last stitch of that row. Then, into the extra chain of the extended stitch, make your foundation stitch. Add as many foundation stitches as you need, counting the extended stitch as a foundation stitch.

Adapting Patterns

How do you change pattern instructions that call for a regular foundation chain and first row so you can use foundation stitches instead?

Look at the instructions for the first row of stitches. Usually, there is a stitch count at the end; 25 sc or 30 dc, for example. If this is the case, simply work that many foundation stitches.

If there is no stitch count listed, look at the number of foundation chains you are directed to work. Usually, if the first row is all sc stitches, you will be asked to work one more chain than the number of single crochets needed, for a turning chain. So if the directions say "ch 15," make 14 foundation single crochets. If the first row is to be double crochet and the pattern says "ch 23," make 20 foundation double crochets.

Other Foundation Stitches

You can work foundation stitches with half double crochet, treble crochet, and every stitch beyond those. Just add a chain at the beginning of the stitch to extend it and work the next stitch into that chain. You can even work some pattern stitches as foundation stitches; experiment!

Creating Foundation Double Crochet

Foundation Double Crochet: Swatch 5

Ch 3.

STEP 1: Yarn over, insert hook in 3rd chain from hook, yarn over and draw up a loop (3 loops on hook), yarn over and pull through 1 loop (1 chain made), [yarn over and pull through 2 loops] 2 times—1 edc; the beginning of a row of foundation double crochet **(Figure 1)**.

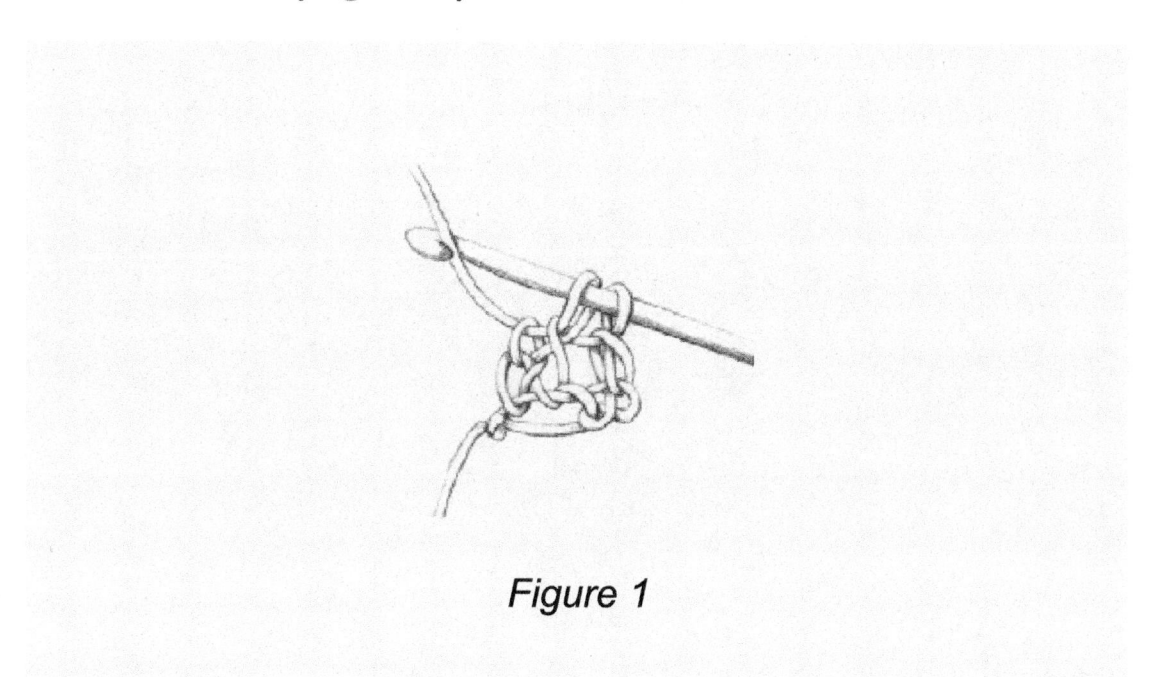

Figure 1

STEP 2: Yarn over, insert hook under the 2 loops of the chain you made in the first edc in Step 1 **(Figure 2)**, yarn over and draw up a loop (3 loops on hook), yarn over and pull through 1 loop (1 chain made), yarn over and pull through 2 loops, yarn over and pull through 2 loops **(Figure 3)**—1 foundation double crochet st.

Figure 2

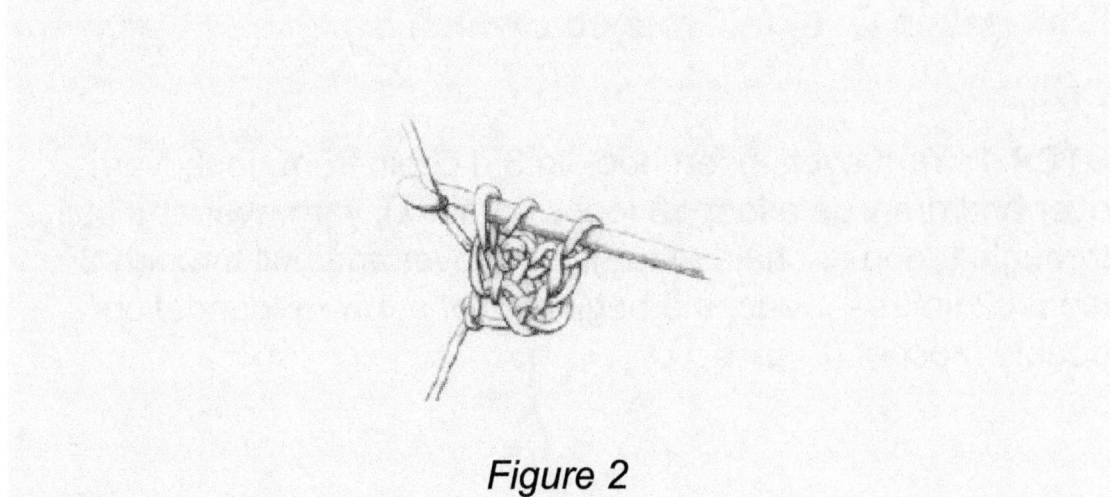

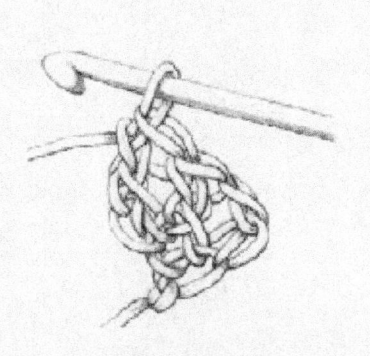

Figure 3

STEP 3: Yarn over, insert hook under the 2 loops of the chain you made in the foundation double crochet st in Step 2 **(Figure 4)**, yarn over and draw up a loop (3 loops on hook), yarn over and pull through 1 loop (1 chain made), [yarn over and pull through 2 loops] 2 times. Rep Step 3 as needed **(Figure 5)**.

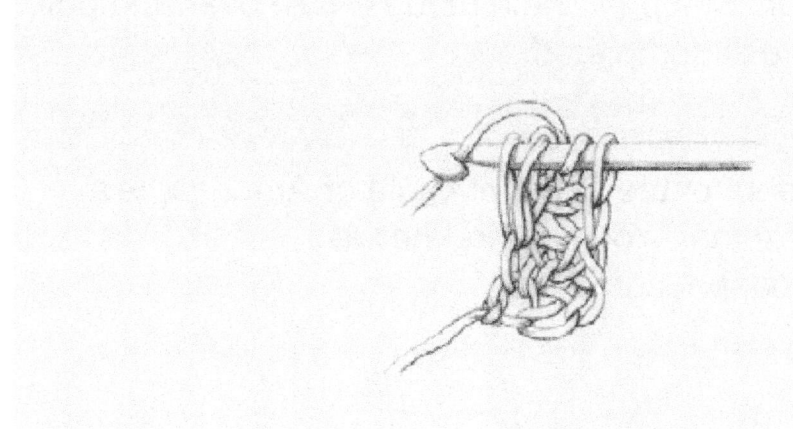

Figure 4

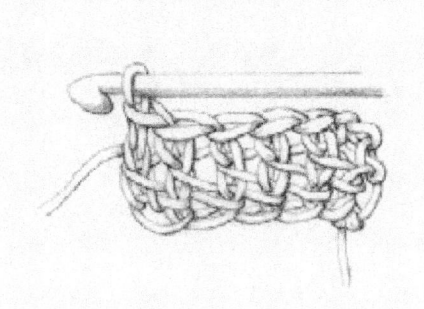

Figure 5

Working Extended Stitches

Extended Double Crochet (edc): Yarn over, insert hook into the next stitch or chain, yarn over and draw up a loop (3 loops on hook), yarn over and pull through 1 loop (1 chain made), [yarn over and pull through 2 loops] 2 times—1 edc completed.

Extended Single Crochet (esc): Insert hook into the next stitch or chain, yarn over and draw up a loop (2 loops on hook), yarn over and pull through 1 loop (1 chain made), yarn over and pull through 2 loops—1 esc completed.

Marty Miller, president of the Crochet Guild of America, is a longtime crochet designer. You can find her at thecrochetdoctor.blogspot.com.

Rosemary Sweater

There is nothing better than the first turn of cool, crisp fall air. Autumn is the season that makes you run for your big sweaters and your wool yarn. This pullover is the perfect mix for early fall days, when it's all you need to wear outside. With its subtle Empire waist and matching sleeve detail, this sweater lets you throw it on over any outfit and stay stylish.

Kathryn Martin

Finished Size

31 (35, 39, 43, 47)" (79 [89, 99, 109, 119] cm) bust circumference. Garment shown measures 35" (89 cm).

Yarn

DK weight (#3 Light)

shown here: Louet KidLin (53% kid mohair, 24% linen, 23% nylon; 120 yds [110 m]/1 3/4 oz [50 g]; 3): #75 pumpkin patch, 8 (9, 10, 11, 12) skeins.

Hook

Sizes I/9 (5.5 mm) and K/10½ (6.5 mm). *Adjust hook size if necessary to obtain the correct gauge.*

Notions

Yarn needle.

Gauge

14 Ldc and 8 rows = 4" (10 cm) with smaller hook.

Notes

- The bodice is worked flat in one piece to the waist. It is then washed, blocked, folded in half, and seamed at the underarms. Finally, the bottom half and sleeves are worked in rounds to the end.

- Turning ch-3 counts as a linked double crochet. Begin working the next linked double crochet by inserting the hook through the second chain of the turning chain.

Stitch Guide

Linked Double Crochet (Ldc):

Note: See page 23 for more details.

SET-UP ST: Insert hook in 2nd ch from hook, yo, draw up a lp, insert hook in 4th ch from hook or in next st, yo, draw up a lp (3 lps on hook), yo, draw through 2 lps, yo, draw through last 2 lps—2 Ldc made, tch counts as first Ldc.

NEXT STITCH: Insert hook in middle horizontal bar of previous stitch, yo, draw up a lp, insert hook in next ch or st, yo, draw up a lp, (3 lps on hook), yo, draw through 2 lps, yo, draw through last 2 lps.

When working in the round, link last Ldc to beg tch as foll:

Work last Ldc until there are 2 lps left on hook, insert hook in 2nd ch of beg ch-3, yo, draw up a lp, yo, pull through all 3 lps on hook, sl st in top of tch to join.

Back

With smaller hook, ch 59 (65, 73, 79, 87).

ROW 1: (WS) Work Ldc set-up st (see Stitch Guide), Ldc in each ch across, turn—57 (63, 71, 77, 85) Ldc sts.

ROW 2: Ch 3 (counts as first Ldc here and throughout), sk first Ldc, Ldc flo in each Ldc across, turn.

Rep Row 2 seven (seven, nine, nine, nine) more times.

Begin armhole shaping

ROW 1: (RS) Ch 5 (counts as Ldc, ch 1), Ldc in 4th ch from hook, Ldc flo to last Ldc, 3 Ldc flo in last Ldc, turn—61 (67, 75, 81, 89) Ldc.

ROWS 2–3: Rep Row 1—69 (75, 83, 89, 97) Ldc.

ROW 4: Ch 3, sk first Ldc, Ldc flo across, turn.

Rep Row 4 ten (ten, twelve, twelve, fourteen) more times.

Right neck shaping

ROW 1: (RS) Ch 3, sk first Ldc, Ldc flo in next 22 (25, 27, 30, 32) Ldc, hdc in next Ldc, sc in next Ldc, sl st in next Ldc, leave rem sts unworked, turn—23 (26, 28, 31, 33) Ldc.

ROW 2: Sl st in first sc, sl st in next hdc, ch 3, sk first Ldc, Ldc flo across, turn.

ROW 3: Ch 3, sk first Ldc, Ldc flo across, turn.

Rep Row 3 two (two, four, four, six) more times.

NEXT ROW: Ch 3, Ldc flo in first Ldc and in each Ldc across—24 (27, 29, 32, 34) Ldc.

NEXT ROW: Lay down working yarn, but do not fasten off. Join new yarn with sl st to beg of previous row. Ch 9 (9, 11, 11, 13). Fasten off. Pick up working yarn, turn. Ch 3, sk first Ldc, Ldc flo across, Ldc in each ch, turn—33 (36, 40, 43, 47) Ldc.

NEXT ROW: Ch 3, sk first Ldc, Ldc flo across, turn.

Rep last row 6 more times.

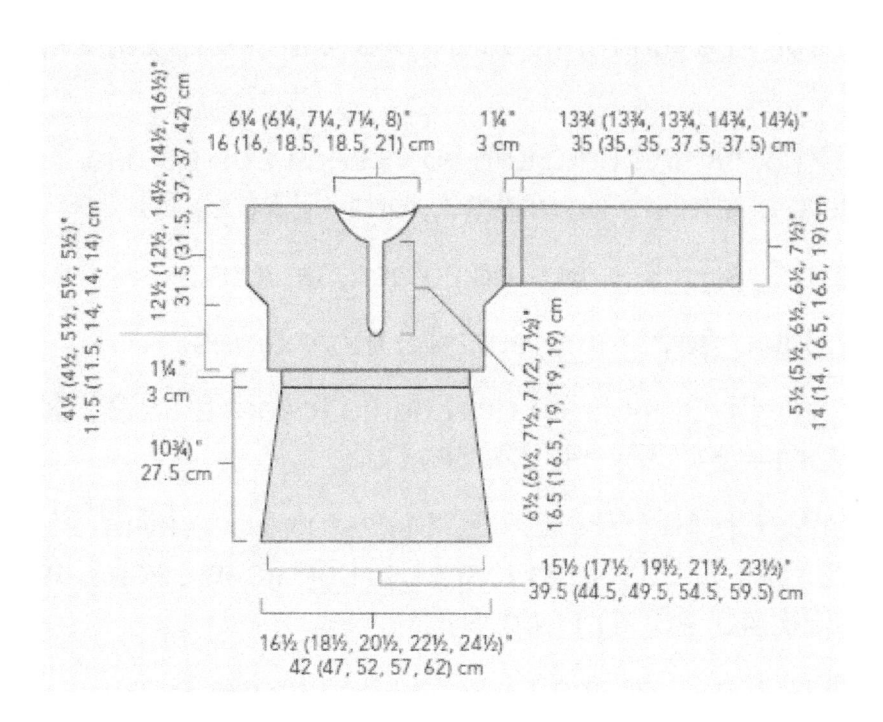

Download the diagram for this project here.

Right-arm and -front shaping

ROW 1: Sl st in each of first 2 Ldc, ch 3, sk next Ldc, Ldc flo across, turn—31 (34, 38, 41, 45) Ldc.

ROW 2: Ch 3, sk first Ldc, Ldc flo to last 2 Ldc, leave rem Ldc unworked, turn—29 (32, 36, 39, 43) Ldc.

ROW 3: Rep Row 1—27 (30, 34, 37, 41) Ldc.

ROW 4: Ch 3, sk first Ldc, Ldc flo across, turn.

Rep Row 4 zero (zero, two, two, two) more times. Lay down working yarn. Do not fasten off.

Left neck shaping

With RS facing and smaller hook, join new yarn in 17th (17th, 21st, 21st, 25th) Ldc from sl st on Row 1 of neck.

ROW 1: Sl st in next Ldc, sc in next Ldc, hdc in next Ldc, dc in next Ldc, Ldc in each rem Ldc across, turn—22 (25, 27, 30, 32) Ldc.

ROW 2: Ch 3, sk first Ldc, Ldc flo in each Ldc across, Ldc flo in next dc, leave rem sts unworked, turn—23 (26, 28, 31, 33) Ldc.

ROW 3: Ch 3, sk first Ldc, Ldc flo across, turn.

Rep Row 3 two (two, four, four, six) more times.

NEXT ROW: Ch 3, sk first Ldc, Ldc flo to last Ldc, 2 Ldc flo in last Ldc, turn—24 (27, 29, 32, 34) Ldc.

NEXT ROW: Ch 10 (10, 12, 12, 14), work Ldc set-up st, Ldc in each ch across, 2 Ldc flo in first Ldc, Ldc flo in each Ldc across, turn—33 (36, 40, 43, 47) Ldc.

NEXT ROW: Ch 3, sk first Ldc, Ldc flo across, turn.

Rep last row 6 times.

Left-arm and -front shaping

ROW 1: Ch 3, sk first Ldc, Ldc flo to last 2 Ldc, leave rem Ldc unworked, turn—31 (34, 38, 41, 45) Ldc.

ROW 2: Sl st in each of first 2 Ldc, ch 3, sk next Ldc, Ldc flo in each Ldc across, turn—29 (32, 36, 39, 43) Ldc.

ROW 3: Rep Row 1—27 (30, 34, 37, 41) Ldc.

ROW 4: Ch 3, sk first Ldc, Ldc flo across, turn.

Rep Row 4 zero (zero, two, two, two) more times. Fasten off and weave in loose ends.

Joining front

With RS facing, pick up working yarn from right-front shaping.

ROW 1: Ch 3, sk first Ldc, Ldc flo across, ch 3, dc in first st on left front to join, Ldc flo in each Ldc across left front side, turn—54 (60, 68, 74, 82) Ldc.

ROW 2: Ch 3, sk first Ldc, Ldc flo in each Ldc to ch-3, Ldc in each ch, Ldc flo in each Ldc across, turn—57 (63, 71, 77, 85) Ldc.

ROW 3: Ch 3, sk first Ldc, Ldc flo across, turn.

Rep Row 3 four more times. Fasten off and weave in loose ends.

Seaming Top Half

With RS facing and smaller hook, join yarn with sl st at left fold of back neck opening. Sc evenly around neck opening. Fasten off and weave in loose ends. Handwash top in cold water with mild soap, let soak at least 15 minutes. Roll top gently in towel to remove excess water, lay out on a blocking surface, pin to schematics, and let dry. It is important to wash top now so that it will be flexible enough in the next step to gather at the waist. Fold top in half with RS together. Using matching yarn, whipstitch (see page 122) side seams together. Weave in loose ends. Turn top RS out.

Waist

Working along bottom edge of bodice, with smaller hook and RS facing, join yarn with sl st at side seam, ch 6.

ROW 1: Sc in 2nd ch from hook and each ch across, sl st in row end of body twice (first sl st joins waist band to body, 2nd counts as tch), turn—5 sc.

ROW 2: Sk both sl sts, sc blo in each sc across, turn.

ROW 3: Ch 1, sc blo across, sl st twice in row end of body, turn.

Rep Rows 2–3 evenly around body opening for a total of 104 (119, 134, 150, 165) rows. Fasten off. Sew waistband ends together with whipstitch.

Lower Body

With smaller hook, join yarn with sl st to WS of waist at seam.

RND 1 (WS): Ch 3, work 92 (106, 120, 134, 148) Ldc evenly around waist, link last Ldc to beg tch (see Stitch Guide), turn—93 (107, 121, 135, 149) Ldc.

RND 2: With larger hook, ch 3, Ldc in first Ldc and in each Ldc to last Ldc, link last Ldc to beg tch, turn—94 (108, 122, 136, 150) Ldc.

RND 3: Ch 3, sk first Ldc, 2 Ldc flo in next Ldc, Ldc flo in each of next 46 (53, 60, 67, 74) Ldc, 2 Ldc flo in next Ldc, Ldc flo in each rem Ldc linking last Ldc to beg tch, turn—96 (110, 124, 138, 152) Ldc.

RND 4: Ch 3, Ldc flo across, sl st in top of tch, turn.

Rep Rnds 3–4 eight more times, then Rnd 3 once more—114 (128, 142, 156, 170) Ldc. **OPTIONAL:** For tunic-length sweater, Rep Rnd 4 ten more times or to desired length, ending with WS row.

LAST RND: Ch 1, sc in each Ldc around, sl st in first sc to join. Fasten off.

Armhole Ribbing

Working along armhole edge of bodice, with smaller hook and RS facing, join yarn with sl st at top of side seam, ch 6.

ROW 1: Sc in 2nd ch from hook and each ch across, sl st in row end of body twice, turn—5 sc.

ROW 2: Sk both sl sts, sc blo in each sc across, turn.

ROW 3: Ch 1, sc blo across, sl st twice in row end of body, turn.

Rep Rows 2–3 evenly around armhole for 48 (48, 56, 56, 65) rows. Fasten off. Sew ends together with whipstitch.

Begin sleeves

With smaller hook, join yarn with sl st to WS of armhole seam.

RND 1 (WS): Ch 3, Ldc evenly around arm for 40 (40, 47, 47, 55) Ldc, link last Ldc to beg tch, turn—41 (41, 48, 48, 56) Ldc.

RND 2: With larger hook, ch 3, Ldc in first Ldc and each Ldc to last Ldc, link last Ldc to beg tch, turn—42 (42, 49, 49, 57) Ldc.

RND 3: Ch 3, Ldc flo in each Ldc linking last Ldc to beg tch, sl st to tch, turn.

Rep Rnd 3 twenty-four (twenty-four, twenty-four, twenty-six, twenty-six) more times.

LAST RND: Ch 1, sc in each Ldc, sl st in first sc. Fasten off.

Finishing

Weave in loose ends. Follow washing and blocking instructions from Seaming Top Half, blocking full sweater according to schematic.

Robyn Chachula is author of *Blueprint Crochet* and *Baby Blueprint Crochet* (Interweave). You can find her at crochetbyfaye.com.

Beyond the Basics

Linked *Crochet*

Working linked crochet will make you feel like a crochet wizard. You work a new stitch in the horizontal bars of the previous stitch, in a sort of mini Tunisian method. When you get to the end of the row of linked double crochet (shown here)—presto! You've made, in effect, two rows of single crochet. Linked crochet is a lot drapier than single crochet, without the bulk. So you can make light spring garments. Because the stitches are linked, there's full coverage, without little peekaboo holes. And —no disrespect to our favorite basic stitch—it's a lot more engaging than single crochet.

To make linked double crochet:

Working on a base row of stitches:

STEP 1: Ch 2, insert hook in second chain and draw up a loop **(Figure 1)**, insert the hook in the stitch below as normal **(Figure 2)**, [yarn over and draw through 2 loops] 2 times. First stitch completed **(Figure 3).**

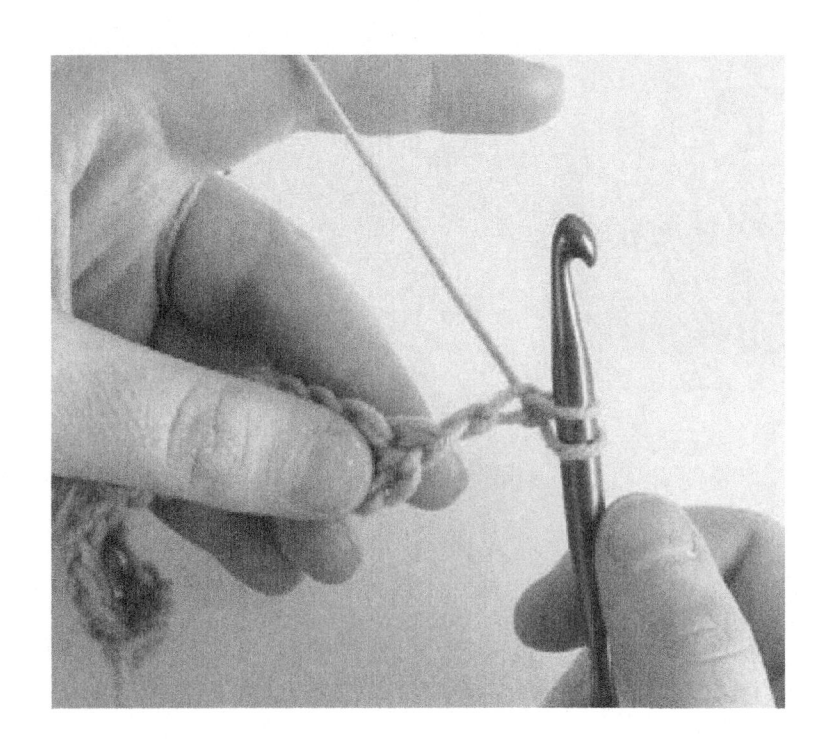

Figure 1

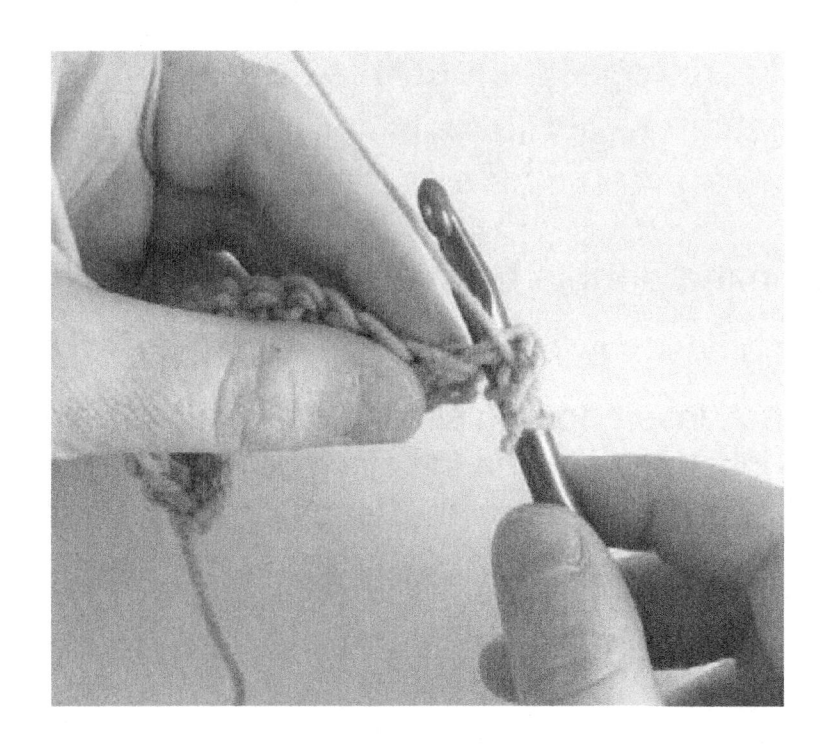

Figure 2

Figure 3

STEP 2: Insert hook in top horizontal bar of stitch just made **(Figure 4)** and draw up loop; insert hook in next stitch as usual and draw up loop (3 loops on hook; **Figure 5**), [yarn over and pull through 2 loops] 2 times.

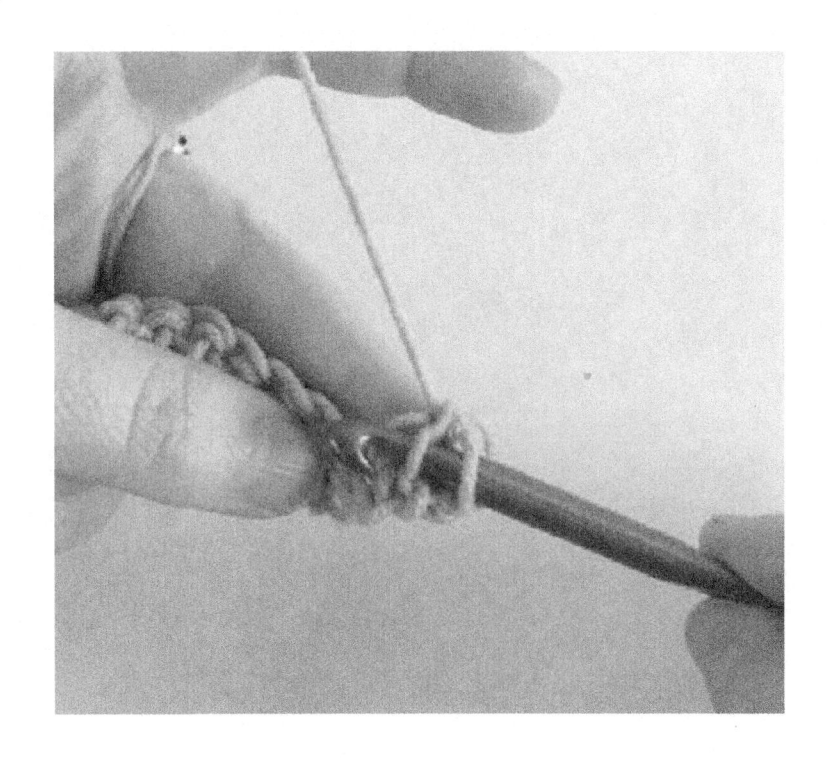

Figure 4

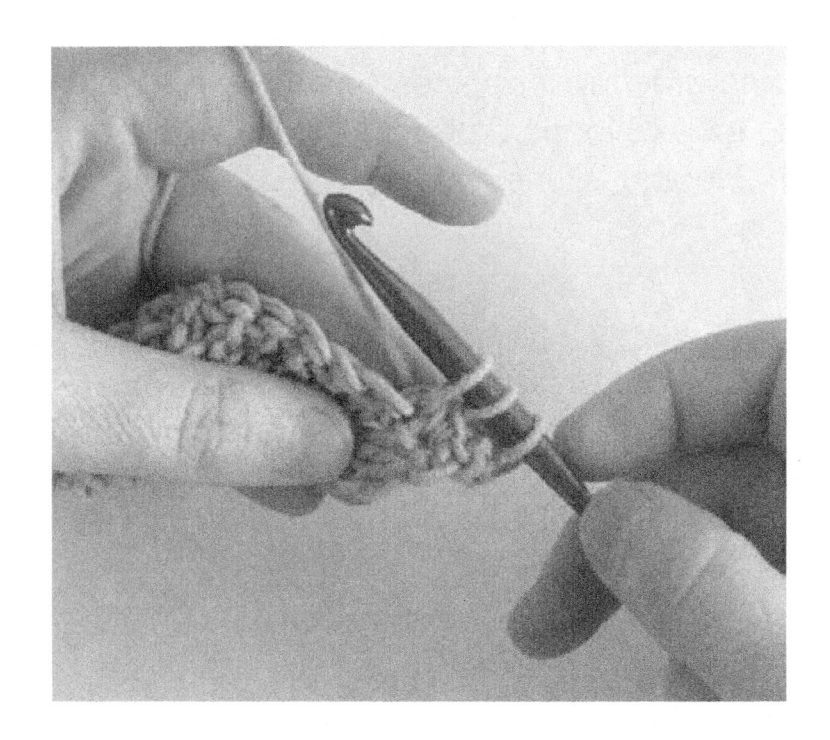

Figure 5

Repeat Step 2 across **(Figure 6)**.

Figure 6

Infinity Wrap

Increases on one side of an infinity motif and decreases on the other side form the curves, with a section of working even in the middle. The self-striping yarn beautifully accentuates the directional geometry. A bobble-and-mesh edging is a playful alternative to fringe. This wrap is worked quite large and can be worn over a coat, as a coat, or even double as an exquisite throw.

Kathryn Martin

Finished Size

32" (81.5 cm) wide and 96" (244 cm) long.

Yarn

Chunky weight (#5 Bulky)

shown here: Plymouth Boku (95% wool, 5% silk; 99 yd [91 m]/1¾ oz [50 g]; 5): #5 plum, 15 balls.

Hook

H/8 (5mm). *Adjust hook size if necessary to obtain the correct gauge.*

Notions

Yarn needle; stitch markers (m).

Gauge

12 dc and 6 rows = 4" (10 cm).

Download the diagrams for this project here.

Stitch Guide

5 dc Popcorn (5-dc pc): Ch 3 (counts as first dc), 4 dc in same st, remove hook from working lp, insert hook in 3rd ch of first dc in group just made, pick up working lp, draw lp through first dc to close, ch 1.

8 dc Cluster (dc8tog): [Yo, insert hook in next st, pull up a lp, yo and draw through 2 lps on hook] 8 times (9 lps on hook), yo, draw through all 9 lps on hook.

Motif

(make 5)

Ch 76.

ROW 1: 8 dc in 2nd ch from hook, dc in each of next 10 sts, [dc in next st, dc2tog (see Glossary) over next 2 sts, dc in each of next 5 sts] 8 times, turn—74 sts.

ROW 2: Ch 1, [dc in next 2 sts, dc2tog over next 2 sts, dc in each of next 3 sts] 8 times, dc in each of next 10 sts, 2 dc in each of next 8 sts, turn—74 sts.

ROW 3: Ch 1, [dc in next st, 2 dc in next st] 8 times, dc in each of next 10 sts, (dc in next st, dc2tog over next 2 sts, dc in each of next 3 sts) 8 times, turn—74 sts.

ROW 4: Ch 1, [dc in next st, dc2tog over next 2 sts, dc in each of next 2 sts] 8 times, dc in each of next 10 sts, [dc in each of next 2 sts, 2 dc in next st] 8 times, turn—74 sts.

ROW 5: Ch 1, [dc in each of next 3 sts, 2 dc in next st] 8 times, dc in each of next 10 sts, [dc2tog over next 2 sts, dc in each of next 2 sts] 8 times, turn—74 sts.

ROW 6: Ch 1, [dc2tog over next 2 sts, dc in next st] 8 times, dc in each of next 10 sts, [dc in each of next 3 sts, 2 dc in next st, dc in next st] 8 times, turn—74 sts.

ROW 7: Ch 1, [dc in each of next 3 sts, 2 dc in next st, dc in each of next 2 sts] 8 times, dc in each of next 10 sts, [dc2tog over next 2 sts] 8 times, turn—74 sts.

ROW 8: Ch 1, dc8tog (see Stitch Guide), dc in each of next 10 sts, [dc in each of next 5 sts, 2 dc in next st, dc in next st] 8 times, turn—75 sts. Fasten off.

Motif finishing

With yarn needle and yarn, close up motif as foll: Sk first 8 sts of Row 8 just worked, sew next 10 sts of Row 8 to row ends (see Figure 1, page 27) using mattress st (see Glossary). There should be 64 sts left on each side of motif. Mark the center point of side (see Figure 1).

Motif Joining

Side A

Join yarn with sl st at marked center of 64 sts (see Figure 1).

Figure 1. Sides A and B–Row 1 of Motif Joining Worked Across 1 Motif

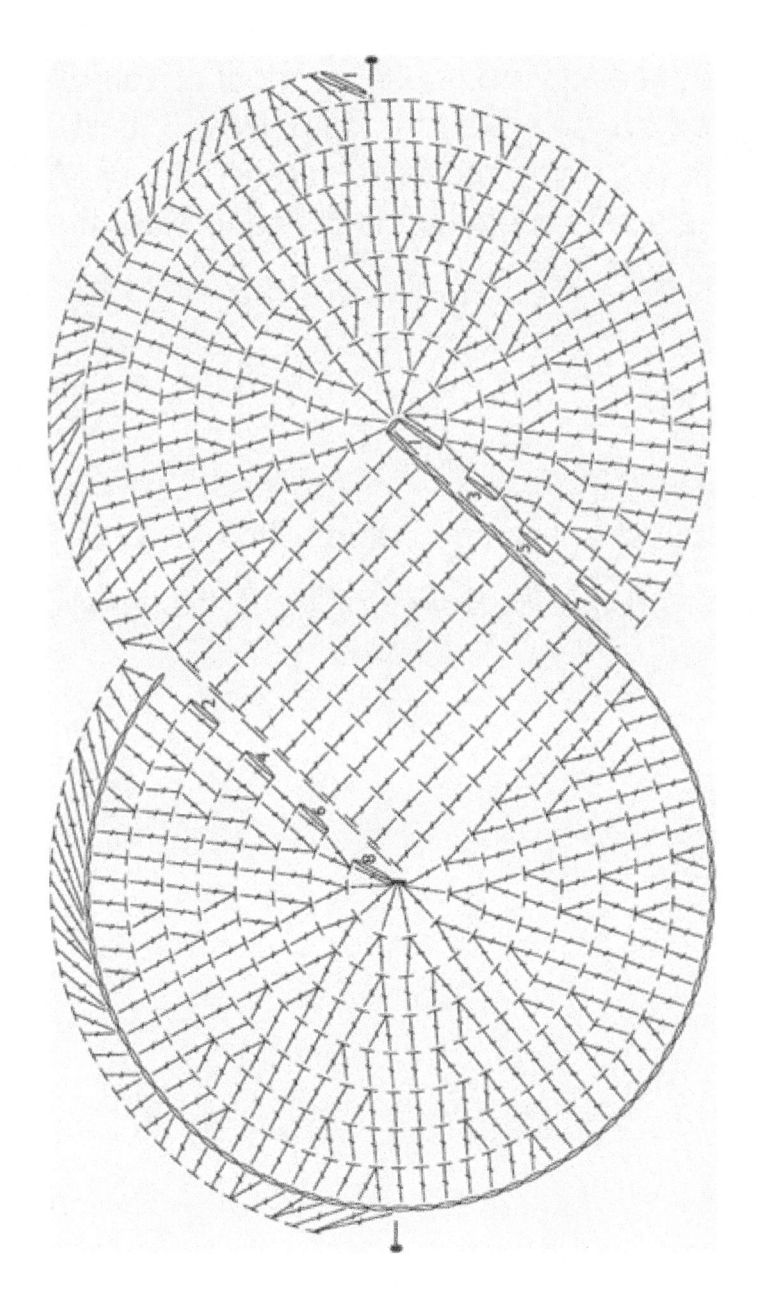

ROW 1: Ch 1, *[dc2tog over next 2 sts, dc in next st] 3 times, dc in next st, [dc in next st, 2 dc in next st] 3 times, [2 dc in next st, dc in next st) 3 times, dc in next st, [dc in next st, dc2tog over next 2 sts] 3 times; working across top edge of each motif without fastening off, rep from * 9 more times, turn—320 sts.

ROWS 2–5: Rep Row 1.

ROW 6: Ch 3 (counts as dc), dc in each st across, turn—320 sts.

ROW 7: Ch 5 (counts as dc, ch 2), sk next 2 sts, *dc in next st, ch 2, sk next 2 sts; rep from * to last st, dc in last st, turn—107 ch-2 sps.

ROW 8: Ch 5, sk next ch-2 sp, dc in next dc, *ch2, sk next ch-2 sp, dc in next dc; rep from * across, turn.

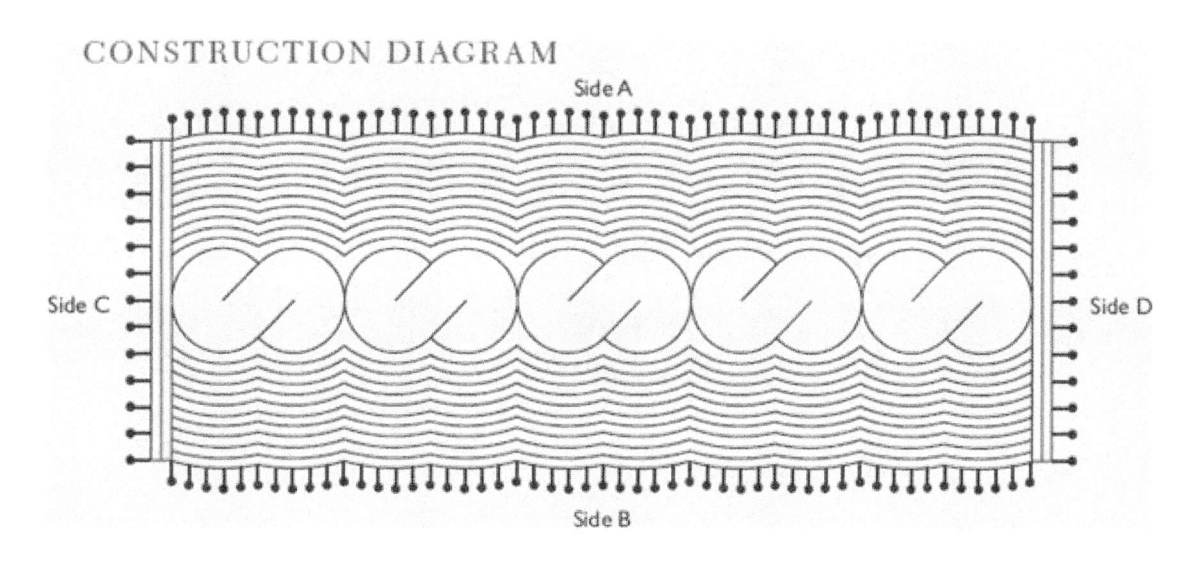

CONSTRUCTION DIAGRAM

Side A

Side C

Side D

Side B

ROWS 9–11: Rep Row 8 three times.

ROW 12: (See Figure 2.) Ch 1, sc in first dc, *ch 6 (counts as ch-3 and beg ch-3 of 5-dc pc), 5-dc pc (see Stitch Guide, page 26) in 3rd ch from hook, sl st blo in next 3 ch and in sc **, ch 2, sc in next dc, ch 2, sc in next dc; rep from * across, ending last rep at **, turn.

Figure 2. Reduced Sample of Sides A and B Pattern—Rows 6–12

Sides C and D
Rows 1–3

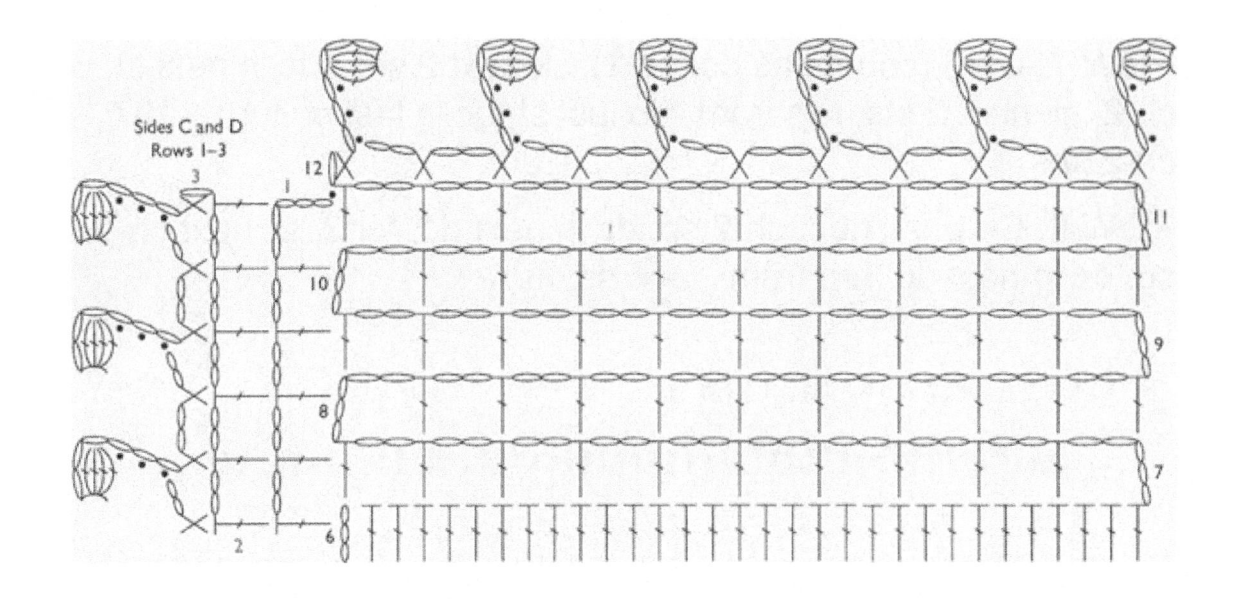

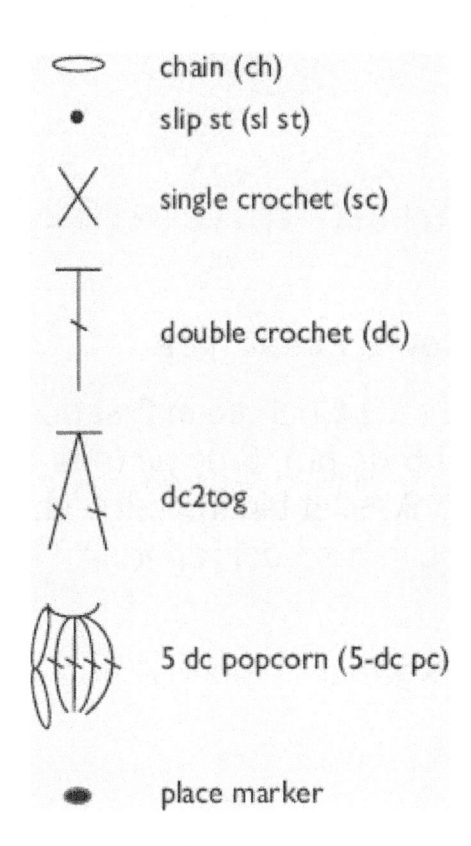

- ⌒ chain (ch)
- • slip st (sl st)
- ✕ single crochet (sc)
- ⊤ double crochet (dc)
- ⋀ dc2tog
- 5 dc popcorn (5-dc pc)
- • place marker

Rep Rows 1–12 for side B.

Finishing for Sides C and D
Along side C:

ROW 1: (See Figure 2.) Join yarn with sl st in last dc at corner, ch 5 (counts as dc, ch 2), dc in each dc along end of rows, *ch 2, dc in end of next dc row; rep from * across, turn.

ROW 2: Rep Row 7 from motif joining.

ROW 3: Rep Row 12 from motif joining. Fasten off.

Rep Rows 1–3 for side D.

Finishing

Weave in loose ends. Block to finished measurements.

Kristin Omdahl is a crochet and knit designer and author of *Wrapped in Crochet, Crochet So Fine,* and *A Knitting Wrapsody,* as well as the instructor on the DVD *Innovative Crochet: Motifs* (all from Interweave). See more of Kristin's work at styledbykristin.com.

Alpine Frost Scarf

With a simple shell pattern that evokes frost on a window, this merino lace scarf keeps away the chill. Easily alter the look by crocheting a wider or longer version.

Pamela Bethel

Finished Size

9" (23 cm) wide and 66" (168 cm) long after blocking.

Yarn

Sockweight (#1 Superfine)

shown here: Skacel Collection Merino Lace (100% merino wool; 1,375 yd [1,257 m]/3½ oz [100 g]; 🔳): #36 off-white, 1 skein.

Hook

Size D/3 (3 mm). *Adjust hook size if necessary to obtain the correct gauge.*

Notions

Yarn needle.

Gauge

4½ reps and 14 rows = 4" (10 cm) in shell patt after blocking.

Stitch Guide

Half-shell (half-sh): (Ch 5, dc).

Shell (sh): (Dc, ch 2, dc, ch 2, dc).

Sh patt

(multiple of 6 sts + 3)

ROW 1: Dc in 6th ch from hook (counts as half-sh), sk 2 ch *sc in next ch, sk 2 ch, sh (see above) in next ch, sk 2 ch; rep from * to last ch, sc in last ch, turn.

ROW 2: Half-sh (see above) in first sc, *sc in center dc of next sh, sh in next sc; rep from * ending with sc in 3rd ch of half-sh from previous row, turn.

Rep Row 2 for patt.

Scarf

Ch 57. Work in sh patt (see Stitch Guide) until scarf measures about 56" (142 cm) (or about 10" [25.5 cm] shorter than desired length). Fasten off and weave in loose ends. Steam-block gently to measurements. Allow to dry.

Amy O'Neill Houck is the author of her own crochet book and lives in Alaska, where she's able to make the most of her woolly stash year-round. She blogs at thehookandi.com.

Beyond the Basics

Learn to Love *Laceweight*
by TRACY ST. JOHN

Have you been itching to make that gorgeous lacy design you saw in the latest issue of *Interweave Crochet*? But then, you looked at the yarn and saw the little yarn-weight ball with the zero on it: Lace! How will you ever finish a project in laceweight yarn?

At first glance, a project calling for such fine yarn and maybe even one of those scary little steel hooks can be intimidating. But if you take a moment to examine the pattern and design, you may find that it is not beyond your abilities. You could even consider a laceweight project a welcome challenge—a chance to build your skills and expand your crochet horizons. All you need is a little education and encouragement to venture into the lovely world of this delicate yarn. Who knows? You might come to love working with laceweight.

    Laceweight yarn has a gauge of thirty-two to forty-two double crochets over four inches of work, according to Craft Yarn Council of America standards. The gauge varies according to the hook size, which can range from size 8 (1.4 mm) steel to size D (3 mm) standard, although larger hooks may be used to create an airier garment.

    Laceweight may appear a bit more like thread than yarn, but it has a good deal more body and heft than thread. Laceweight yarns are much softer and more pliable than crochet cotton, and they are incomparable for delicacy and drape in the finished fabric. They are available in countless fiber blends, textures, and colors. The level of detail that can be achieved at this fine gauge is phenomenal.

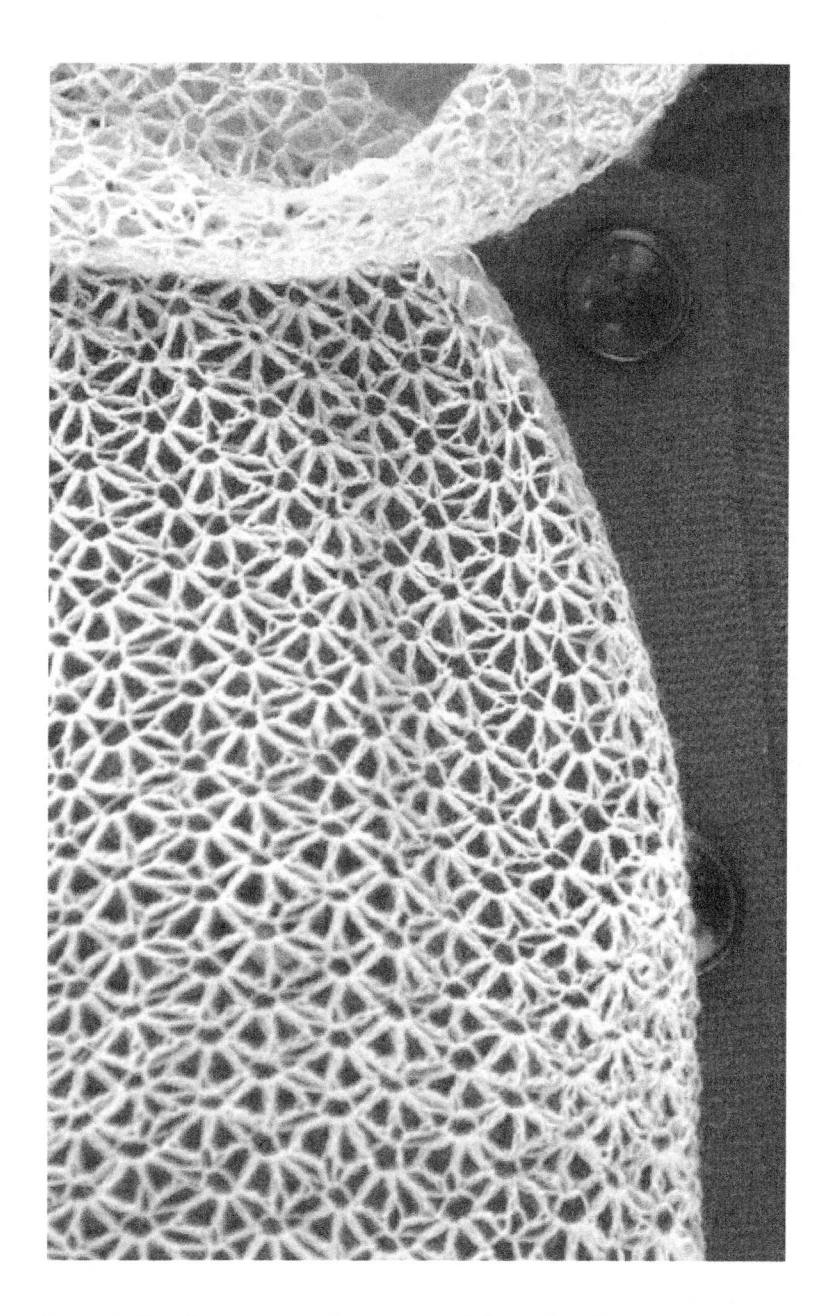

Now, about that scary, tiny steel hook. Despite the name, steel hooks are not lethal weapons. Specifically developed for use with thin yarn, hooks of such a fine gauge need to be made of strong material to keep them from bending. The numbering system for these hooks is different from that of their larger counterparts. For instance, steel size 8 (1.4 mm) distinguishes itself from the standard size H/8 (5 mm); the larger the number in U.S. steel sizes, the smaller the hook. It's just the opposite of standard hook sizes (though the millimeter sizing reliably reflects diminishing sizes).

The steel hook has the same shape and serves the same purpose as any of the other hooks in your toolbox, though the handle may be narrower. Many crocheters find it helpful to make the steel hook handle a little larger and easier to grasp. Slip-on grips, similar to pencil grips, are available, as are ergonomic handles into which you can slide the hook. Some hooks are designed with a larger handle. You can make a larger handle out of polymer clay, felted wool, or even a foam hair curler and duct tape. It doesn't have to be pretty, just comfortable in your hand.

A finished laceweight project often appears complicated and intricate, but the actual pattern and process is made up of the same stitches that you use in heavier-weight yarn. Because the yarn is so fine and the stitches are so small, it is possible to include many stitches in an inch of work, which allows beautiful detail not possible with heavier yarn.

Many laceweight patterns are charted with symbols as well as written out; this visual reference helps to show the overall pattern. Before launching into the laceweight project, practice the pattern with DK or worsted-weight yarn and an appropriate hook size. Once you have familiarized yourself with the pattern on a larger scale, it is much easier to see how all those little details come together to form the design. You will be able to see exactly where to insert your hook or how those clusters are constructed; the confidence to try the design with the tiny yarn and hook will soon follow. (Also, after seeing the stitch pattern in the heavier yarn, you may decide the heavier-weight sample would make a lovely design for a different day.)

Pamela Bethel

Dragonfly Shawl, page 34.

  Once you have developed a sense of what gauge change can do, you will see that very simple stitch patterns can look quite spectacular when worked in miniature; let the delicacy of the yarn do the work for you. The result is simple but stunning.
  The sheer number of stitches in a laceweight project can be intimidating. Even a skinny scarf in laceweight can feel like a long-term commitment when you think of all those tiny stitches. But many lace patterns are repetitive and easy to memorize, making it possible to speed along a row without constantly referring to a pattern or chart. So, although a laceweight project

might not be ideal for a movie theater, it might be great to work on while chatting with your crochet group. You could break a project of great scope into daily segments. You could also keep on hand another project in a larger gauge for an "instant gratification" break. Whatever method works best for you, just remember that this gorgeous lace is absolutely worth the effort.

Symbol charts help you visualize the laceweight project.

The lacy fabric in progress can look more like a used tissue than the lovely lace in the photograph. The reasons for the limp-rag syndrome can vary: Some crocheters are hesitant to work with as much tension as usual for fear of breaking the yarn; multiple hook insertions can lead to sloppy-looking holes; sometimes the yarn slips on the slippery steel hook, and the stitch just doesn't turn out right. Often, there is no fault on the part of the crocheter; the laceweight simply needs to be blocked to show its shape.

Whatever the challenge, blocking the fabric when finished will transform the used tissue into lace. To block, fill a basin with cool water and submerge the project, letting the fibers soak for a few minutes. Resist the urge to squeeze it in the water. Just let the fabric float as irregularities smooth away and the fibers fluff up, minimizing holes or inconsistent stitches. Drain the water, gently squeeze out the excess (never wring it), and roll it jelly roll–style in a towel to remove most of the saturation. Lay the piece on a flat surface and shape it to the desired measurements; some designs also benefit from being pinned into place while drying. Voilà! Lovely lace.

It feels good to complete a crochet project of any kind. Completing a laceweight project feels better than good—you'll feel euphoric, knowing you can handle designs more satisfying and challenging than you ever thought you could.

Tracy St. John lives in Montana, where she teaches, designs, and crochets.

Dragonfly Shawl

Just like the dragonfly that creates a symphony of elegance with a dance in flight, this shawl emulates that harmony through variances in stitch density coupled with an edging of webbed lace and pointed winged scallops—an extraordinary heirloom-quality piece your family will treasure for years to come.

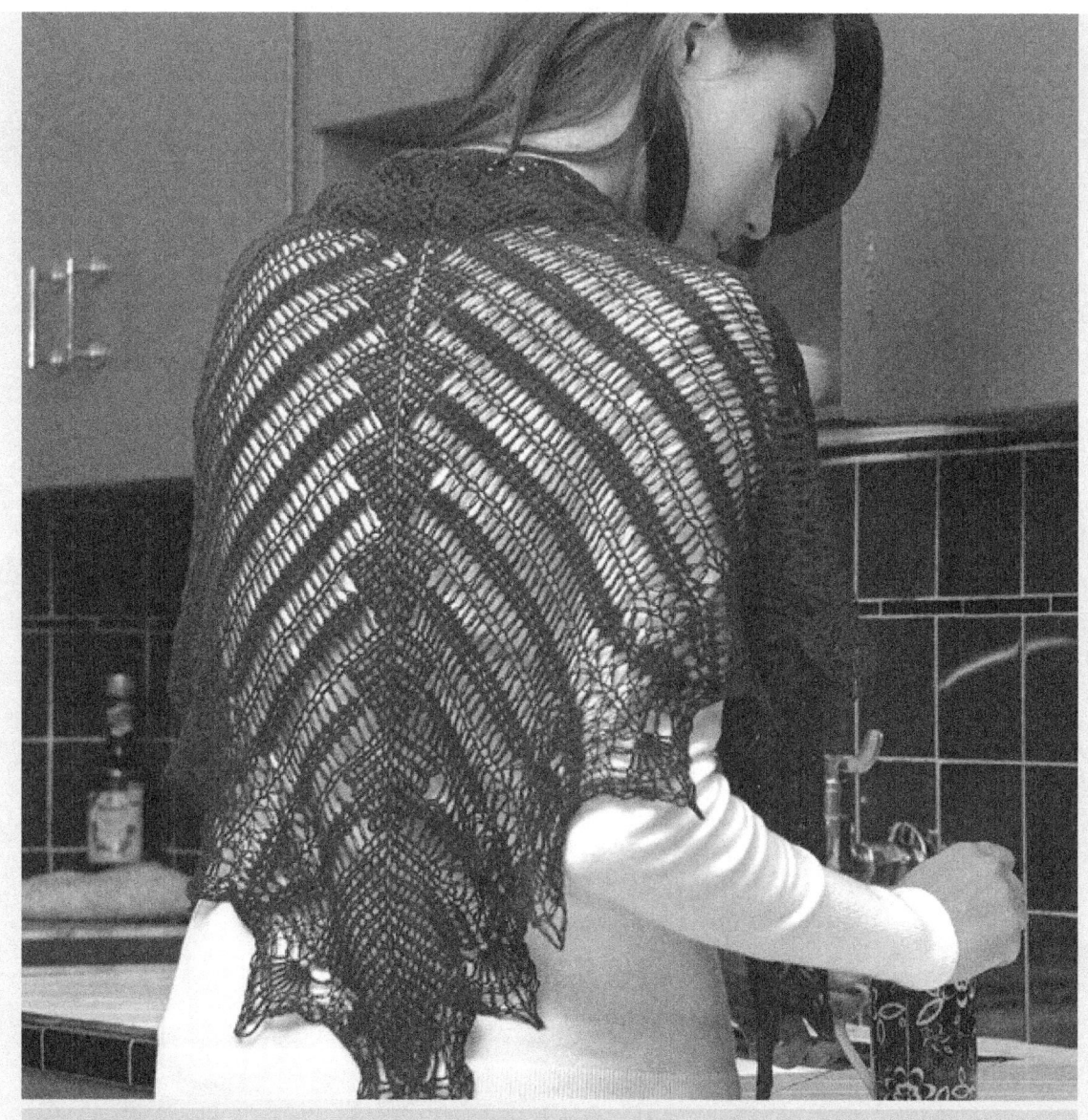

Pamela Bethel

Finished Size

About 32" (81.5 cm) long and 60" (152.5 cm) wide, blocked.

Yarn

Fingering weight (#0 Lace)

shown here: Jade Sapphire Lacey Lamb (100% extrafine lambswool; 825 yd [754 m]/2 oz [60 g]; **0**): #115, 2 balls.

Hook

Size D/3 (3.25 mm). *Adjust hook size if necessary to obtain the correct gauge.*

Notions

Yarn needle, stitch marker (m).

Gauge

3 sh, 5 SMK plus 3 ch-5 sps, and 13 rows = 4" (10 cm) before blocking.

Download the diagrams for this project here.

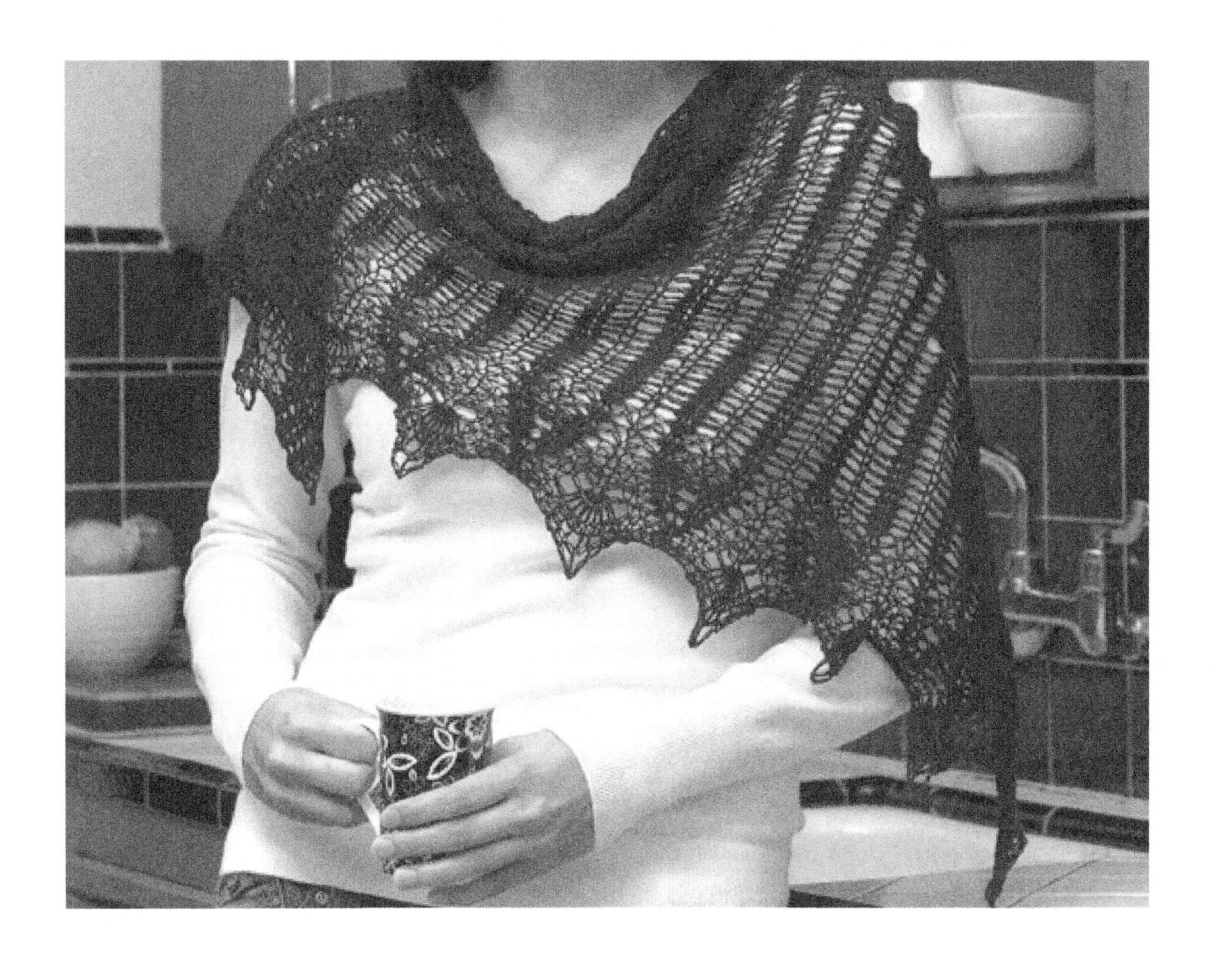

Notes

- "Tip" refers to center ch-5 sp of each trp-ch5 at tip of shawl. In Row 3, place marker (pm) in center ch-5 sp to mark tip; move m up to center ch-5 sp on each row.
- Dc-sh, BP-sh, FP-sh, and half-sh are referred to as sh.
- Blocking is required to obtain finished shape.

+ Shawl's height and width build on a ratio of about 1:2 and are customizable, as edging will work with any measurement as long as there is an even number of sh on each side of the shawl.

Stitch Guide

(see stitch diagrams on pages 37 and 38):

Dc sh (dc-sh): (3 dc, ch 1, dc, ch 1, 3 dc) in same st.

Front post sh (FP-sh): 3 dc in first ch-1 sp of same sh, ch 1, FPdc (see page 85) around next st (st is BPdc or dc from last row), ch 1, 3 dc in 2nd ch-1 sp of same sh, leave outer dc of sh unworked.

Back post sh (BP-sh): 3 dc in first ch-1 sp of same sh, ch 1, BPdc (see page 85) around next st (st is FPdc from previous row), ch 1, 3 dc in 2nd ch-1 sp of same sh, leave outer dc of sh unworked.

Half sh (half-sh): Dc in first ch-1 sp of next sh, ch 1, BPdc around next st, ch 1, dc in next ch-1 sp leaving outer dc of sh unworked.

Solomon's knot (SMK; see Glossary): Draw lp on hook to ¼"–½" (6 mm–1.3 cm), yo and draw through lp on hook (long ch made), sc in ch just made by inserting hook between thread found at back and 2 lps at front of ch to complete st.

Single ch 5 (s-ch5): (Sc, ch 5, sc) in same sp.

End ch 5 (end-ch5): (Sc, ch 2, tr) in same sp (counts as 1 ch-5 sp).

Double ch 5 (dbl-ch5): (Sc, [ch 5, sc] 2 times) in same sp (counts as 2 ch-5 sps).

Double end ch 5 (dbl-end-ch5): (Sc, ch 5, sc, ch 2, tr) in same sp (counts as 2 ch-5 sps).

Triple ch 5 (trp-ch5): (Sc, [ch 5, sc] 3 times) in same sp (counts as 3 ch-5 sps).

Cluster (cl): *Note:* Worked over ch-1 sp, post st, then ch-1 sp of same half-sh. Yo, insert hook in first sp of same half-sh and pull up lp, yo and draw through 2 lps on hook, [yo, insert hook in next st or sp and pull up lp, yo and draw through 2 lps on hook] 2 times, yo and draw through 4 lps on hook.

Sequence patt:

Dc sh sequence (dc-sh-seq): SMK, sk next 2 ch-5 sps, dc-sh in next ch-5 sp, SMK, sk next 2 ch-5 sps.

Front post sh sequence (FP-sh-seq): SMK, sk next SMK, FP-sh in next sh, SMK, sk next SMK.

Back post sh sequence (BP-sh-seq): SMK, sk next SMK, BP-sh in next sh, SMK, sk next SMK.

Half sh sequence (half-sh-seq): SMK, sc back lp only (blo) in next SMK, SMK, half-sh in next sh, SMK, sc blo in next SMK, SMK, dc in next ch-5 sp.

Front post edging sequence (FP-edge-seq): SMK, sk next 2 SMK, FP-sh in next half-sh, SMK, sk next 2 SMK, s-ch5 in next dc.

Shawl

ROW 1: Ch 2, end-ch5 (see Stitch Guide, page 36) in 2nd ch from hook, turn.

ROW 2: Ch 1, (sc, [ch 5, sc] 4 times, ch 2, tr) in ch-5 sp, turn—5 ch-5 sps.

ROW 3: Ch 1, s-ch5 (see Stitch Guide) in each of first 2 ch-5 sps, trp-ch5 (see Stitch Guide) in next ch-5 sp, place marker (pm) in center ch-5 sp of trp-ch5 to mark tip of shawl (see Notes), s-ch5 in next ch-5 sp, end-ch5 in last ch-5 sp, turn—7 ch-5 sps.

ROW 4: Ch 1, dbl-ch5 (see Stitch Guide) in first ch-5 sp, s-ch5 in each ch-5 sp to tip, trp-ch5 in tip, s-ch5 in rem ch-5 sps to last ch-5 sp, dbl-end-ch5 (see Stitch Guide) in last ch-5 sp, turn—11 ch-5 sps.

ROW 5: Ch 1, s-ch5 in each ch-5 sp to tip, trp-ch5 in tip, s-ch5 in rem ch-5 sps to last ch-5 sp, end-ch5 in last ch-5 sp, turn—13 ch-5 sps.

ROW 6: Rep Row 4—17 ch-5 sps.

ROW 7: Ch 1, s-ch5 in first ch-5 sp, dc-sh-seq (see Stitch Guide), s-ch5 in each ch-5 sp to tip, trp-ch5 in tip, s-ch5 in each of next 2 ch-5 sps, dc-sh-seq, end-ch5 in last ch-5 sp, turn—2 sh, 4 SMK, 9 ch-5 sps.

ROW 8: Ch 1, dbl-ch5 in first ch-5 sp, FP-sh-seq (see Stitch Guide), s-ch5 in each ch-5 sp to tip, trp-ch5 in tip, s-ch5 in each ch-5 sp to next SMK, FP-sh-seq, dbl-end-ch5 in last ch-5 sp, turn—13 ch-5 sps.

ROW 9: Ch 1, *s-ch5 in each ch-5 sp to first SMK, BP-sh-seq (see Stitch Guide)*, s-ch5 in each ch-5 sp to tip, trp-ch5 in tip; rep from * to *, s-ch5 in each ch-5 sp to last ch-5 sp, end-ch5 in last ch-5 sp, turn—15 ch-5 sps.

ROW 10: Ch 1, dbl-ch5 in first ch-5 sp, *s-ch5 in each ch-5 sp to first SMK, FP-sh-seq*, s-ch5 in each ch-5 sp to tip, trp-ch5 in tip; rep from * to *, s-ch5 in each ch-5 sp to last ch-5 sp, dbl-end-ch5 in last ch-5 sp, turn—19 ch-5 sps.

ROWS 11–12: Rep Rows 9–10—25 ch-5 sps.

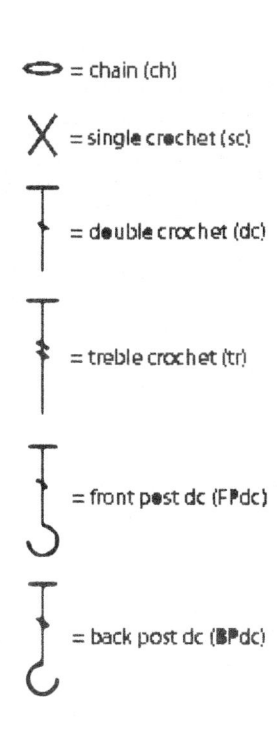

- ⬯ = chain (ch)
- ✕ = single crochet (sc)
- ┬ = double crochet (dc)
- ┬ = treble crochet (tr)
- ┬ = front post dc (FPdc)
- ┬ = back post dc (BPdc)

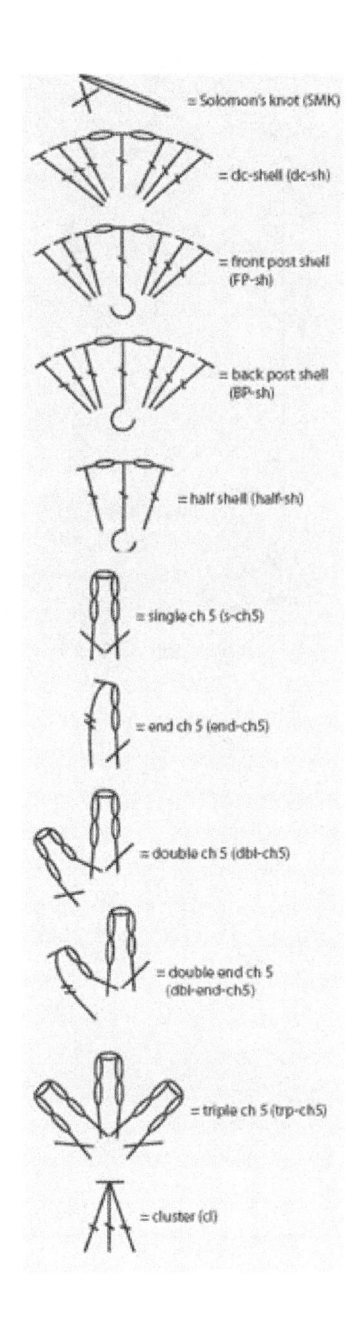

Legend:
- = Solomon's knot (SMK)
- = dc-shell (dc-sh)
- = front post shell (FP-sh)
- = back post shell (BP-sh)
- = half shell (half-sh)
- = single ch 5 (s-ch5)
- = end ch 5 (end-ch5)
- = double ch 5 (dbl-ch5)
- = double end ch 5 (dbl-end-ch5)
- = triple ch 5 (trp-ch5)
- = cluster (cl)

ROW 13 (2 SH INC): Ch 1, s-ch5 in each ch-5 sp to first SMK, BP-sh-seq, s-ch5 in next ch-5 sp, dc-sh-seq, s-ch5 in each ch-5 sp to tip, trp-ch5 in tip, s-ch5 in each of next 2 ch-5 sps, dc-sh-seq, s-ch5 in next ch-5 sp, BP-sh-seq, s-ch5 in each ch-5 sp to last ch-5 sp, end-ch5 in last ch-5 sp, turn—17 ch-5 sps, 4 sh, 8 SMK.

SHAWL
ROWS 1–30

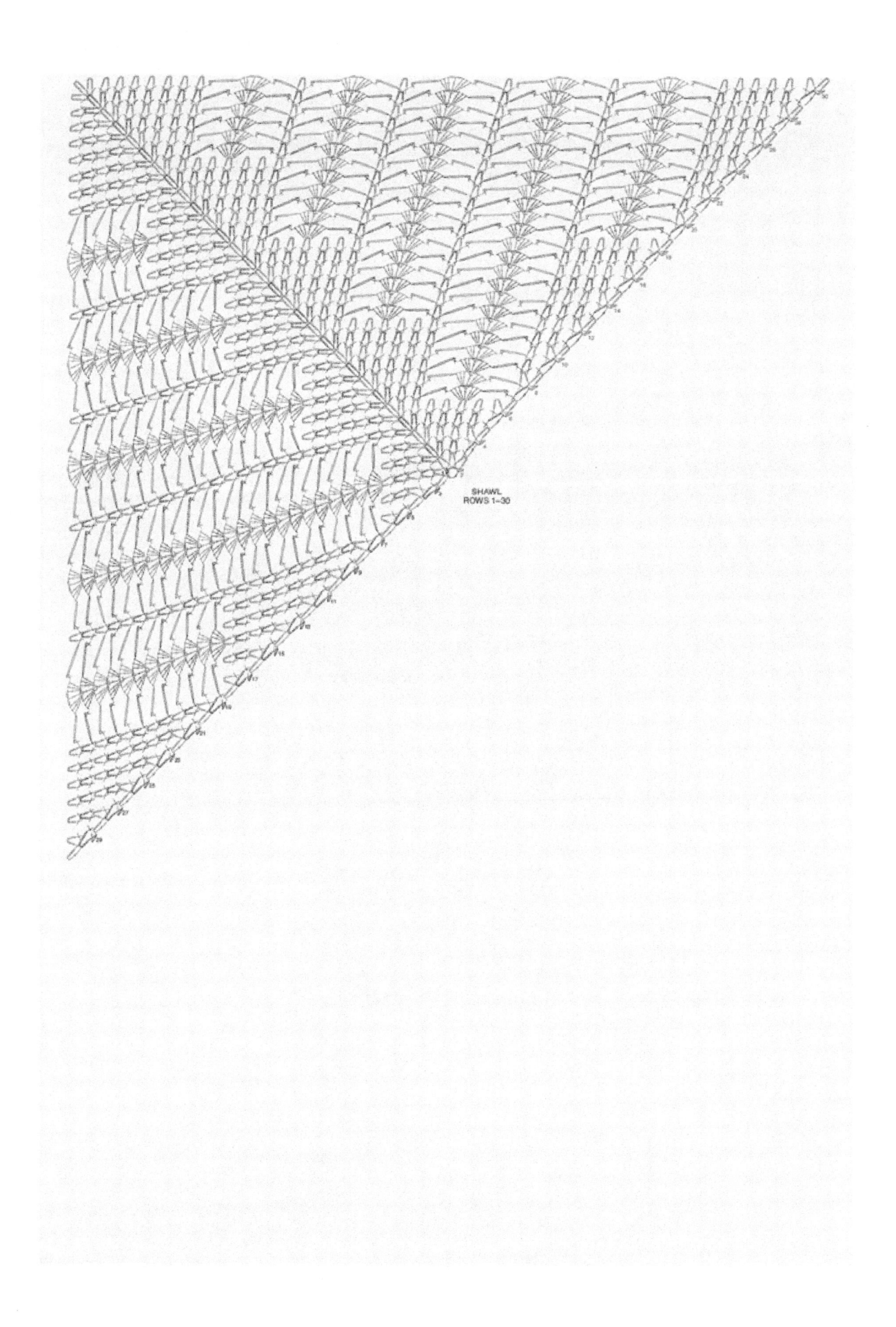

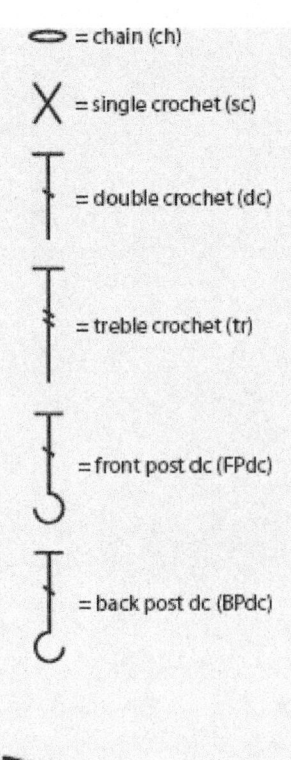

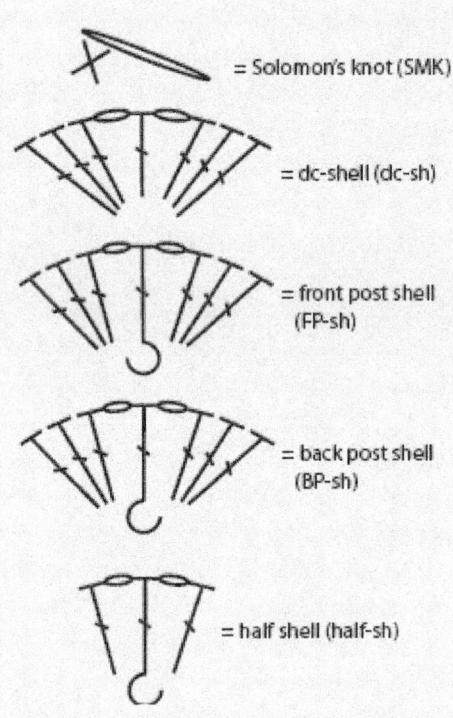

- ⬭ = chain (ch)
- ✕ = single crochet (sc)
- † = double crochet (dc)
- ‡ = treble crochet (tr)
- = front post dc (FPdc)
- = back post dc (BPdc)
- = Solomon's knot (SMK)
- = dc-shell (dc-sh)
- = front post shell (FP-sh)
- = back post shell (BP-sh)
- = half shell (half-sh)

= single ch 5 (s-ch5)

= end ch 5 (end-ch5)

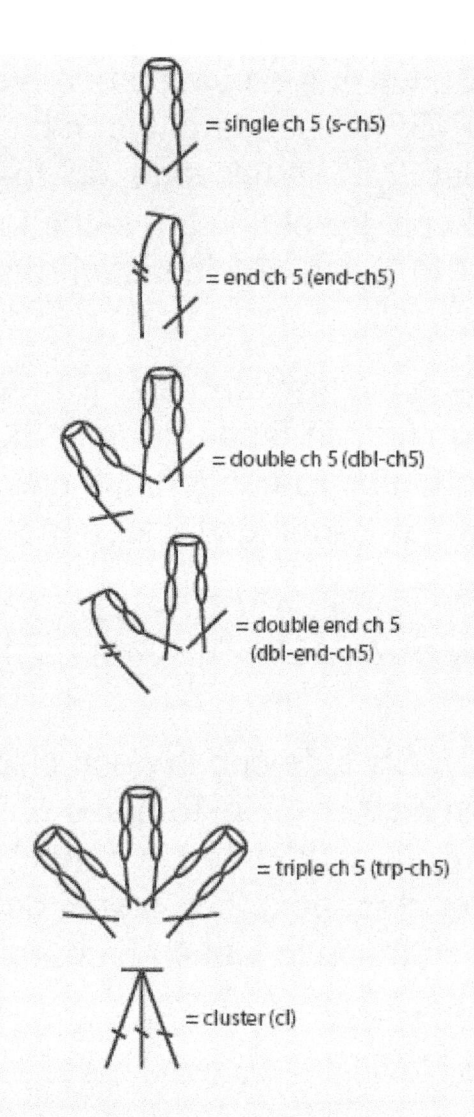

= double ch 5 (dbl-ch5)

= double end ch 5 (dbl-end-ch5)

= triple ch 5 (trp-ch5)

= cluster (cl)

ROW 14: Ch 1, dbl-ch5 in first ch-5 sp, *s-ch5 in each ch-5 sp to first SMK, [FP-sh-seq, s-ch5 in next ch-5 sp] through first ch-5 sp after last SMK on this side*, s-ch5 in rem ch-5 sps to tip, trp-ch5 in tip; rep from * to *, s-ch5 in rem ch-5 sps to last ch-5 sp, dbl-end-ch5 in last ch-5 sp, turn—21 ch-5 sps.

ROW 15: Ch 1, *s-ch5 in each ch-5 sp to first SMK, [BP-sh-seq, s-ch5 in next ch-5 sp] through first ch-5 sp after last SMK on this side*, s-ch5 in rem ch-5 sps to tip, trp-ch5 in tip; rep from * to *, s-ch5 in rem ch-5 sps to last ch-5 sp, end-ch5 in last ch-5 sp, turn—23 ch-5 sps.

ROWS 16–18: Rep Rows 14–15; then rep Row 14—33 ch-5 sps.

ROW 19 (4 SH INC): Ch 1, s-ch5 in first ch-5 sp, *dc-sh-seq, s-ch5 in next ch-5 sp, [BP-sh-seq, s-ch5 in next ch-5 sp] through first ch-5 sp after last SMK on this side, dc-sh-seq*, s-ch5 in each of next 2 ch-5 sps, trp-ch5 in tip, s-ch5 in each of next 2 ch-5 sps; rep from * to *, end-ch5 in last ch-5 sp, turn—15 ch-5 sps, 8 sh, 16 SMK.

ROW 20: Ch 1, dbl-ch5 in first ch-5 sp, *[FP-sh-seq, s-ch5 in next ch-5 sp] through first ch-5 sp after last SMK on this side*, s-ch5 in rem ch-5 sps to tip, trp-ch5 in tip, s-ch5 in each ch-5 sp to next SMK, rep from * to * ending with dbl-end-ch5 in last ch-5 sp, turn—19 ch-5 sps.

ROWS 21–24: [Rep Row 15; then Row 14] 2 times—31 ch-5 sps.

ROW 25 (2 SH INC): Ch 1, *s-ch5 in each ch-5 sp to first SMK, [BP-sh-seq, s-ch5 in next ch-5 sp] to first s-ch5 after last SMK on this side*, dc-sh-seq, s-ch5 in each of next 2 ch-5 sps, trp-ch5 in tip, s-ch5 in each of next 2 ch-5 sps, dc-sh-seq, rep from * to *, s-ch5 in rem ch-5 sps to last ch-5 sp, end-ch5 in last ch-5 sp, turn—23 ch-5 sps, 10 sh, 20 SMK.

ROWS 26–30: Rep Rows 14–15 two times; then rep Row 14—39 ch-5 sps.

Rep Rows 19–30 until shawl measures about 20–23" (51–58.5 cm) from beg to center of working row, ending on Row 30 with an even number of sh on each side of shawl. Do not fasten off.

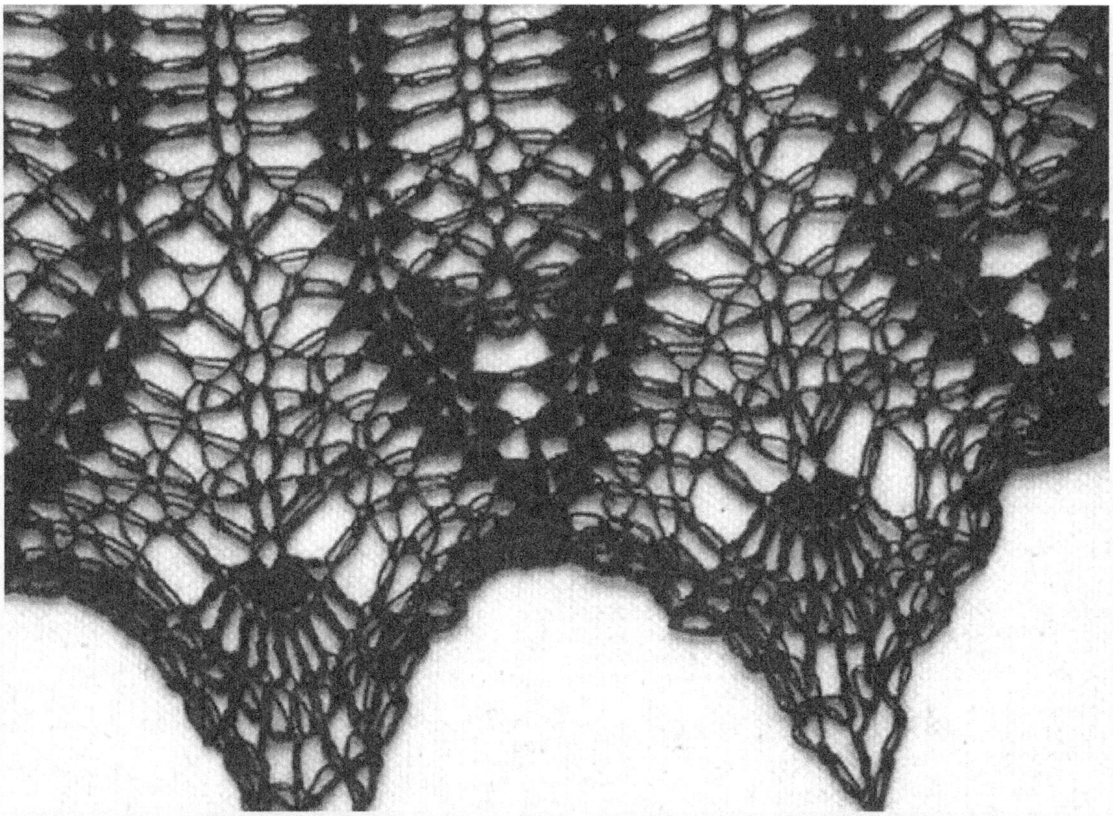

Edging

ROW 1: Ch 1, *s-ch5 in each ch-5 sp to last ch-5 sp before first SMK, dc in next ch-5 sp, [half-sh-seq (see Stitch Guide, page 36)] through first ch-5 sp after last SMK on this side*, s-ch5 in rem ch-5 sps to tip, trp-ch5 in tip, rep from * to *, s-ch5 in rem ch-5 sps to last ch-5 sp, end-ch5 in last ch-5 sp, turn.

ROW 2: Ch 1, dbl-ch5 in first ch-5 sp, *s-ch5 in each ch-5 sp to first dc, s-ch5 in dc, rep FP-edge-seq (see Stitch Guide) through last dc*, s-ch5 in each ch-5 sp before tip, trp-ch5 in tip, rep from * to *, s-ch5 in rem ch-5 sps to last ch-5 sp, dbl-end-ch5 in last ch-5 sp, turn.

ROWS 3–4: Rep Rows 1–2.

ROW 5: Ch 1, *s-ch5 in each ch-5 sp to first SMK, [SMK, sc blo in next SMK, SMK, BP-sh in next sh, sk next SMK, s-ch5 in next ch-5 sp, sk next SMK, BP-sh in next sh, SMK, sc blo in next SMK, SMK, s-ch5 in next ch-5 sp] to first ch-5 sp after last SMK on this side*, s-ch5 in rem ch-5 sps to tip, trp-ch5 in tip, rep from * to *, s-ch5 in rem ch-5 sps to last ch-5 sp, end-ch5 in last ch-5 sp, turn.

ROW 6: Ch 1, dbl-ch5 in first ch-5 sp, *s-ch5 in each ch-5 sp to first SMK, [SMK, sc in sc bet next 2 SMK, SMK, FP-sh in next sh, s-ch5 in next ch-5 sp, FP-sh in next sh, SMK, sc in sc bet next 2 SMK, SMK, s-ch5 in next ch-5 sp] to first ch-5 sp after last SMK on this side*, s-ch5 in rem ch-5 sps to tip, trp-ch5 in tip, rep from * to *, s-ch5 in rem ch-5 sps to last ch-5 sp, dbl-end-ch5 in last ch-5 sp, turn.

ROW 7: Ch 1, *s-ch5 in each ch-5 sp to first SMK, [SMK, (sc blo in next SMK, SMK) 2 times, BP-sh in next sh, sk next ch-5 sp, BP-sh in next sh, SMK, (sc blo in next SMK, SMK) 2 times, s-ch5 in next ch-5 sp] to first ch-5 sp after last SMK on this side*, s-ch5 in rem ch-5 sps to tip, trp-ch5 in tip, rep from * to *, s-ch5 in rem ch-5 sps to last ch-5 sp, end-ch5 in last ch-5 sp, turn.

ROW 8: Ch 1, dbl-ch5 in first ch-5 sp, *s-ch5 in each ch-5 sp to first SMK, [SMK, (sc in sc bet next 2 SMK, SMK) 2 times, FP-sh in each of next 2 sh, SMK, (sc in sc bet next 2 SMK, SMK) 2 times, s-ch5 in next ch-5 sp] to first ch-5 sp after last SMK on this side*, s-ch5 in rem ch-5 sps to tip, trp-ch5 in tip, rep from * to *, s-ch5 in rem ch-5 sps to last ch-5 sp, dbl-end-ch5 in last ch-5 sp, turn.

ROW 9: Ch 3 (counts as dc), (2 dc, ch 1, dc, ch 1, 3 dc) in first ch-5 sp, sk next ch-5 sp, [dc-sh in next ch-5 sp, sk next ch-5 sp] 2 times, SMK, sc in next ch-5 sp, SMK, sk next ch-5 sp, sc in next ch-5 sp, SMK, sk next ch-5 sp, 9 dc in next ch-5 sp, *SMK, sk next SMK, [sc blo in next SMK, SMK] 2 times, skipping first (3 dc, ch-1 sp and post st of next sh), 3 dc in 2nd ch-1 sp of that sh, ch 1, dc in sp bet same sh and next sh, ch 1, 3 dc in first ch-

1 sp of next sh (last 7 dc and 2 ch-1 sps count as sh on next row), [SMK, sc blo in next SMK] 2 times, SMK, sk next SMK, 9 dc in next ch-5 sp*, rep from * to * to 15 ch-5 sps before tip, [SMK, sk next ch-5 sp, sc in next ch-5 sp] 2 times, SMK, sk next 2 ch-5 sps, dc-sh in next ch-5 sp, SMK, sk next 2 ch-5 sps, sc in next ch-5 sp, SMK, sk next ch-5 sp, sc in next ch-5 sp, SMK, sk next 2 ch-5 sps, 3 dc in next ch-5 sp, 9 dc in tip, 3 dc in next ch-5 sp (tip formed), SMK, sk next 2 ch-5 sps, sc in next ch-5 sp, SMK, sk next ch-5 sp, sc in next ch-5 sp, SMK, sk next 2 ch-5 sps, dc-sh in next ch-5 sp, SMK, sk next 2 ch-5 sps, [sc in next ch-5 sp, SMK, sk next ch-5 sp] 2 times, 9 dc in next ch-5 sp, rep from * to * to last 10 ch-5 sps, SMK, sk next ch-5 sp, [sc in next ch-5 sp, SMK, sk next ch-5 sp] 2 times, dc-sh in next ch-5 sp, [sk next ch-5 sp, dc-sh in next ch-5 sp] 2 times, turn.

ROW 10: Ch 1, s-ch5 in first dc, FP-sh in each of first 3 sh, * [SMK, sc blo in next SMK] 2 times, SMK, sk next SMK, tr in next dc, [ch 1, tr in next dc] 8 times, SMK, sk next SMK, [sc blo in next SMK, SMK] 2 times, FP-sh in next sh*, rep from * to * through last sh on this side [SMK, sc blo in next SMK] 2 times, SMK, sk next SMK, tr in next dc, [ch 1, tr in next dc] 6 times, (ch 1, tr) 3 times in next dc, [ch 1, tr in next dc] 7 times, SMK, sk next SMK, [sc blo in next SMK, SMK] 2 times, FP-sh in next sh, rep from * to * to last 2 sh, FP-sh in each of last 2 sh, end-ch5 in last dc of last sh, turn.

ROW 11: Ch 1, s-ch5 in first ch-5 sp, BP-sh in each of next 2 sh, half-sh in next sh, *[SMK, sc blo in next SMK] 2 times, SMK, sk next SMK, sc in next tr, [SMK, sc in next tr] 8 times, SMK, sk next SMK, [sc blo in next SMK, SMK] 2 times, half-sh in next sh*, rep from * to * through last sh on this side, [SMK, sc blo in next SMK] 2 times, SMK, sk next SMK, sc in next tr, [SMK, sk next ch-1 sp, sc in next tr] 16 times, SMK, sk next SMK, [sc blo in next SMK, SMK] 2 times, half-sh in next sh, rep from * to * to last 2 sh, BP-sh in each of last 2 sh, end-ch5 in last ch-5 sp, turn.

ROW 12: Ch 1, dbl-ch5 in first ch-5 sp, FP-sh in each of next 2 sh, sc in first dc of next half-sh, ch 2, cl (see Stitch Guide), ch 2, sc in last dc of same half-sh, *[SMK, sk next SMK, sc in next sc] 4 times, [SMK, sk next SMK, dc in next sc] 2 times, SMK, sk next SMK, tr in next sc, [SMK, sk next SMK, dc in next sc] 2 times, [SMK, sk next SMK, sc in next sc] 4 times, SMK, sc in first dc of next half-sh, ch 2, cl, ch 2, sc in last dc of same half-sh*, rep from * to * through last half sh on this side, [SMK, sk next SMK, sc in next sc] 8 times, [SMK, sk next SMK, dc in next sc] 2 times, SMK, sk next SMK, tr in next sc, [SMK, sk next SMK, dc in next sc] 2 times, [SMK, sk next SMK, sc in next sc] 8 times, SMK, sk next SMK, sc in first dc of next half-sh, ch 2, cl, ch 2, sc in last dc of same half-sh, rep from * to * to last 2 sh, FP-sh in each of last 2 sh, dbl-end-ch5 in last ch-5 sp, turn.

ROW 13: Ch 1, s-ch5 in each of first 2 ch-5 sps, BP-sh in each of next 2 sh, ch 2, sc in top of next cl, ch 2, *2 sc blo in each of next 3 SMK, sc in next sc, SMK, sk next SMK, sc in next sc, [SMK, sk next SMK, sc in next dc] 2 times, work 2 SMK, sk next SMK, tr in next tr, 2 SMK, sk next SMK, [sc in next dc, SMK, sk next SMK] 2 times, sc in next sc, SMK, sk next SMK, sc in next sc, 2 sc blo in each of next 3 SMK, ch 2, sc in next cl, ch 2*, rep from * to * through last cl on this side, 2 sc blo in each of next 3 SMK, sc in next sc, [SMK, sk next SMK, sc in next sc] 5 times, [SMK, sk next SMK, sc in next dc] 2 times, 2 SMK, sk next SMK, tr in next tr, 2 SMK, sk next SMK, sc in next dc, SMK, sk next SMK, sc in next dc, [SMK, sk next SMK, sc in next sc] 6 times, 2 sc blo in each of next 3 SMK, ch 2, sc in top of next cl, ch 2, rep from * to * to last 2 sh, BP-sh in last 2 sh, s-ch5 in next ch-5 sp, end-ch5 in last ch-5 sp. Fasten off and weave in loose ends. Block to measurements.

Lisa Naskrent designs and crochets in Macomb, Illinois. You can see more of her work at crochetgarden.com.

Beyond the Basics

Symbolcraft
by SANDY WISEHEART

The International Language of Crochet

Symbolcraft, as it is known to some, is a way of diagramming the individual crochet stitches that produce the fabric structure; it lets you see how the stitches fit together to form a particular pattern. Each crochet stitch has a unique symbol; groups of symbols are linked together to illustrate rows, rounds, and motifs. The symbols for some of the basic stitches used in this issue are shown below.

The symbols are logical in their representation: a chain stitch is shown as an oval; half double crochet is shown with a single crossbar, representing the single yarnover drawn through all the loops in that stitch; double crochet has two crossbars; treble crochet has three. This makes it easier to puzzle out new symbols in diagrams just from the way they are constructed.

CIRCULAR DIAGRAM

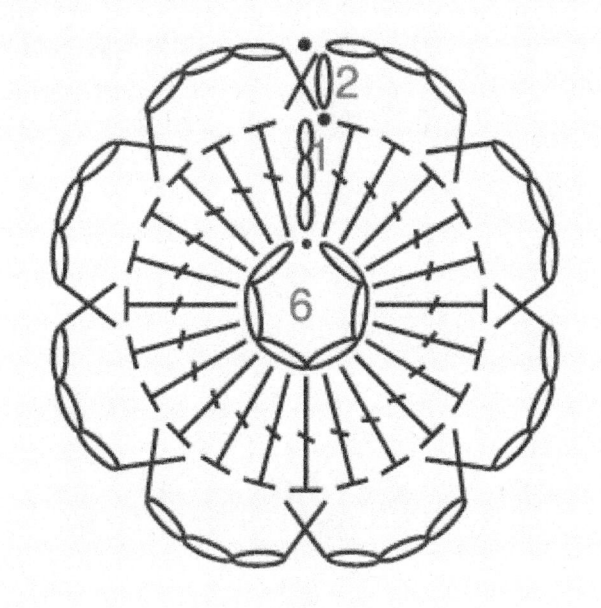

ROW BY ROW DIAGRAM

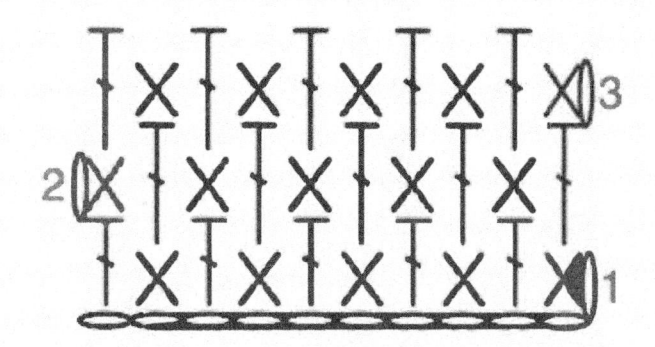

BASIC STITCHES

- slip stitch (sl st)
- chain (ch)
- single crochet (sc)
- half double crochet (hdc)
- double crochet (dc)
- treble crochet (tr)

CLUSTER STITCHES

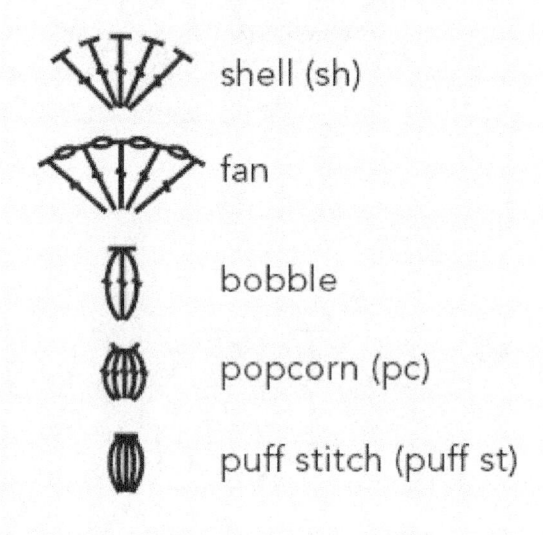

- shell (sh)
- fan
- bobble
- popcorn (pc)
- puff stitch (puff st)

    The logical format of the symbols also makes it easy to diagram combinations of stitches, as in the symbols for cluster stitches at right. At a glance, you can see that the shell stitch consists of five double crochet stitches worked into a single stitch. Looking at the diagram, it is easy to grasp the difference between this shell stitch and the fan stitch below it: the double crochet stitches in the fan are separated by chain stitches, whereas there are no chain stitches in the shell. Likewise, you can see the difference between a bobble stitch (several incomplete double crochet stitches connected by a single yarnover through all the final loops), a popcorn stitch (several completed double crochet stitches pulled together into a cup shape by connecting the first and last stitch), and a puff stitch (multiple loops on the hook pulled together with a single yarnover).

From individual stitches and stitch combinations, you can build diagrams for entire stitch patterns. There are two kinds of diagrams: those that represent part of a repeating pattern worked in rounds or rows and those that represent an entire motif (such as a granny square or flower). Both types of diagrams show the right side of the fabric, and both assume that the crocheter is right-handed.

For crochet worked in rows, the diagrams are read from bottom to top; rows are read alternately from right to left, then left to right in the exact order that the stitches are worked. Row numbers are placed next to the first stitch of each row to indicate which direction the row is worked.

Written out in words, the same pattern would read as follows:

FOUNDATION CH: Ch 11.

ROW 1: Sc in 2nd ch from hook, dc in next ch, *sc in next ch, dc in next ch; rep from * to end, turn.

ROW 2: Ch 1, *sc in dc, dc in sc; rep from * to end, turn.

ROW 3: Rep Row 2.

The foundation ch "row" is not marked with a row number; it is read from left to right. The final ch symbol of the foundation ch is vertical rather than horizontal, indicating that this ch is the turning ch.

The row numbers indicate that Row 1 begins at the right side and is read from right to left. Row 2 begins on the left side and is read from left to right. Each stitch symbol stands directly above the stitch in the row below to indicate that the stitches are worked into the top loops of the stitches of the previous row, rather than in the spaces between stitches.

Diagrams for crochet worked in the round are usually circular. Circular diagrams are generally read from the center outward; rounds are read counterclockwise, the same direction as the stitches are worked. However, there is an exception: some granny square motifs require the fabric to be turned at the end of each round; diagrams for these motifs should be read alternately counterclockwise, then clockwise. The stitch diagram will indicate whether or not the fabric should be turned. Round numbers will appear on alternate sides of the joining point if the fabric is to be turned, on the same side of the joining point if the fabric is not turned.

For the circular diagram on page 42, the round numbers are to the right of the joining points indicating that all rounds are worked counterclockwise. The number in the very center of the motif specifies the initial number of chain stitches in the foundation ring.

The written instructions for this diagram would read as follows:

FOUNDATION CH: Ch 6, join with sl st in first ch to form a ring.

RND 1: Ch 3 (counts as first dc), work 23 dc in ring, join with sl st to top of beg ch-3.

RND 2: Ch 1, sc in top of beg ch-3 from previous rnd, ch 3, *skip 2 dc, sc in next dc, ch 3; rep from * around, ending with sl st in top of first sc. Fasten off.

Stitch diagrams are just like roadmaps: just follow the symbols, one by one, from beginning to end. If you can read the language of symbolcraft, you can read the entire world of crochet.

Sandi Wiseheart, incorrigible crafter and blogger, lives in Toronto. Read her blog at sandiwiseheart.com.

Boteh Scarf

This simple motif reminds designer Kathy Merrick of Persian carpet *Boteh* (Old Persian for "cluster of leaves"). They can look like leaves, pine cones, pears, or paisleys. Each motif flows gracefully into the next, resulting in a swirled effect, and this lightweight wool yarn lends excellent drape to the whole project.

Kathryn Martin

Finished Size

About 4½" (11.5 cm) wide at widest points and 72" (183 cm) long.

Yarn

Sportweight (#2 Fine)

shown here: Lorna's Laces Shepherd Sock (80% superwash wool, 20% nylon; 215 yd [190 m]/1¾ oz [50 g]; **2**): chino, 2 skeins.

Hook

Size F/5 (4 mm). *Adjust hook size if necessary to obtain the correct gauge.*

Notions

Yarn needle.

Gauge

24 sts and 15 rows = 4" (10 cm) in hdc.

Download the diagram for this project here.

Notes

- This is a modular scarf made of curved triangular pieces joined by rows of double-treble crochet worked down the angled (decreased) side of each piece.

- To keep your rows of hdc even, be sure to work the stitch directly below the turning chain at the beginning of each row. When you reach the end of the row, do not work a stitch in the turning chain from the row below.

Stitch Guide

Dtr: Yo 3 times, insert hook in next st, yo and draw up a lp (5 lps on hook), [yo and draw through first 2 lps on hook] 4 times.

First Triangle

(see stitch diagram)

Ch 17.

ROW 1: Hdc in 3rd ch from hook and in each ch across, turn—15 hdc.

ROW 2: (WS) Ch 2, work 1 row hdc, turn.

ROW 3: (RS) Ch 2, hdc in each st across to last hdc, turn, leaving last hdc unworked.

ROW 4: (WS) Ch 2, hdc in each hdc of previous row.

Rep Rows 2 and 3, leaving the last st unworked on each RS row, until you have a row with only 1 st—29 rows total. Hdc in next st, then turn and work 1 hdc in st just worked; turn to work down the side (dec) edge of piece as foll:

DTR ROW: Ch 5, dtr (see Stitch Guide) in tch of Row 28 then work 1 dtr in tch of every other row including fdn ch—15 dtr; turn.

Second Triangle

(see stitch diagram)

ROW 1: Ch 2, work 1 row hdc, turn.

Ch 2. Work as for first triangle, beg with Row 2. Work second triangle 15 times for a total of 16 triangles. Fasten off.

Finishing

Join yarn and work 1 row hdc evenly (about 2 hdc for every 3 rows) around the entire scarf. Fasten off. Weave in loose ends. Steam-block lightly to smooth out scarf if needed.

Kathy Merrick is the author of *Crochet in Color* (Interweave). Find more of her work at kathrynmerrick.com.

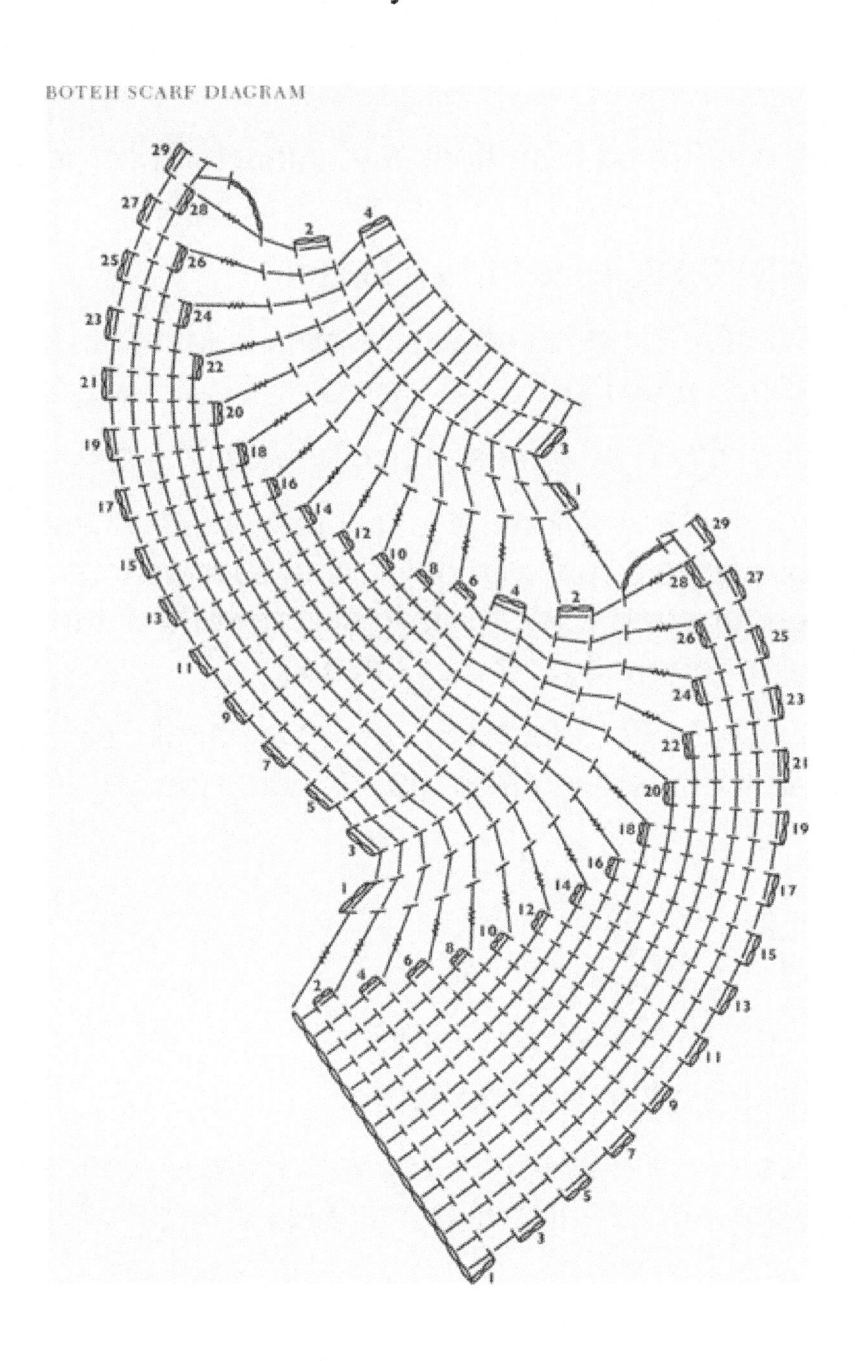

BOTEH SCARF DIAGRAM

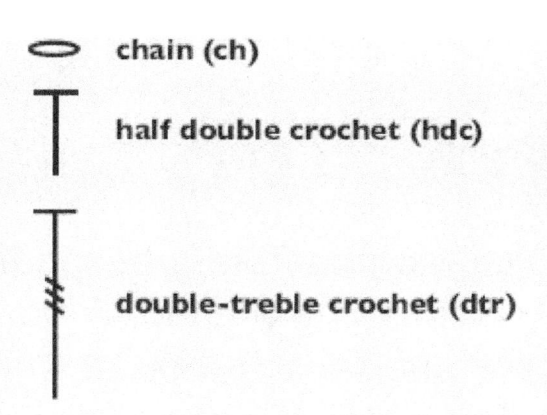

⊖ chain (ch)

┬ half double crochet (hdc)

┬ double-treble crochet (dtr)

Moorish Mosaic Afghan

A single motif that morphs from a hexagon to an octagon is the core of this stunning afghan. A gorgeous interplay of color gives the blanket the look of Moorish tiles. Two supporting motifs—a small square and a triangle—are the mortar that hold the octagons together. A chart on page 50 will let you follow Lisa's brilliant color scheme, or you can devise your own. As a bonus, the superwash wool means you can wrap yourself in your masterpiece daily.

Joe Coca

Finished Size

About 40" (101.5 cm) wide and 48" (122) long.

Yarn

Worsted weight (#4 Medium)

shown here: Mission Falls 136 Merino Superwash (100% merino superwash wool; 136 yd [124 m]/1¾ oz [50 g]; 4): #027 macaw (turquoise green; MC), 7 balls; #012 raisin (dark red; A), #002 stone (light gray; B), #013 curry (tan; C), #531 sprout (dark green; D), and #019 mist (light green; E), 3 balls each.

note: This yarn is unavailable. Suggested substitution: Cascade 220 superwash sport.

Hook

Size I/9 (5.5 mm). *Adjust hook size if necessary to obtain the correct gauge.*

Notions

Yarn needle; 8 stitch markers (m).

Gauge

Radius of octagon (center to edge) or edge of 1 square = about 4" (10 cm).

Download the diagrams for this project here.

Notes

+ To change colors, insert hook in indicated st to join, drop old color, yo with new color and draw through lp on hook.

Stitch Guide

Beg cluster (beg-cl): Ch 3, yo, insert hook in indicated sp and pull up lp, yo and draw through 2 lps on hook (2 lps on hook), yo, insert hook in same sp and pull up lp, yo and draw through 2 lps on hook, yo and draw through all 3 lps on hook.

Cluster (cl): Yo, insert hook in indicated sp and pull up lp, yo and draw through 2 lps on hook, [yo, insert hook in same sp and pull up lp, yo and draw through 2 lps on hook] 2 times, yo and draw through all 4 lps on hook.

COLOR CHART FOR LARGE MOTIF

Octagon

ROUND NUMBER	1	2	3	4	5	6	7	8	9	10	11	12	13	14	15	16	17	18	19	20	21	22	23	24	25	26	27	28	29	30
1	D	A	D	MC	B	D	MC	C	B	C	E	A	E	MC	B	C	B	B	E	D	A	C	C	A	B	E	MC	E	MC	C
2	A	C	B	A	C	B	MC	A	MC	C	D	D	A	D	B	D	A	E	C	A	B	MC	B	MC	E	E	D	E	MC	B
3	D	C	B	A	D	D	MC	C	B	C	D	MC	E	MC	B	D	A	A	E	D	A	C	E	A	B	E	MC	E	MC	C
4	A	C	B	A	D	A	MC	B	B	C	D	B	B	B	B	D	A	B	C	A	B	MC	E	D	E	E	D	E	MC	MC
5	D	D	B	B	B	D	MC	C	MC	C	C	A	E	MC	B	C	E	B	E	D	A	C	C	A	B	E	MC	B	C	C
6	A	MC	D	A	D	D	MC	B	MC	C	D	B	E	B	B	D	D	B	C	A	B	MC	C	A	E	E	D	MC	C	C
7	A	MC	D	A	D	D	MC	A	MC	C	D	MC	E	D	B	D	D	C	D	B	MC	C	A	E	E	D	B	C	C
8	B	MC	B	A	D	D	MC	B	MC	C	MC	D	E	B	D	D	E	MC	A	E	D	C	A	C	E	A	E	MC	C
9	A	E	B	A	D	D	C	A	MC	MC	A	E	MC	B	D	MC	A	C	D	B	MC	B	A	E	A	D	E	MC	C
10	A	E	B	C	B	D	B	B	D	A	MC	D	E	B	C	B	D	E	C	A	B	MC	E	A	E	MC	D	E	MC	C
11	A	E	B	C	D	D	D	C	D	D	MC	MC	E	MC	B	B	MC	B	C	D	B	MC	E	A	E	B	D	B	MC	C
12	D	E	B	C	D	D	B	B	A	A	MC	B	E	B	C	C	A	E	C	A	MC	C	A	E	MC	D	MC	MC	MC
13	A	E	B	C	C	D	D	A	MC	D	MC	MC	E	D	B	C	A	A	E	D	B	C	C	A	B	B	MC	E	MC	MC
14	A	E	B	C	D	D	B	C	B	A	MC	D	E	MC	C	A	A	E	C	A	A	MC	C	A	E	MC	D	E	MC	C

Octagon motif

NOTE: *See diagram on page 53.*

RND 1: (RS) Ch 4, sl st in 4th ch from hook to form ring, beg-cl (see Stitch Guide) in ring, ch 3, [cl, ch 3] 5 times in ring, sl st in first ch-3 sp to join—6 cl, 6 ch-3 sps.

RND 2: Ch 1, 6 sc in each ch-3 sp around, sl st in first sc to join—36 sc.

RND 3: Ch 1, sc in first 5 sc, 2 sc in next sc, [sc in next 5 sc, 2 sc in next sc] 5 times, sl st in first sc to join—42 sc.

RND 4: Ch 1, sc around, sl st in first sc to join.

RND 5: (Beg-cl, [ch 3, cl] 2 times) in first sc, sk next 2 sc, sc in next sc, sk next 2 sc, *(cl, [ch 3, cl] 2 times) in next sc, sk next 2 sc, sc in next sc, sk next 2 sc; rep from * around, sl st in first ch-3 sp to join—14 ch-3 sps, 7 sc.

NOTE: *If changing colors at end of Rnd 6, change colors in first sl st of Rnd 7 instead of sl st at end of Rnd 6.*

RND 6: Ch 1, 7 sc in each of first 2 ch-3 sps, sc in next sc, *7 sc in each of next 2 ch-3 sps, sc in next sc; rep from * around, sl st in first sc to join—105 sc.

RND 7: Sl st in next sc, ch 1, sc in same sc and in next 11 sc, ch 1, sk next 3 sc, *sc in next 12 sc, ch 1, sk next 3 sc; rep from * around, sl st in first sc to join—84 sc, 7 ch-1 sps.

RND 8: Ch 1, sc in first 11 sc, sc2tog (see Glossary) over next sc and ch-1 sp, *sc in next 11 sc, sc2tog over next sc and ch-1 sp; rep from * around, sl st in first sc to join—84 sc.

RND 9: Ch 1 (bring ch to height of a dc, does not count as a st), dc in same sc, hdc in next 2 sc, sc in next 5 sc, hdc in next 2 sc, dc in next 3 sc, *hdc in next 2 sc, sc in next 5 sc, hdc in next 2 sc, dc in next 3 sc; rep from * around omitting last dc on last rep, sl st in first dc to join—84 sts.

RND 10: Ch 1, sc in first 20 sts, 2 sc in next st, *sc in next 20 sts, 2 sc in next st; rep from * around, sl st in first sc to join—88 sc.

RND 11: Ch 1, sc in first 10 sc, 3 sc in next sc, *sc in next 10 sc, 3 sc in next sc; rep from * around, sl st in first sc to join, place marker (pm) in center sc of each 3-sc group to mark corners—104 sc.

RND 12: Ch 1, sc around working 3 sc in each corner moving m up to center sc of each new 3-sc corner group, sl st in first sc to join—120 sc.

RND 13: Ch 1, sc around moving m up, sl st in first sc to join.

RND 14: Rep Rnd 12—136 sc. Fasten off.

Square motif

NOTE: *See diagram on page 52.*

RND 1: (RS) With color indicated (see diagram on page 52), ch 5 (counts as tr), 19 tr in fifth ch from hook, join with sl st in top of beg ch-5 changing to MC—20 tr.

RND 2: Ch 1 (does not count as st throughout), sc in first 4 sts, (2 hdc, dc, 2 hdc) in next st, *sc in next 4 sts, (2 hdc, dc, 2 hdc) in next st; rep from * 2 more times, sl st in first sc to join—16 sc, 16 hdc, 4 dc.

RND 3: Ch 1, sc in first 6 sts, 3 sc in next st, pm in center sc of 3-sc group made to mark corner, *sc in next 8 sts, 3 sc in next st marking center sc of 3-sc group made to mark corner; rep from * 2 more times, sc in last 2 sts, sl st in first sc to join—44 sc.

RND 4: Ch 1, sc around working 3 sc in each corner moving m up, sl st in first sc to join—52 sc.

RNDS 5–6: Rep Rnd 4—68 sc. Fasten off.

Triangle motif

NOTE: *See diagram on page 52.*

ROW 1: With MC, ch 5 (counts as tr), 10 tr in fifth ch from hook, turn—11 tr.

ROW 2: (RS) Ch 1, 2 sc in first tr, sc in next 4 tr, (2 hdc, dc, 2 hdc) in next tr, sc in next 4 tr, 2 sc in last tr, turn—12 sc, 4 hdc, 1 dc.

ROW 3: Ch 1, 2 sc in first sc, sc in next 7 sts, 3 sc in next st, pm in center sc of 3-sc group just made to mark corner, sc in next 7 sts, 2 sc in last sc, turn—21 sc.

ROW 4: Ch 1, 2 sc in first sc, sc in each sc to corner, 3 sc in corner, sc in each sc to last sc, 2 sc in last sc—25 sc.

ROWS 5–6: Rep Row 4—33 sc. Fasten off.

Afghan

Foll chart for each rnd's color, make 30 octagon motifs (see Stitch Guide on page 50). Referring to diagram on page 52 for each square's center color, make 20 square motifs (see Stitch Guide). Make 4 square motifs each using colors A–E for Rnd 1 and using MC for Rnds 2–6 for all motifs. Using MC make 18 triangle motifs (see Stitch Guide).

Joining

Using layout chart and MC, weave outer lps of corresponding sc tog on WS.

Edging

With A and RS facing, join yarn in first sc of any corner octagon, *sc in next 50 sc around 3 sides of corner octagon, working along next side, work 16 sc across edge of each octagon and 17 sc evenly across edge of each triangle to next corner octagon; rep from * 3 times, sl st in first sc to join. Fasten off.

CONSTRUCTION DIAGRAM

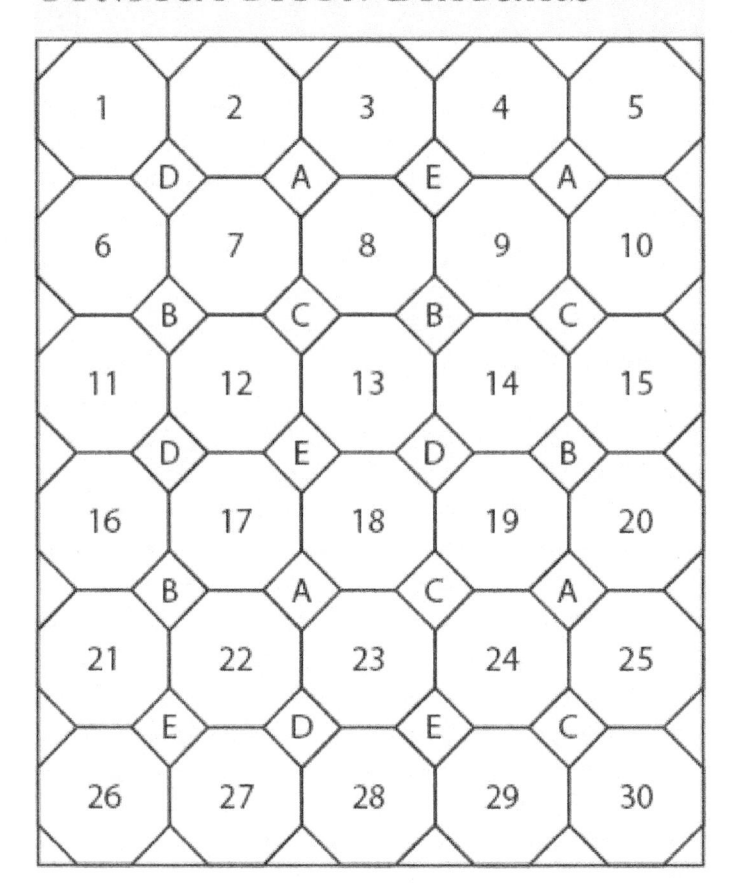

TRIANGLE MOTIF

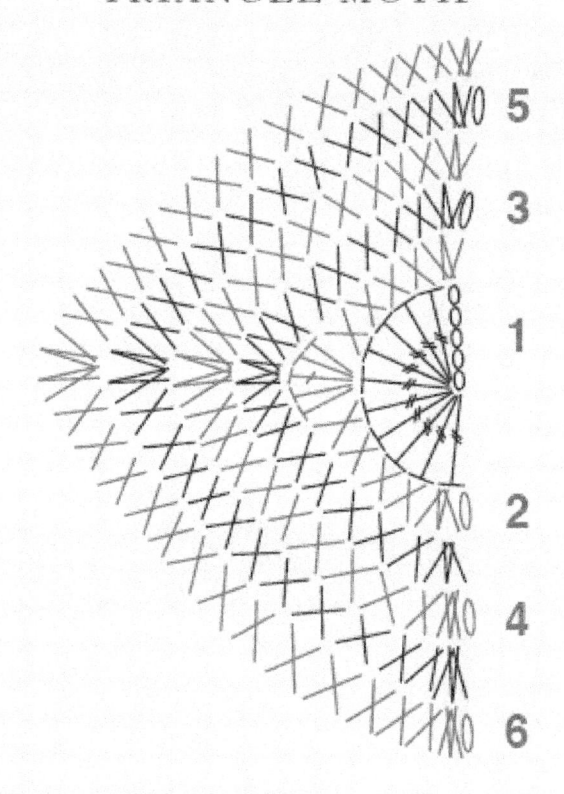

SQUARE MOTIF

OCTAGON MOTIF

- slip st (sl st)
- ◯ chain (ch)
- ✕ single crochet (sc)

- half double crochet (hdc)
- double crochet (dc)
- sc2tog (see Stitch Guide, page 50)
- beginning cluster (beg-cl)
- cluster (cl)

Big Bow Cardigan

Designer Julia Vaconsin wanted to create a fashionable garment that's easy enough for a beginner crocheter to make. The built-in scarf extends from the collar of the jacket and can be flung around your neck like a traditional scarf or tied in a bow. The jacket itself is worked from side to side, starting with the right sleeve. The sleeves are worked simply, without shaping. An asymmetrical closure adds interest to this warm, flattering cardigan that's made for enjoying the winter outdoors.

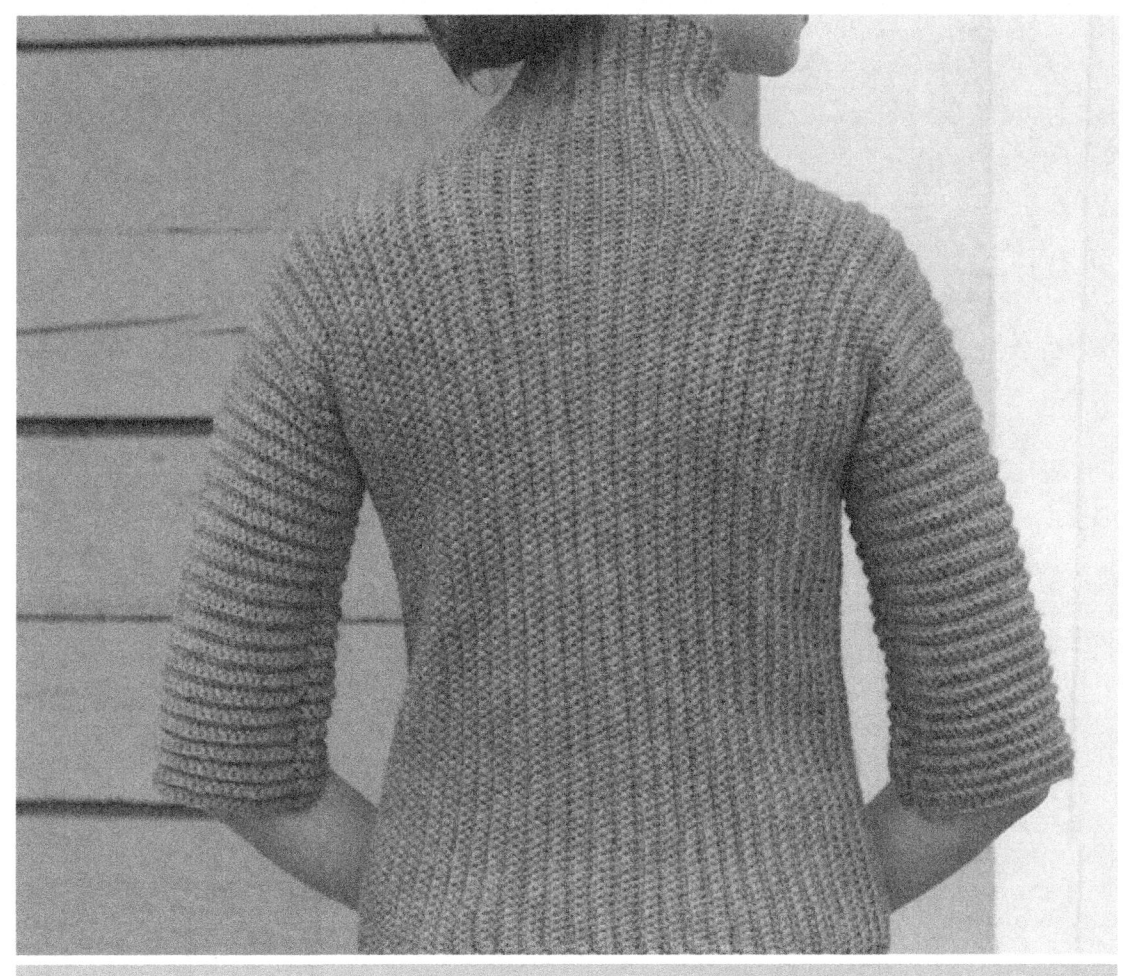

Pamela Bethel

Finished Size

35½ (41, 44½, 48, 51½)" (90 [104, 113, 122, 131] cm) bust circumference. Garment shown measures 35½" (90 cm) and is shown with 1½" (4 cm) positive ease.

Yarn

Worsted weight (#4 Medium)

shown here: Naturally Naturelle Aran 10 Ply (100% wool; 186 yd [170 m]/3½ oz [100 g]; (**4**)): #152, 7 (8, 10, 11, 12) skeins. Yarn distributed by Fiber Trends.

Hook

Size H/8 (5 mm). *Adjust hook size if necessary to obtain the correct gauge.*

Notions

Yarn needle; six (six, six, seven, seven) 1" (3 cm) buttons.

Gauge

17 sts and 14 rows = 4" (10 cm) in sc blo.

Note

+ Garment is worked from right sleeve cuff to left sleeve cuff. All sts are worked through back loop only (blo).

Cardigan

Right sleeve

Ch 55 (59, 65, 69, 75).

ROW 1: Sc in 2nd ch from hook and in each ch across, turn—54 (58, 64, 68, 74) sc.

ROWS 2–42 (46, 48, 50, 52): Ch 1, sc blo across, turn.

Right front and back

Ch 59 (61, 63, 65, 67).

ROW 1: (RS) Sc in 2nd ch from hook and in each ch, sc blo across sc, fsc (see Glossary) 58 (60, 62, 64, 66), turn—170 (178, 188, 196, 206) sts.

ROWS 2–18 (22, 24, 26, 28): Ch 1, sc blo across, turn.

Cont right front and front collar

ROW 1: (RS) Sc blo in next 85 (89, 94, 98, 103) sts (half of the body sts), fsc 22 for collar, turn—107 (111, 116, 120, 125) sts.

ROWS 2–22 (24, 26, 28, 30): Ch 1, sc blo across, turn.

NEXT ROW (BUTTON AND KEYHOLE ROW): Ch 1, sc blo in next 7 (11, 10, 6, 11) sts, *ch 4, sk next 4 sts, sc blo in next 10 (10, 11, 10, 10) sts; rep from * 5 (5, 5, 6, 6) more times, ch 10 for keyhole, sk next 10 sts, sc blo to end, turn.

NEXT ROW: Ch 1, sc blo to keyhole, work 10 sc in keyhole sp, sc blo in each sc and work 4 sc in each ch-4 sp across, turn. Work 2 rows even in sc. Fasten off.

16½ (17, 17¾, 18½, 19)"
42 (43, 45, 47, 48.5) cm

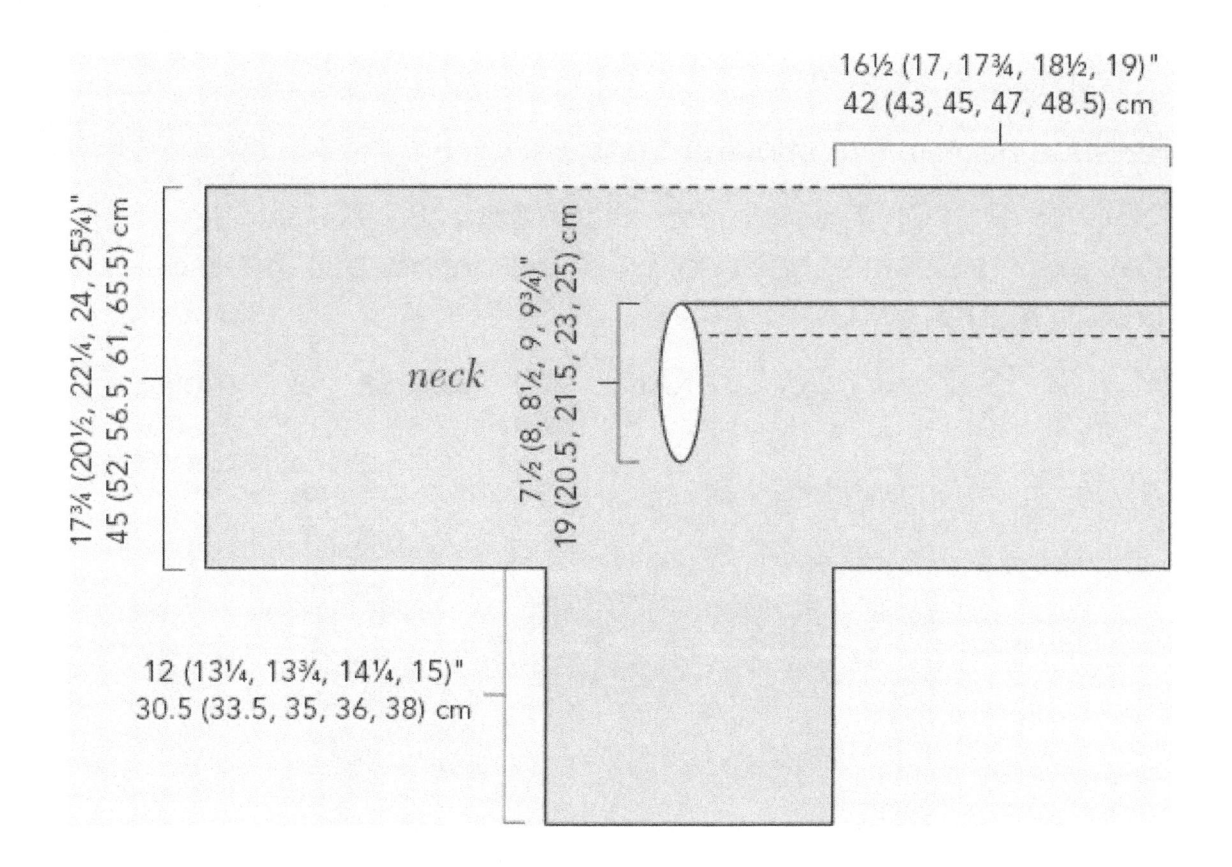

17¾ (20½, 22¼, 24, 25¾)"
45 (52, 56.5, 61, 65.5) cm

neck

7½ (8, 8½, 9, 9¾)"
19 (20.5, 21.5, 23, 25) cm

12 (13¼, 13¾, 14¼, 15)"
30.5 (33.5, 35, 36, 38) cm

Left front

Ch 86 (90, 95, 99, 104).

ROW 1: Sc in 2nd ch from hook and in each ch across, turn—85 (89, 94, 98, 103) sc.

ROWS 2–8: Ch 1, sc blo across, turn.

Set aside, but do not fasten off.

Back and back collar

ROW 1: With separate ball of yarn, ch 23, sc in 2nd ch from hook and in each ch across, then with RS of back facing and beg at neck edge cont in sc blo along right back, turn—107 (111, 116, 120, 125) sc.

ROWS 2–26 (28, 30, 32, 34)**:** Ch 1, sc blo across, turn.

RS of back will be facing. Do not fasten off, yarn will be used for scarf.

Left front and back

Replace hook in live st of left front.

ROW 1: (RS) Ch 1, sc blo across left front (85 [89, 94, 98, 103] sts), sk first 22 sts of back collar, sc blo across back to end—170 (178, 188, 196, 206) sc.

ROW 2–18 (22, 24, 26, 28): Ch 1, sc blo across. Fasten off.

Left sleeve

With RS facing, join yarn to work left sleeve over middle 54 (58, 64, 68, 74) sts as foll:

ROW 1: Leave first 57 (59, 61, 63, 65) sts of row unworked, pull up lp in 58th (60th, 62nd, 64th, 66th) st, ch 1, sc blo in next 54 (58, 64, 68, 74) sts, leave rem 58 (60, 62, 64, 66) sts unworked, turn—54 (58, 64, 68, 74) sc.

ROWS 2–42 (46, 48, 50, 52): Ch 1, sc blo across, turn. Fasten off.

Left (back) scarf

With RS facing insert hook in live st at upper edge of back collar. Work scarf as foll:

ROW 1: Ch 1, sc blo across 22 sts, turn.

ROW 2: Ch 1, sc blo across, turn.

ROWS 3–106: Rep Row 2. Fasten off.

Right (front) scarf

ROW 1: With RS facing, count 23 sts down right front from neck edge (where keyhole is), pull up lp in this st, ch 1, sc blo in next 22 sts to end of row (collar)—22 sts.

ROW 2: Ch 1, sc blo across, turn—22 sts.

ROWS 3–86: Rep Row 2. Fasten off.

Finishing

Wash and block garment to schematic measurements. Sew side and sleeve seams. Sew seam for right-back collar. Sew first 10 rows of scarf to upper edge of left front. Sew on buttons opposite buttonholes.

Luna Sweater

This sweater is richly textured with faux cables accomplished with short single crochets and back-loop-only single crochets, with a punctuating double crochet. The sweater is worked in vertical rows from top to hem, with the ribbing worked at the same time as the main body pattern.

Joe Coca

Finished Size

33 (37, 41, 45½, 50, 54)" (89 [94, 104, 115.5 127, 137] cm) bust circumference. Garment shown measures 33" (84 cm); modeled with 1" (2.5 cm) ease.

Yarn

Worsted weight (#4 Medium)

shown here: Mission Falls 136 Merino Superwash (100% merino wool, 136 yd [124 m]/1¾ oz [50 g]; **4**): #019 mist, 8 (9, 10, 11, 12, 14) skeins. Yarn distributed by CNS Yarns.

note: This yarn is unavailable. Suggested substitution: Cascade 220 superwash.

Hook

Sizes G/6 (4 mm) and F/5 (3.75 mm). *Adjust hook size if necessary to obtain the correct gauge.*

Gauge

16 sts and 19 rows = 4" (10 cm) in main body patt with larger hook, blocked.

note: Stitch gauge, especially at armhole, changes slightly after blocking due to weight of garment.

Notes

- Garment is worked in rows vertically.
- Ribbing is worked at same time as main body patt. Do not turn or chain bet ribbing and main body section of same row.
- Row 4 of main body patt includes a dc worked in sc 4 rows below. When there isn't sufficient room to work dropped st, work a sc blo instead.

+ Number of sc blo worked at end of row will vary according to location in garment.

+ Upper back of garment is about 1" (2.5 cm) wider than upper front of garment.

Stitch Guide

Short single crochet (ssc): Insert hook from bottom to top under horizontal bar below front lp of next sc, yo and pull up lp, yo and draw through 2 lps (see sidebar, page 62).

Main body patt:

NOTE: *On Row 4, final sts of a row should always be sc blo. The number of sc blo at end of a Row 4 will fluctuate throughout.*

Ch 21 for gauge swatch. Foundation row: Sc in 2nd ch from hook and each ch across.

ROW 1: Ch 1, ssc across, turn.

ROW 2: (RS) Ch 1, sc back lp only (blo) across, turn.

ROW 3: Ch 1, ssc across, turn.

ROW 4: Ch 1, sc blo in first 2 sc, *with yarn in front, dc in next sc 4 rows below, sk sc behind dc just worked, with yarn in back, sc blo in next 4 sc; rep from * to end, turn (see sidebar, page 62).

ROWS 5–6: Ch 1, ssc across, turn.

Rep Rows 1–6 for patt.

Rib patt:

ROW 1: Sl st blo across, turn.

ROW 2: (RS) Ch 1, sc blo across.

Short single crochet (ssc) is worked in the horizontal bar below the top 2 lps normally worked into. With the WS of the previous row facing you, insert hook from bottom to top under horizontal bar below front lp of next sc, yo and pull up lp, yo and draw through 2 lps.

Row 4 of Main body patt The faux cables are worked with the RS facing and into the top 2 lps of the row 4 rows below (Ssc make the top 2 lps both visible on the RS of the fabric). To create the faux cable work with yarn in front, dc in next sc 4 rows below, sk sc behind dc just worked.

Joe Coca

Continue with yarn in back, sc blo in next indicated number of sts.

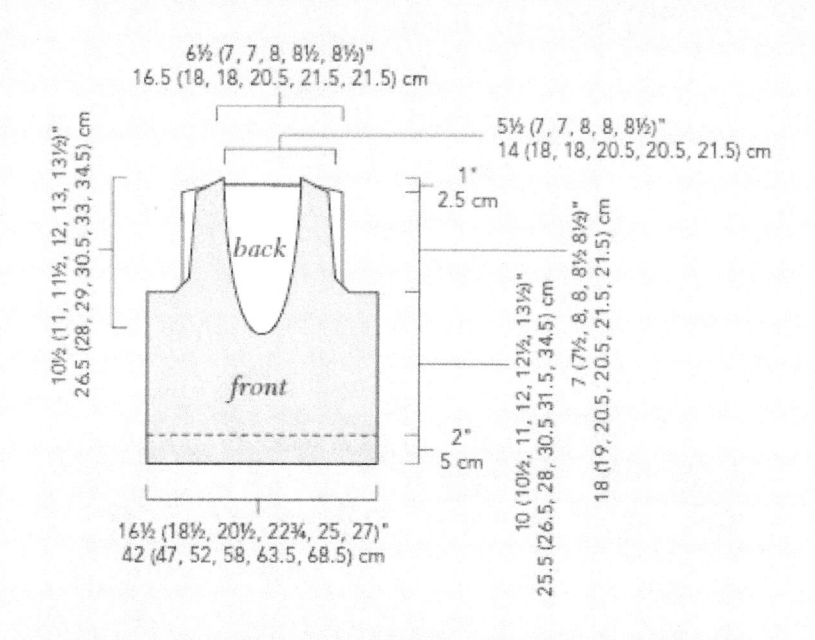

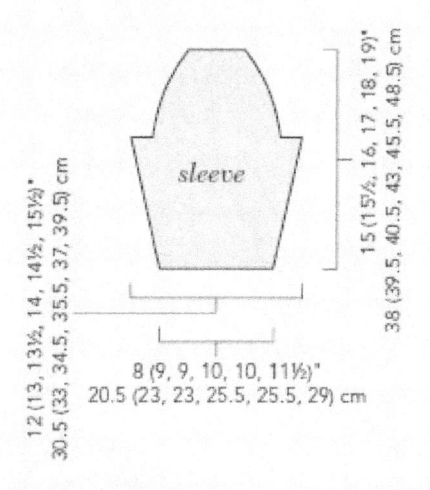

Back

Back beg at left side seam. With larger hook, ch 54 (56, 58, 62, 66, 70).

ROW 1: (RS) Sc in 2nd ch from hook and in each ch across, turn—53 (55, 57, 61, 65, 69) sc.

ROW 2: Work main body patt Row 1 (see Stitch Guide) to last 10 sts, work rib patt Row 1 (see Stitch Guide) to end, turn—43 (45, 47, 51, 55, 59) ssc, 10 sl sts.

ROW 3: Work rib patt Row 2 in first 10 sts, work main body patt Row 2 to end, turn—53 (55, 57, 61, 65, 69) sc.

ROW 4: Work main body patt Row 3 to last 10 sts, work rib patt Row 1.

ROW 5: Work rib patt Row 2 in first 10 sts, work main body patt Row 4.

ROW 6: Work main body patt Row 5 to last 10 sts, work rib patt Row 1.

ROW 7: Work rib patt Row 2 in first 10 sts, work main body patt Row 6.

Size 37" (94 cm) only:

Rep Rows 2–3.

Size 41" (104 cm) only:

Rep Rows 2–5.

Size 45½" (115.5 cm) only:

Rep Rows 2–7.

Sizes 50 (54)" (127 [137] cm) only:

Rep Rows 2–7. Rep Rows 2–3.

Shape armhole

All sizes:

ROW 1: (WS) Ch 2, sc in 2nd ch from hook, work in main body patt to last 10 sts, work in rib patt across, turn—54 (56, 58, 62, 66, 70) sts.

ROW 2: Work rib patt in first 10 sts, work main body patt to last st, 2 sc in last st—55 (57, 59, 63, 67, 71) sts.

Rep Rows 1–2 two (two, two, three, five, six) times—59 (61, 63, 69, 77, 83) sts.

Shape shoulder

ROW 1: (WS) Ch 18 (20, 22, 20, 16, 14), sc in 2nd ch from hook and in each ch across, cont in main-body patt to last 10 sts, work in rib patt to end, turn—76 (80, 84, 88, 92, 96) sts.

ROW 2: Work rib patt across first 10 sts, cont in main body patt to last st, 2 sc in last st—77 (81, 85, 89, 93, 97) sts.

ROW 3: Ch 2, sc in 2nd ch from hook, cont in main body patt to last 10 sts, cont in rib patt to end, turn—78 (82, 86, 90, 94, 98) sts.

Rep Rows 2–3. Rep Row 2—81 (85, 89, 93, 97, 101) sts. Work 5 (7, 9, 9, 9, 9) rows even in patt.

Shape neck

ROW 1: (RS) Work rib patt in first 10 sts, cont in main body patt to last 5 sts, turn leaving rem sts unworked—76 (80, 84, 88, 92, 96) sts.

Work 30 (32, 34, 36, 34, 40) rows even in patt.

Shape shoulder

ROW 1: (WS) Ch 6, sc in 2nd ch from hook and in each ch, work in main body patt to last 10 sts, work in rib patt to end, turn—81 (85, 89, 93, 97, 101) sts.

Work 4 (6, 8, 6, 8, 8) rows even in patt.

NEXT ROW: Work in rib patt across first 10 sts, work in main body patt to last 2 sts, sk next st, sc in last st—80 (84, 88, 92, 96, 100) sts.

NEXT ROW: Ch 1, sk first st, work in main body patt to last 10 sts, work in rib patt to end, turn—79 (83, 87, 91, 95, 99) sts. Rep last 2 rows 2 (4, 2, 2, 2, 2) times—75 (79, 83, 87, 91, 95) sts.

Shape armhole

ROW 1: (RS) Work in rib patt across first 10 sts, work in main body patt to last 17 (19, 21, 19, 15, 13) sts, turn leaving rem sts unworked—58 (60, 62, 68, 76, 82) sts.

ROW 2: Ch 1, sk first st, work in main body patt to last 10 sts, work in rib patt to end, turn—57 (59, 61, 67, 75, 81) sts.

ROW 3: Work in rib patt across first 10 sts, work in main body patt to last 2 sts, sk next st, sc in last st—56 (58, 60, 66, 74, 80) sts.

ROWS 4–5 (5, 5, 7, 11, 13): Rep last 2 rows—53 (55, 57, 61, 65, 69) sts.

Rep Rnd 2. Work 7 (9, 11, 15, 15, 15) rows even in patt. Fasten off.

Front

Front beg at right side seam. With larger hook, ch 54 (56, 58, 62, 66, 70).

ROW 1: (RS) Sc in 2nd ch from hook and in each ch across, turn—53 (55, 57, 61, 65, 69) sc.

ROW 2: Work main body patt to last 10 sts, work rib patt to end, turn.

ROW 3: Work rib patt across first 10 sts, work main body patt to end, turn.

Rep Rows 2–3 two (three, four, five, six, six) times.

Shape armhole

ROW 1: (WS) Ch 2, sc in 2nd ch from hook, work main body patt to last 10 sts, work rib patt to end, turn—54 (56, 58, 62, 66, 70) sts.

ROW 2: Work rib patt across first 10 sts, work main body patt to last st, 2 sc in last st—55 (57, 59, 63, 67, 71) sts.

Rep Rows 1–2 three (three, three, four, six, seven) times—61 (63, 65, 71, 79, 85) sts.

Shape right shoulder

ROW 1: (WS) Ch 16 (18, 20, 18, 14, 12), sc in 2nd ch from hook and in each ch, work main body patt to last 10 sts, work rib patt to end, turn—76 (80, 84, 88, 92, 96) sts.

ROW 2: Work rib patt across first 10 sts, work main body patt to last st, 2 sc in last st—77 (81, 85, 89, 93, 97) sts.

ROW 3: Ch 2, sc in 2nd ch from hook, work main body patt to last 10 sts, work rib patt to end, turn—78 (82, 86, 90, 94, 98) sts.

Rep Rows 2–3. Rep Row 2—81 (85, 89, 93, 97, 101) sts. Work 5 (5, 7, 7, 7, 7) rows even in patt.

Shape neck

ROW 1: (RS) Work rib patt across first 10 sts, work main body patt to last 3 (3, 3, 2, 3, 2) sts, turn leaving rem sts unworked—78 (82, 86, 91, 94, 99) sts.

ROW 2: Ch 1, sl st in first 3 (2, 2, 3, 3, 3) sts, work main body patt to last 10 sts, work rib patt to end, turn—75 (80, 84, 88, 91, 96) sts.

Rep Rows 1–2 five (seven, seven, eight, seven, nine) times. Rep Row 1 one (zero, one, zero, zero, zero) times—42 (45, 46, 48, 49, 51) sts. Work 2 (3, 2, 3, 3, 3) rows even in patt.

NEXT ROW: (WS) Ch 4 (3, 4, 4, 4, 4), sc in 2nd ch from hook and in each rem ch, work main body patt to last 10 sts, work rib patt to end, turn—45 (47, 49, 51, 52, 54) sts.

NEXT ROW: (RS) *Work rib patt across first 10 sts, work main body patt to last st, esc (see Glossary) in last st, work 2 (2, 1, 1, 2, 1) more esc, sc in last worked esc, turn*—48 (50, 51, 53, 55, 56) sts.

Rep last 2 rows 5 (7, 7, 8, 7, 8) times. Rep from * to * 1 (0, 1, 0, 0, 0) time—81 (85, 89, 93, 97, 101) sts. Work 4 (3, 6, 3, 7, 5) rows even in patt.

Shape left shoulder

NEXT ROW: (RS) Work rib patt across first 10 sts, work main body patt to last 2 sts, sk next st, sc in last st—80 (84, 88, 92, 96, 100) sts.

NEXT ROW: Ch 1, sk first st, work main body patt to last 10 sts, work rib patt to end, turn—79 (83, 87, 91, 95, 99) sts.

Rep last 2 rows 2 times—75 (79, 83, 87, 91, 95) sts.

Shape armhole

ROW 1: (RS) Work rib patt across first 10 sts, work main body patt to last 15 (17, 19, 17, 13, 11) sts, turn leaving rem sts unworked—60 (62, 64, 70, 78, 84) sts.

ROW 2: Ch 1, sk first st, work main body patt to last 10 sts, work rib patt to end, turn—59 (61, 63, 69, 77, 83) sts.

ROW 3: Work rib patt across first 10 sts, work main body patt to last 2 sts, sk next st, sc in last st—58 (60, 62, 68, 76, 82) sts.

Rep last 2 rows 2 (2, 2, 3, 5, 6) times. Rep Row 1—53 (55, 57, 61, 65, 69) sts. Work 7 (9, 11, 15, 15, 13) rows even in patt. Fasten off.

Sleeve

NOTE: *Sleeve is worked vertically, it begs and ends without rib patt. When there is no rib patt (Row 4 of main body patt) do not work dc st and work only in sc blo. When inc and dec, number of sts changes at beg (ribbing portion).*

Work dc evenly above previous dcs rather than working exact number of sc blo at beg or row. If end of a row pulls, make last st of each row in both lps of st.

With larger hook, ch 5 (5, 8, 9, 4, 4).

ROW 1: (RS) Sc in 2nd ch from hook and in each ch across, turn—4 (4, 7, 8, 3, 3) sc.

ROW 2: Work main body patt to last st, esc in last st, work 3 (3, 2, 2, 2, 2) more esc, sc in last worked esc, turn—8 (8, 10, 11, 6, 6) sts.

ROW 3: Ch 5 (5, 4, 4, 4, 4), sc in 2nd ch from hook and in each ch, work main body patt to end, turn—12 (12, 13, 14, 9, 9) sts.

ROWS 4–5: Rep Rows 2–3—20 (20, 19, 20, 15, 15) sts.

Shape cap

ROW 1: Ch 2, sc in 2nd ch from hook, work main body patt to last st, esc in last st, work 3 (3, 2, 2, 2, 2) more esc, sc in last worked esc, turn—25 (25, 23, 24, 19, 19) sts.

ROW 2: Ch 5 (5, 4, 4, 4, 4), sc in 2nd ch from hook and in each ch, work main body patt to last st, 2 sc in last st, turn—30 (30, 27, 28, 23, 23) sts.

Rep last 2 rows 1 (1, 2, 2, 3, 3) times—40 (40, 43, 44, 47, 47) sts.

NEXT ROW: *Ch 2, sc in 2nd ch from hook, work main body patt to last 10 sts, work rib patt to end, turn*—41 (41, 44, 45, 48, 48) sts.

NEXT ROW: Work rib patt across first 10 sts, work main body patt to last st, 2 sc in last st—42 (42, 45, 46, 49, 49) sts.

Rep last 2 rows 8 (9, 9, 10, 11, 13) times. Rep from * to *—59 (61, 64, 67, 72, 76) sts. Work 4 (4, 2, 4, 4, 2) rows even in patt.

NEXT ROW: *Work rib patt across first 10 sts, work main body patt to last 2 sts, sk next st, sc in last st*—58 (60, 63, 66, 71, 75) sts.

NEXT ROW: Ch 1, sk first st, work main body patt to last 10 sts, work rib patt to end, turn—57 (59, 62, 65, 70, 74) sts. Rep last 2 rows 8 (9, 10, 11, 11, 13) times. Rep from * to *—40 (40, 41, 42, 47, 47) sts. Discontinue rib patt as foll:

ROW 1: Ch 1, sk first st, work main body patt to last 4 (4, 3, 3, 3, 3) sts, turn leaving rem sts unworked—35 (35, 37, 38, 43, 43) sts.

ROW 2: Ch 1, sl st in first 4 (4, 3, 3, 3, 3) sts, work main body patt to last 2 sts, sk, next st, sc in last st, turn—30 (30, 33, 34, 39, 39) sts.

Rep last 2 rows 1 (1, 1, 1, 2, 2) times—20 (20, 25, 26, 15, 15) sts.

NEXT ROW: *Ch 1, work main body patt to last 4 (4, 3, 3, 3, 3) sts, turn leaving rem sts unworked*—16 (16, 22, 23, 12, 12) sts.

NEXT ROW: Ch 1, sl st in first 4 (4, 3, 3, 3, 3) sts, work main body patt to end, turn—12 (12, 19, 20, 9, 9) sts. Rep last 2 rows 1 (1, 2, 2, 1, 1) times, then rep from * to * 0 (0, 0, 1, 1, 1) time—4 (4, 7, 8, 3, 3) sts. Fasten off.

Finishing

Immerse all pieces completely in water, gently remove water, roll in towel to remove excess water, lay flat to dry, moving ribbing into shape, if necessary. Ribbing biases slightly. Allow to dry completely.

Seaming

With yarn needle, seam shoulders and set in sleeves. Seam sides of sleeves and sides of body.

Trim

With smaller hook, join yarn at shoulder seam.

RND 1: Ch 1, sc evenly around neckline, sl st in first sc to join.

RND 2: Ch 1, sc in each sc around, skipping sts at lower depth of neckline where necessary to accommodate curve, sl st in first sc to join. Fasten off and weave in loose ends. Block again, if necessary.

Kim Guzman has turned her love of crochet and knitting into a full-time career. You can find her work at www.kimguzman.com

Back to Basics

Weaving in *Ends*

After investing countless hours with hook and yarn in hand, fussily perfecting every stitch of a crochet project you've been envisioning—you want to be sure to finish it with as much finesse as invested in each stitch. After the seaming is done, you will have some, possibly many, dangling ends. Tuck those in professionally following these easy steps.

The first step actually comes when you start the project and every time you start a new color or ball of yarn: Leave at least 6 inches of yarn for every yarn end. A frequent rookie error is leaving stubby little tails. This bit of frugality never pays off, as little ends have a way of wiggling out later. So, you've done that, right?

Fastening off: On the last stitch, do not make a turning chain. Cut the yarn, leaving at least 6 inches. Draw the end through the last loop on the hook and pull snugly to tighten.

Weaving in loose ends: Thread the yarn tail on a blunt-ended tapestry needle; for thread or laceweight yarn, use a smaller needle with a blunt end. For bulky yarn, split fastened-off ends in half and weave in both new ends separately.

For all weights of yarn, work ends on the wrong side of the project. Where possible, weave ends into seam allowances. For solid fabric, you have other options: Weave the end in straight down the work or work the yarn in a zigzag, until the yarn is nearly used up. Work the last few stitches in the opposite direction, making sure the ends are securely fastened in and cannot be pulled back out. To ensure that the woven-in ends are not visible from the right side, weave the needle through the crochet fabric on the wrong side, and then turn the fabric over and make sure you can't see the needle from the right side. For lace fabric, work down through the solid stitch area, without carrying the yarn across open lace areas.

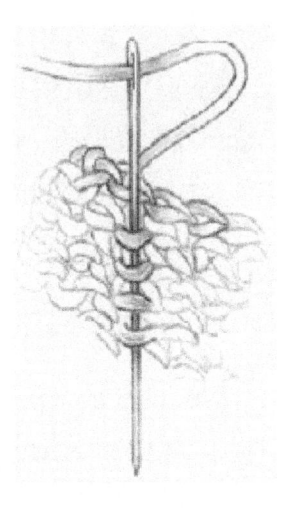

for solid fabric, work the ends into the yarns on the wrong side

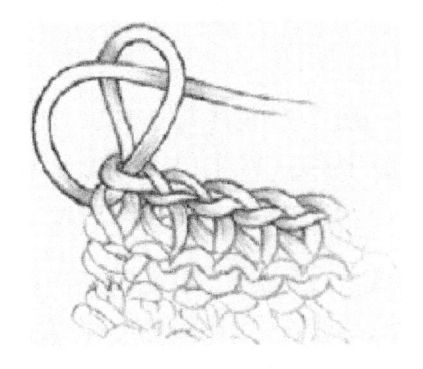

draw end through last loop on hook

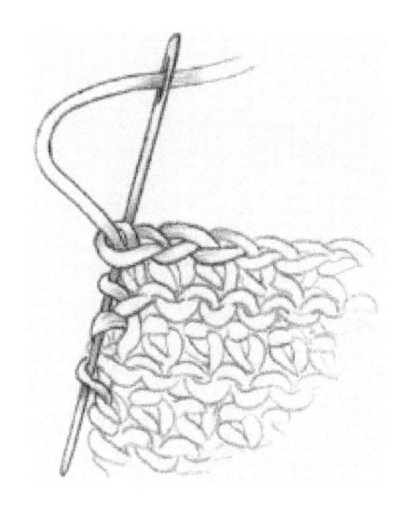

where possible, weave ends into seam allowances

When the end is woven in, trim the yarn close to the fabric. Repeat for all loose ends.

Tunisian Vest

Basic Tunisian crochet—aka afghan stitch—blossoms into an elegant honeycomb pattern when it's combined with its alter ego, Tunisian purl. Work two colors of tweedy yarn on alternate rows and you get a distinguished fabric that's ideal for a classic man's vest. In this instance, the colorwork pattern is limited to the fronts, while the back is worked in simple Tunisian crochet in a solid color. If you're unfamiliar with Tunisian crochet, find out how to do it in the primer on page 70.

© Chris Hartlove

Finished Size

39½ (44, 48, 51¾, 56½)" (100.5 [112, 122, 131.5, 143.5] cm) chest circumference, buttoned. Vest shown measures 44" (112 cm).

Yarn

DK weight (#3 Light)

shown here: Jo Sharp DK Tweed (85% wool, 10% silk, 5% cashmere; 147 yd [135 m]/1¾ oz [50 g]; 3): #405 Emporio (burgundy; MC), 6 (6, 7, 8, 9) balls; #403 emerald (green; CC), 2 (2, 2, 2) balls. Yarn distributed by JCA Inc.

Hook

Tunisian hook size H/8 (5 mm); crochet hook size H/8 (5 mm). *Adjust hook size if necessary to obtain correct gauge.*

Notions

Tapestry needle; five (five, six, six, six) ⅞" (2.2 cm) buttons.

Gauge

17 sts and 16 rows = 4" (10 cm) in tweed pattern stitch on size H/8 (5 mm) afghan hook.

Notes

- In Tunisian crochet, the RS of the piece is always facing.
- One forward row (F-Row) and one reverse row (R-Row) equals one row of Tunisian Crochet.
- It is assumed that the R-Row is always worked the same way and the instructions for the R-Row are usually omitted in the instructions.

- Always work the first stitch of every forward row into the second vertical thread from the edge.
- Always work the last st of every row as Tss, inserting hook under the final vertical thread plus the thread just behind it, before pulling through a loop.

Stitch Guide

Tunisian Simple Stitch (Tss):

FORWARD ROW: *Insert needle from right to left through second vertical strand and pull up a loop; rep from *. Do not turn work at end of row.

REVERSE ROW: Yo, pull through first st on hook, *yo, pull through 2 sts; rep from *—1 loop rem on hook.

Repeat these two rows for one row of pattern.

Tunisian Purl Stitch (Tps): With yarn in front (yfwd), insert hook from right to left under next vertical thread, yo and pull a loop through. Anchor the working thread in front of work with your thumb as you wrap and pull a loop through.

Tweed Pattern Stitch:

ROW 1-FORWARD: With A, *Tss, Tps; rep from * across, end Tss.

ROW 1-REVERSE: Yo, pull through first st on hook, *yo, pull through 2 sts; rep from * across.

ROW 2-FORWARD: With B, *Tps, Tss; rep from * across, end Tss.

ROW 2-REVERSE: Yo, pull through first st on hook, *yo, pull through 2 sts; rep from * across.

Repeat Rows 1 and 2 for pattern.

Bind Off:

AT BEG OF ROW: Form st as usual, then pull through loop on hook (forms a slip st).

AT END OF ROW: Leave the designated number of sts unworked (these sts will not be worked again).

Dec: Insert hook under two vertical strands at the same time, yarn over, and draw a loop through both strands.

Inc: Insert hook from front to back under horizontal strand that lies between loop on hook and first vertical strand, yarn over, and draw a loop through.

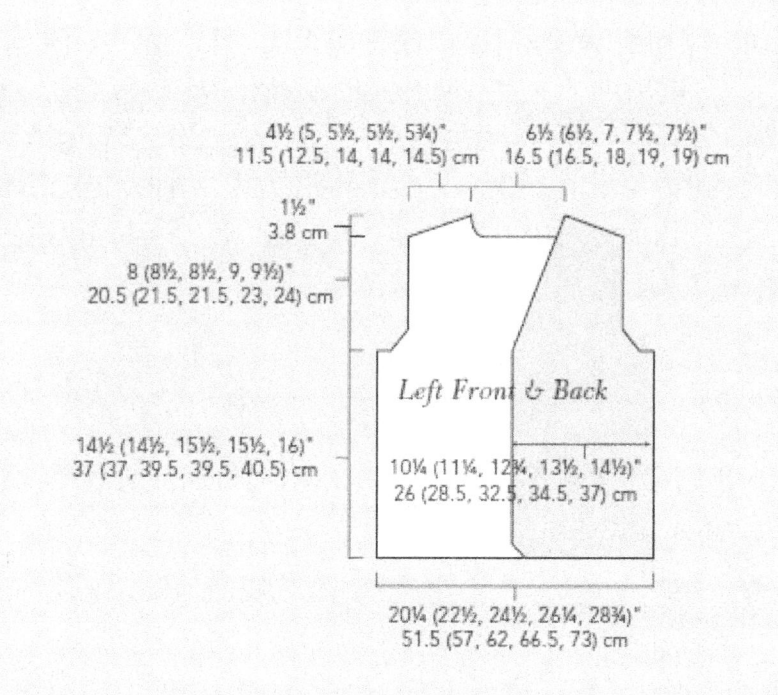

4½ (5, 5½, 5½, 5¾)"
11.5 (12.5, 14, 14, 14.5) cm

6½ (6½, 7, 7½, 7½)"
16.5 (16.5, 18, 19, 19) cm

1½"
3.8 cm

8 (8½, 8½, 9, 9½)"
20.5 (21.5, 21.5, 23, 24) cm

Left Front & Back

14½ (14½, 15½, 15½, 16)"
37 (37, 39.5, 39.5, 40.5) cm

10¼ (11¼, 12¾, 13½, 14½)"
26 (28.5, 32.5, 34.5, 37) cm

20¼ (22½, 24½, 26¼, 28¾)"
51.5 (57, 62, 66.5, 73) cm

Back

With afghan hook and MC, loosely ch 86 (96, 104, 112, 122).

FOUNDATION ROW: Skipping the first ch, pull up a loop under single thread on back of each ch—86 (96, 104, 112, 122) sts. Beg with a reverse row, work in Tss until piece measures 14½ (14½, 15½, 15½, 16)" (37 [37, 39.5, 39.5, 40.5] cm) from beg, or desired length to underarm.

Shape armholes

NOTE: *Shaping is worked on F-Rows only.*

BO 5 (5, 5, 7, 8) sts (see Stitch Guide), work in patt to last 5 (5, 5, 7, 8) sts; work R-Row as usual—76 (86, 94, 98, 106) sts rem. Cont in patt, dec 1 st each end of every row 1 (4, 4, 4, 4) time(s), then every other row 4 (4, 4, 5, 8) times—66 (70, 78, 80, 82) sts rem. Cont even until armhole measures 8 (8½, 8½, 9, 9½)" (20.5 [21.5, 21.5, 23, 24] cm).

Shape shoulders and neck

BO 3 (3, 4, 4, 4) sts, work 16 (18, 20, 20, 21) sts in Tss, BO next 28 (28, 30, 32, 32) sts for back neck, work 16 (18, 20, 20, 21) sts in Tss, BO 3 (3, 4, 4, 4) sts—16 (18, 20, 20, 21) sts rem each shoulder. Working each side separately, at armhole edge, BO 3 sts 4 (2, 0, 0, 0) times, then BO 4 sts 1 (3, 5, 5, 4) time(s), then BO 5 sts 0 (0, 0, 0, 1) time.

Right Front

With MC, ch 36 (40, 46, 50, 54). Work foundation row as for back. Beg tweed patt st.

Shape center front

Inc 1 st at the beg of the first 8 F-Rows—44 (48, 54, 58, 62) sts. Cont in patt until piece measures the same as back to armhole.

Shape armhole and V-neck

Shape armhole as for back, working shaping at end of F-Row. *At the same time,* dec 1 st at neck edge (beg of F-Row) every other row 13 (8, 17, 18, 13) times, then every 3rd row 2 (6, 0, 0, 4) times—19 (21, 24, 24, 25) sts rem for shoulder. Work even in patt until armhole measures 8 (8½, 8½, 9, 9½)" (20.5 [21.5, 21.5, 23, 24] cm) from beg of shaping.

Shape shoulders

At armhole edge, BO 3 sts 5 (3, 0, 0, 0) times, then BO 4 sts 1 (3, 6, 6, 5) time(s), then BO 5 sts 0 (0, 0, 0, 1) time.

Left Front

Work as for right front, reversing shaping; work armhole and shoulder shaping at beg of F-Rows, neck shaping at end of F-Rows.

Finishing

With yarn threaded on a tapestry needle, sew shoulder and side seams.

Edging

Mark position of 5 (5, 6, 6, 6) buttonholes, evenly spaced on left center front, with first one ½" (1.3 cm) below beg of neck shaping, last one 1" (2.5 cm) above center front notch, and the others evenly spaced between.

RND 1: With crochet hook, beg at left side seam, join MC and work sl st around lower body, front, and neck edges, ending at left side seam.

RND 2: Ch 1, skip first st, sl st into back loop of next st and every foll st, working (ch 3, skip 3 sts) for buttonholes at each marker on left front.

Beg at underarm seam, work edging around armholes. Weave in loose ends. Sew buttons to right front, opposite buttonholes. Block lightly.

Kathleen Power Johnson has been designing and teaching crochet for twenty-five years.

Beyond the Basics

Tunisian Crochet *Primer*
by KATHLEEN POWER JOHNSON

Tunisian crochet, also called afghan stitch, is cousin to both knitting and crochet. As you might expect—given the family connections—the tool used for Tunisian crochet resembles both a crochet hook and a knitting needle. The afghan hook, as it's generally called, is a knitting needle with a crochet hook on one end.

Every "row" of the basic Tunisian stitch is made by working two rows: the first row (worked from right to left and called the forward row) creates a series of stitches on the hook/needle, the second row (worked from left to right and called the reverse row) binds off the stitches until only one stitch remains. The right side of the fabric is always facing you and the right and wrong sides of the fabric are clearly different.

Tunisian Simple Stitch

Like regular crochet, every project worked in Tunisian crochet begins with a foundation chain from which a row of stitches is picked up and held along the shank of the hook/needle. To work a practice swatch, make a chain of twenty stitches. Then work the first row as follows:

- **Foundation Row (pick up stitches):** Insert the hook through the top loop of the second chain from the hook **(Figure 1)**, yarn over and draw a loop through (2 stitches on hook). *Insert the hook into the top loop of the next chain stitch and draw a loop through, leaving it on the hook. Repeat from *, drawing 1 loop through each chain stitch. When you reach the end of the chain, you should have 20 loops on your hook—one for each chain stitch.

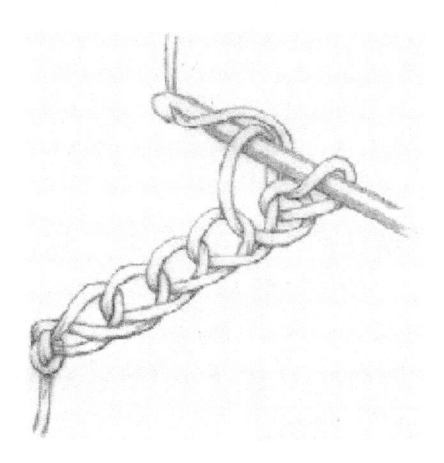

Figure 1

- **Reverse Row (complete the stitch):** Yarn over the hook and draw a loop through the first loop on the hook **(Figure 2)**. This single stitch is the equivalent of 1 turning chain; it brings the hook up to the level of the next row. *Yarn over and bring the hook through 2 stitches **(Figure 3)**. Repeat from * to end of row. As you work from left to right, you'll bind off a stitch each time you draw a loop through the 2 loops on the hook. You will end with 1 loop on the needle—this loop counts as the first stitch of the next row.

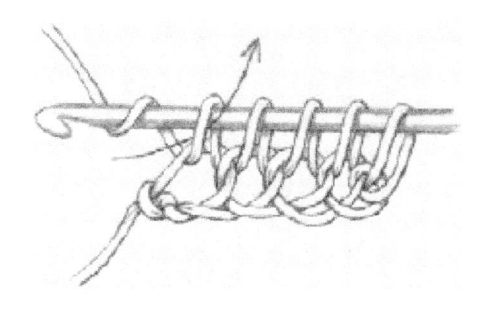

Figure 2

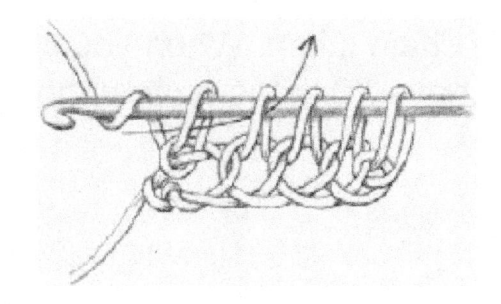

Figure 3

- **Forward Row (pick up stitches):** *Bring the hook from right to left under the first vertical bar created by the first 2 rows **(Figure 4)** and draw a loop through **(Figure 5)**, leaving it on the hook. Rep from * to end of row, drawing up a loop from under the last vertical strand.

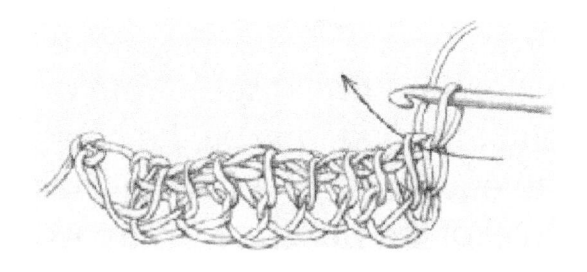

Figure 4

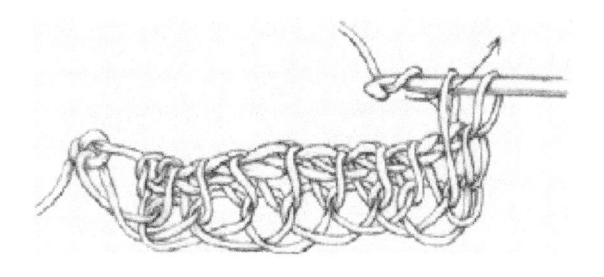

Figure 5

Work a forward row followed by a reverse row for Tunisian simple stitch. After a few rows, look closely at the fabric you've made. You'll see a series of short stacked vertical lines, separated by what looks like sideways Vs or chain stitches.

Tunisian Purl Stitch

Just like knitting, Tunisian crochet can be worked with "purl" rows for a more textured effect. The yarn is held in front of the work on the first forward row to create horizontal bumps. The second row of the sequence, a reverse row, is worked just as for Tunisian simple stitch.

- **Forward Row (pick up stitches):** Bring the yarn to the front of your work, holding it below and in front of the hook. *Insert the hook from right to left through the first vertical strand, as in the second pass of the forward row of the simple stitch. Yarn over by bringing the yarn up, behind, and then over the hook from back to front **(Figure 6)**. Draw a loop through, leaving it on the hook. Repeat from *. As you work from one vertical strand to the next, the yarn you're working with will lie over the vertical strand being worked.

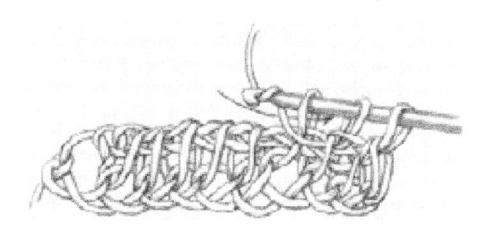

Figure 6

- **Reverse Row (complete the stitch):** Work as for the reverse row of Tunisian simple stitch.

When you look at the fabric made with Tunisian purl stitch, you'll still see the vertical lines made in simple stitch, but this time they will be interrupted by short horizontal bumps made from the strand of yarn that crosses over the vertical strands as you work.

Increasing

To increase a stitch at the beginning of a forward row (worked right to left), pick up an extra loop by inserting the hook from front to back under the horizontal strand that lies between the loop on the hook and the first vertical strand **(Figure 7)**, then yarn over and pull a loop through. Work as usual in the next vertical strand. To increase at the other end of the row, pull an extra loop by inserting the hook under the last horizontal strand in the row, just before the last vertical strand.

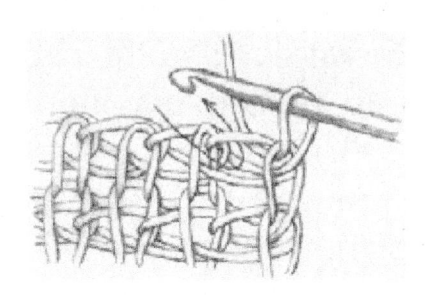

Figure 7

Decreasing

To decrease a stitch, insert the hook under two vertical strands at the same time **(Figure 8)**, yarn over and draw a loop through both strands.

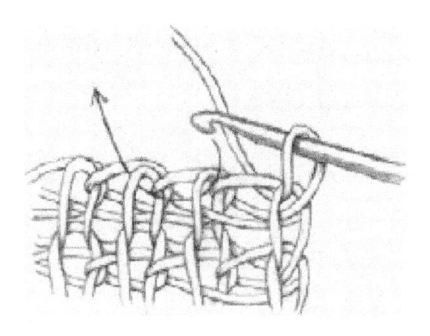

Figure 8

Come-and-Play Cardigan

You can come and play with colors as you crochet this granite stitch children's cardigan. Three bright and cheerful hues are perfect for boys and girls alike. For a different look, you can replace these colors with three soft pastels, three neutrals, or three earth tones.

Kathryn Martin

Finished Size

25½ (27½, 29½, 30½)" (65 [70, 75, 77.5] cm) chest circumference, to fit 2 (4, 6, 8) years old. Garment shown measures 27½" (70 cm).

Yarn

Worsted weight (#4 Medium)

shown here: Plymouth Yarn Encore Worsted (75% acrylic, 25% wool; 200 yds [183 m]/3½ oz [100 g]; 【4】): #4045 blue (A), 1 (2, 2, 2) skeins; #0174 red (B), 1 (1, 2, 2) skeins; #0054 green (C), 1 (1, 2, 2) skeins.

Hook

H/8 (5 mm) and J/10 (6 mm). *Adjust hook size if necessary to obtain correct gauge.*

Notions

Separating zipper, 12 (14, 16, 16)" (30.5 [35.5, 40.5, 40.5] cm); yarn needle; sewing needle; matching sewing thread.

Gauge

16 sts and 16 rows = 4" (10 cm) in granite st with larger hook.

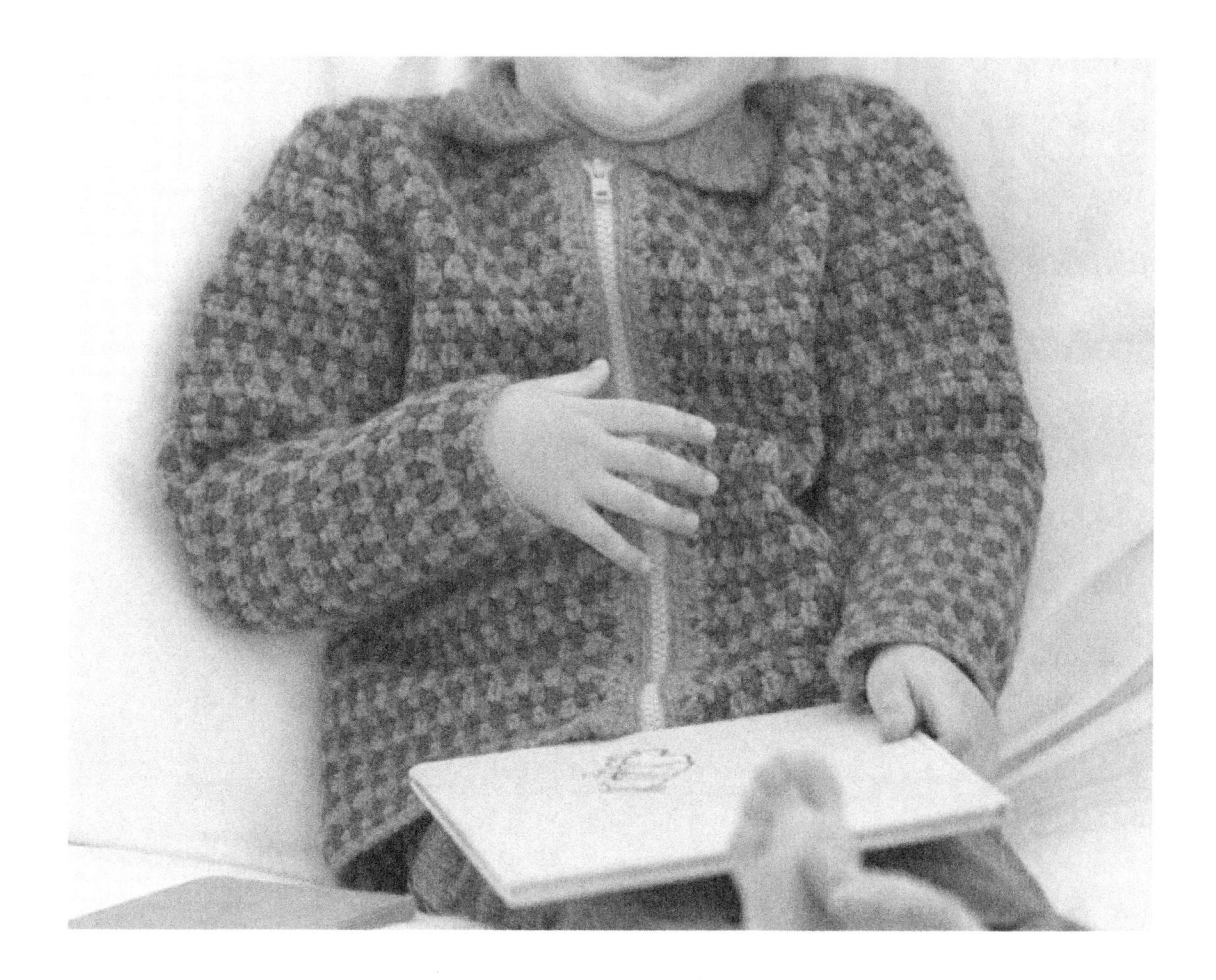

Notes

- Stitch totals given at the end of a row include each chain-one and single crochet.

Stitch Guide

Granite st (worked over an even number of sts):

Always start and end each row with a sc.

ROW 1: Sc in 2nd ch from hook, *ch 1, sk next ch, sc in next ch; rep from * to last ch, sc in last ch.

ROW 2: Ch 1 (does not count as st), sc in first sc, *ch 1, sk next sc, sc in ch-sp*; rep from * ending with sc in last st.

Rep Row 2 for patt.

Color Pattern:

1 row with A, 1 row with B, 1 row with C. Rep these 3 rows for patt.

Double increase (dbl inc):

Inc 2 by working (sc, ch 1, sc) in st indicated.

Decrease (dec):

Edge dec: Work sl sts at beg of row and sk sts at end of row (sl sts and skipped sts are not worked in next row).

Double dec (dbl dec): Dec 2 sts by working sc3tog (see Glossary) over (ch-sp, sc, ch-sp).

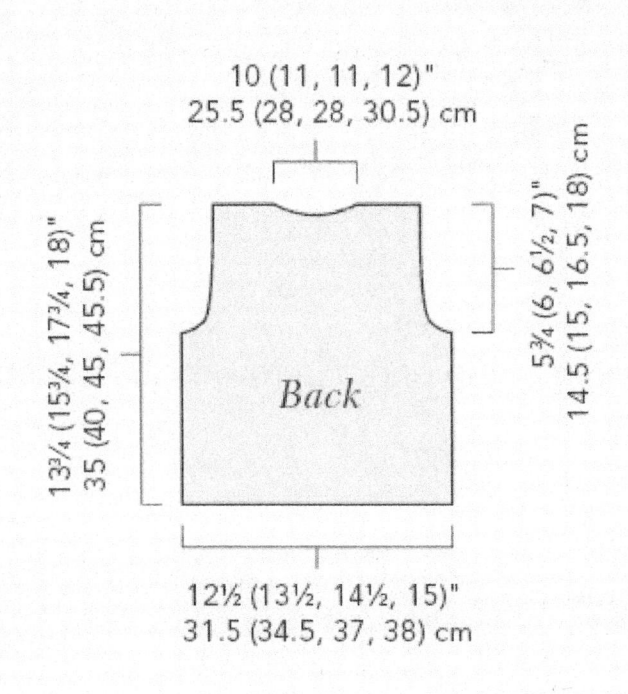

Back

10 (11, 11, 12)"
25.5 (28, 28, 30.5) cm

5¾ (6, 6½, 7)"
14.5 (15, 16.5, 18) cm

13¾ (15¾, 17¾, 18)"
35 (40, 45, 45.5) cm

12½ (13½, 14½, 15)"
31.5 (34.5, 37, 38) cm

2½ (2¾, 3, 3¼)"
6.5 (7, 7.5, 8.5) cm

12 (14, 16, 16)"
30.5 (35.5, 40.5, 40.5) cm

Left Front

6 (6½, 7, 7½)"
15 (16.5, 18, 19) cm

10½ (12, 13, 14)"
26.5 (30.5, 33, 35.5) cm

2¾ (3, 3¼, 3½)"
7 (7.5, 8.5, 9) cm

8¾ (9½, 10½, 11½)"
22 (24, 26.5, 29) cm

Sleeve

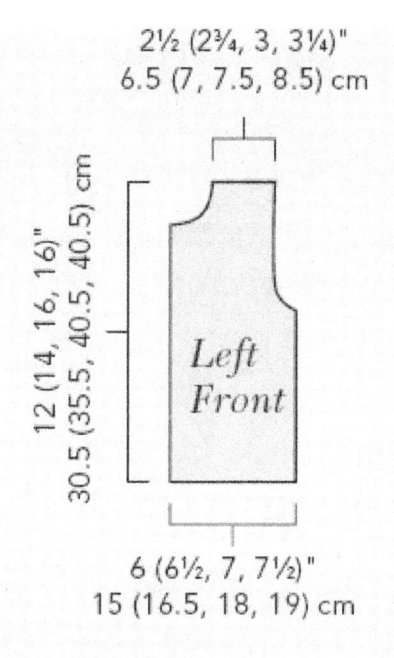

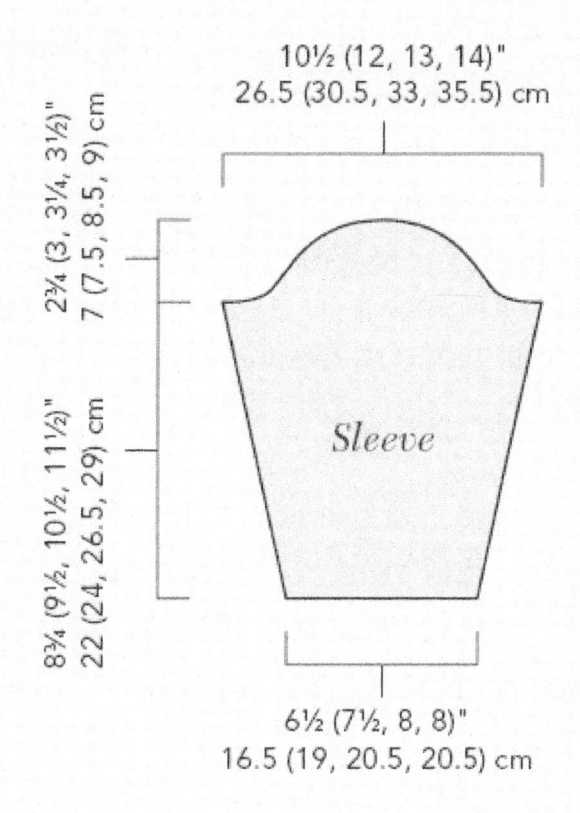

6½ (7½, 8, 8)"
16.5 (19, 20.5, 20.5) cm

Back

With larger hook and A, ch 51 (55, 59, 61).

ROW 1: Work Row 1 of granite st patt (see Stitch Guide, page 74), turn.

ROW 2: Join B. Work Row 2 of granite st patt, turn.

Cont in st patt and color patt until piece measures 7¾ (9¼, 10½, 10½)" (19.5 [23.5, 26.5, 26.5] cm).

Shape armhole

ROW 1: (RS) Sl st in first 3 (3, 4, 4) sts, ch 1, cont in est patt to last 3 (3, 4, 4) sts, leave rem sts unworked, turn—44 (48, 50, 52) sts.

Sizes 27½ (29½)" (70 [75] cm) only

On next row, sl st in first st, ch 1, cont in est patt to last st, turn, leaving rem st unworked—46 (48) sts.

All sizes

Work 1 edge dec (see Stitch Guide) at each side every 2nd row, 2 times, then every 4th row 1 (1, 1, 2) time(s)—38 (40, 42, 44) sts. Cont in patt until piece measures 13½ (15¼, 17, 17½)" (34 [39, 43, 44.5] cm).

Shape back neck

ROW 1: (RS) Work 12 (13, 14, 15) sts in est patt, sl st in next 14 sts, work rem 12 (13, 14, 15) sts in patt, turn.

Cont working each side of neck separately.

Left neck and shoulder

ROW 1: Work 9 (10, 11, 12) sts in est patt, dbl dec (see Stitch Guide) over rem 3 sts, turn—10 (11, 12, 13) sts.

Work even in patt for 1 (1, 2, 1) rows. Fasten off.

Right neck and shoulder

ROW 1: Join yarn in first st of Row 1 of back neck, dbl dec over first 3 sts, cont in est patt across, turn—10 (11, 12, 13) sts. Work even in patt for 1 (1, 2, 1) rows. Fasten off.

Left Front

With larger hook and A, ch 25 (27, 29, 31). Work granite st in color patt until work measures 7¾ (9¼, 10½, 10½)" (19.5 [23.5, 26.5, 26.5] cm).

Shape armhole

ROW 1: (RS) Sl st in each of first 3 (3, 4, 4) sts, ch 1, cont in granite st patt across, turn—21 (23, 24, 26) sts.

ROW 2: Work even in patt, turn. Work 1 edge dec (see Stitch Guide) at armhole edge every RS row 2 (3, 3, 2) times—19 (20, 21, 24) sts.

Work 1 edge dec at armhole edge every 4th row 1 (1, 1, 2) time(s)—18 (19, 20, 22) sts. Work even in patt until work measures 12 (14, 16, 16)" (30.5 [35.5, 40.5, 40.5] cm), ending with WS row.

Shape front neck:

NEXT ROW: (RS) Work in patt, using edge dec, dec 2 (2, 2, 3) sts for neck—16 (17, 18, 19) sts. On foll row, work granite st patt to last 4 sts, dbl dec, sc in last st—14 (15, 16, 17) sts.

Work in granite st patt to last 4 sts, dbl dec, sc in last st every 2nd row 2 times—10 (11, 12, 13) sts. Cont in granite st patt until piece measures same length as back. Fasten off.

Right Front

With larger hook and A, ch 25 (27, 29, 31). Work in granite st and color patt until piece measures 7¾ (9¼, 10½, 10½)" (19.5 [23.5, 26.5, 26.5] cm).

Shape armhole

ROW 1: (RS) Work in patt to last 3 (3, 4, 4) sts, turn, leaving rem sts unworked—21 (22, 24, 26) sts.

Work 1 edge dec at armhole edge 2 (3, 3, 2) times—19 (20, 21, 24) sts. Then work 1 edge dec st every 4th row at armhole edge 1 (1, 1, 2) time(s)—18 (19, 20, 22) sts. Work even in patt until work measures 12 (14, 16, 16)" (30.5 [35.5, 40.5, 40.5] cm).

Shape front neck

Using edge dec, dec 2 (2, 2, 3) sts at beg of row for neck—16 (17, 18, 19) sts. On foll row, dbl dec at neck—14 (15, 16, 17) sts. Dbl dec at neck edge every 2nd row 2 times—10 (11, 12, 13) sts.

Cont until piece measures same length as back. Fasten off.

Sleeves

With larger hook and A, ch 27 (31, 33, 33). Foll the color patt.

Size 27½" (70 cm) only:

Work 3 rows in patt st.

NEXT ROW: Work 14 sts in patt, [2 sc in next st] twice, work in patt across—32 sts.

All sizes:

Work 7 (7, 7, 5) rows even in patt.

NEXT ROW: Dbl inc in first st (see Stitch Guide, page 74), work in patt to last st, dbl inc—30 (36, 36, 36). Cont in patt, double inc at each end every 8th (8th, 8th, 6th) row 3 (3, 4, 5) times—42

(48, 52, 56) sts. Work even in patt until work measures 8¾ (9½, 10½, 11½)" (22 [24, 26.5, 29] cm).

Shape sleeve cap

ROW 1: Sl st in first 3 (5, 5, 5) sts, work in patt to last 3 (5, 5, 5) sts, turn, leaving rem sts unworked—36 (38, 42, 46) sts.

Using edge dec, dec 2 sts at each edge every 2nd row 3 times—24 (26, 30, 34) sts. Work 2 (2, 2, 1) row(s) even in patt. Using edge dec, dec 2 sts at each side every 2nd row 3 (1, 1, 1) time(s)—12 (22, 26, 30) sts.

Size 25½" (65 cm) only:

Fasten off.

Sizes 27½ (29½, 30¾)" (70 [75, 77.5] cm) only:

Work 1 (1, 2) row(s) even in patt. Using edge dec, dec 2 sts at each side every 2nd row 2 (3, 4) times—14 (14, 14) sts.

Size 29½" (75 cm) only:

Work 1 row even in patt.

Sizes 27½ (29½, 30¾)" (70 [75, 77.5] cm) only:

Fasten off.

Finishing

With smaller hook, A, and WS facing, join yarn with sl st to right-front neck edge.

ROW 1: Ch 1, sc in each st to hem edge, turn.

ROW 2: Ch 1, sc in first st, sc in each st to neck edge. Fasten off.

Rep Rows 1–2 for left front, beg with hem edge. Block pieces lightly, if needed. With yarn needle and A, sew shoulder seams and side seams.

Collar

ROW 1: With smaller hook, A, and WS facing, join yarn with sl st to left-front neck edge, ch 1, sc in same st, sc in each st across to right-front neck edge, turn.

ROW 2: Ch 1, sc in each sc across, turn.

Rep Row 2 until collar measures 2¼ (2¾, 2¾, 3¼)" (6 [7, 7, 8] cm). Fasten off and weave in loose ends. Block collar. With sewing needle and matching sewing thread, sew in zipper. With yarn needle and A, sew sleeve seams. Sew sleeves in armholes.

Annette Petavy dreams up crochet designs at her home near Lyon, France. See more of her work at annettepetavy.com.

Beyond the Basics

Finding *Closure*
by DORA OHRENSTEIN

A crocheted garment isn't finished until you put on the perfect closure. For those without sewing experience, that part can be scary. To get over the hurdle myself, I consulted my friend Leslie Johnson, a graduate of New York's famed Fashion Institute of Technology. The detailed steps she taught me make attaching closures very methodical and clear, never to be feared again. The methods involve handsewing only, no machines. If you can master these few simple steps, you'll be able to choose whether to use buttons, a zipper, a frog, or any number of other cool closures to give your garments a professional look.

Stabilizing the Fabric

The first step before attaching closures is to stabilize the edge of the crocheted fabric. This not only makes sewing easier, but also creates a more stable fabric for attaching the closure. Without it, the weight of a zipper or another closure could pull the fabric out of shape.

To stabilize, first work a row of single crochet along the edge **(Figure 1). NOTE:** In these samples, contrasting yarn is used to make the technique visible; you'll want to make yours invisible by using the same color as the garment.

Figure 1

Then work a row of surface crochet chain stitches on the wrong side of the crochet piece, along the bottom edge of the row just completed **(Figure 2)**.

Figure 2

Once these steps are done, you're ready to attach the closure of your choice.

Zippers

Zippers are fabulous for outerwear, making them more chic or adding a sporty touch. Zippers are much easier to install than many people think. The method of inserting a zipper depends on the zipper's function and how you want it to look. The most common use for a zipper in knitwear is to close the front of a jacket or cardigan. For this, you'll need a separating zipper, which opens all the way to the bottom, rather than a standard zipper, which remains attached at the bottom. A separating zipper is what you'll typically find on outerwear.

Decide if you want the zipper to be visible from the outside of the garment. If so, consider whether you want the zipper to be the same color as the garment, or contrasting. Choose a zipper that matches the weight of the fabric and the function of the garment—a heavier one for a jacket or a daintier one for a sweater. In either case, use a plastic zipper; avoid metal, which can snag fabric. Be sure the zipper is the correct length because it is difficult to shorten a separating zipper. It's best to make the garment to suit one of the available lengths. (If you are using a standard zipper, for a side closure on a skirt, for instance, you can shorten it easily: sew a few stitches across the zipper's teeth, right where you want the bottom of the zipper to close, then cut the zipper to a point about one inch longer.)

To sew in a zipper, first stabilize the edges of the fabric as described on page 77. Then pin the zipper to the garment. With the zipper closed, lay the front side of it down on the wrong side of the garment, over the surface crochet stitches. Pin the bottom of the zipper to the bottom of the garment. The top of the zipper should be about half an inch from the top of the opening so it doesn't cause the edge of the fabric to pull away from the body.

For a visible zipper, allow the teeth and just a bit of zipper fabric to extend beyond the edge of the crochet fabric.

To make the zipper invisible from the front, line up the teeth right at the edge of the crochet fabric.

Now, using sewing thread that matches the color of the fabric, handsew the zipper in place. Use a backstitch (see page 107) and sew right along the surface crochet stitches to get an even, straight line of stitches **(Figure 3)**.

Figure 3

At the top of the zipper, fold the zipper fabric down on the diagonal as shown **(Figure 4)**, cut off any excess fabric, and sew along the diagonal.

Figure 4

In this sample of an invisible separating zipper, you'll see that the zipper tab at the top protrudes, as it must **(Figure 5)**.

Figure 5

This inset zipper is visible, showing the surface crochet stitches in a contrasting color **(Figure 6)**.

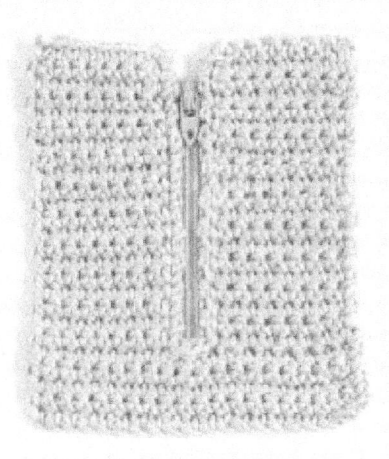

Figure 6

Hook and Eye

A fine-looking invisible closure, less bulky than a zipper, can be made using hooks and eyes. Rather than sewing these bits of metal right on to the crochet fabric, sew them to a piece of ribbon. Grosgrain ribbon works well for jackets or cardigans. If your crocheted fabric is more delicate, use a lighter-weight ribbon such as satin or silk, ⅜" (1 cm) or ⅝" (1.5 cm) in width. Cut the ribbon two inches longer than the opening on the garment. Pin the ribbon to the crocheted fabric on both sides of the opening, with one inch extending at top and bottom. Place pins at regular intervals along the ribbon only where you want the hooks and eyes to be **(Figure 1)**. Line up pins exactly from one side to the other. The top- and bottom-most hook and eye should be half an inch or less away from the top and bottom edges.

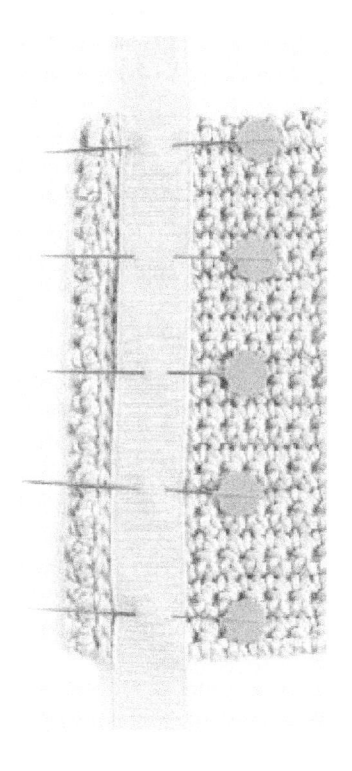

Figure 1

Remove the ribbon from the crochet and sew the hooks and eyes in place following the pins **(Figure 2)**. The hooks are sewn facedown **(Figure 3)**, the eyes faceup. Line up the metal loops at the bottom of each hook and eye right at the edge of the ribbon. To stabilize the hooks and eyes, make a few stitches at the bottom of each, between the metal loops. Then sew down the metal loops **(Figure 4)**.

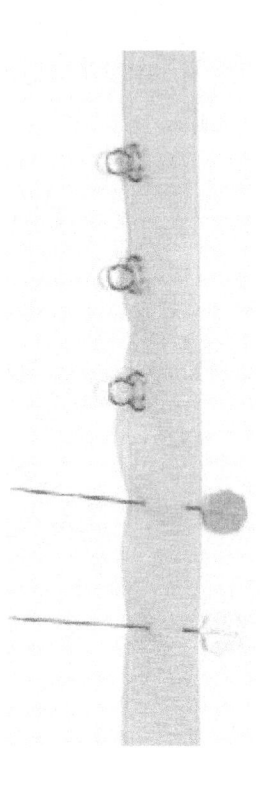

Figure 2

Figure 3

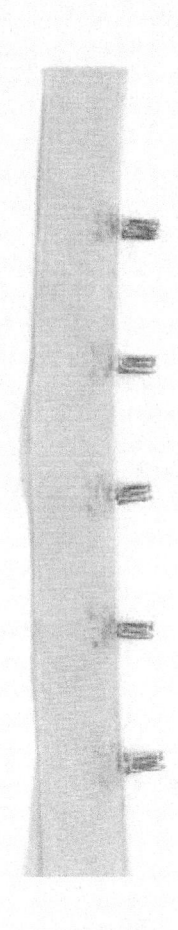

Figure 4

Pin the ribbon to the wrong side of the crochet fabric, with the hooks facing up. Hooks are a bit longer than eyes, so pin the ribbon on the hook side farther from the edge than on the eye side. Cut the ribbon to same length as crochet fabric with a seam allowance. Fold seam and pin in place.

Using thread that matches the ribbon, handsew with small whipstitches **(Figure 5).** Pick up only a few strands of the yarn so that the sewing thread will not show on the garment's right side. Sew all along the edges of the ribbon: top, bottom, and both sides.

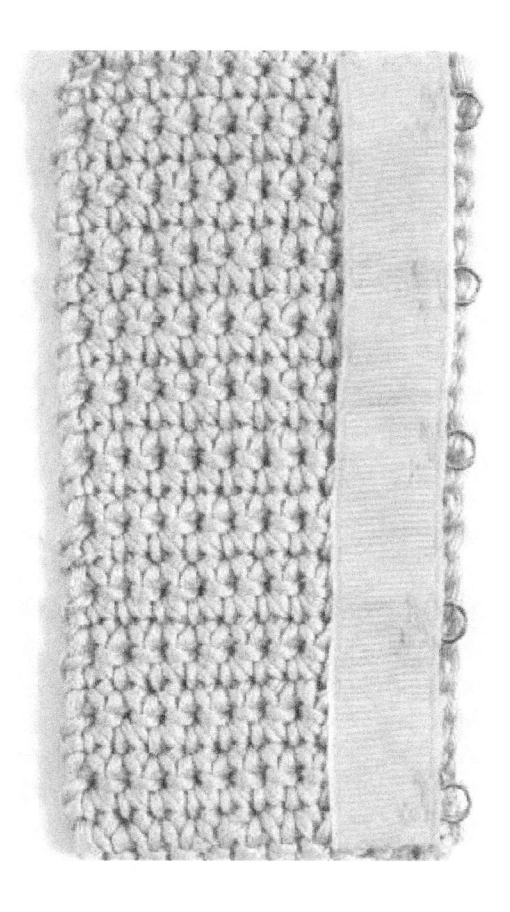

Figure 5

Dora Ohrenstein is the founder and editor of CrochetInsider.com and author of *Creating Crochet Fabric* (Lark Books).

Stone Path Hat

Whether your winter time with family is spent trekking along the timberland trails or strolling along the boulevard, this hat will keep everyone, even the tot on your shoulders, warm and fashionable.

Kathryn Martin

Finished Size

18½ (19, 20, 21, 22)" (47 [48, 51, 53, 56] cm) head circumference. Choose size that is ½–2" (1–5 cm) smaller than actual head circumference. Length: 6½–7 (7–7½, 7½–7¾, 7½–8, 8–8½)" (16.5–18 [18–19, 19–19.5, 19–20, 20–21.5] cm). Hat shown is size 20" (51 cm).

Yarn

Sockweight (#1 Superfine)

shown here: Schoeller Stahl Baby Micro (51% virgin wool, 49% acrylic; 107 yd [97.5 m]/¾ oz [25 g]; **1**): #01 white, 3 (3, 4, 4, 4) balls. Yarn distributed by Skacel.

Hook

Size E/4 (3.5 mm). *Adjust hook size if necessary to obtain correct gauge.*

Notions

Yarn needle.

Gauge

22 sts and 21 rows = 4" (10 cm) in main body patt.

Download the diagram for this project here.

Note

+ Hat is worked in rnds from top down. The brim is optional and is added at the end. When working around FPtr sts of cable, pry sts apart as the latter two may be "buried" beneath. The term "post st(s)" refers to both FPdc and FPtr. In first rnd of brim, because all post sts are worked around posts of sc, pay attention to placement of non-post sts.

Stitch Guide

(See stitch diagram on page 83)

Front post double crochet (FPdc): Yo, insert hook from front to back to front around post of st indicated and pull up a lp, [yo, draw through first 2 lps on hook] twice.

Front post treble crochet (FPtr): Yo twice, insert hook from front to back to front around post of st indicated and pull up a lp, [yo, draw through 2 lps on hook] 3 times.

Cable (uses posts of next 4 sts): Sk next 2 sts, FPtr around next 2 sts, working in front of both FPtr just made, FPtr around first skipped st, FPtr around 2nd skipped st.

Popcorn (pc): Work 5 sc in st indicated, drop lp from hook, insert hook in top of first sc, pick up dropped lp and pull through lp on hook, ch 1 to close.

Adjustable ring: Place slipknot on hook, leaving 4" tail. Wrap tail around your fingers to form a ring. Work sts of first rnd into ring. At end of first rnd, pull tail to tighten ring.

Main body pattern: (multiple of 34 [35, 37, 38, 40] sts)

RND 1: Ch 1, FPdc around first FPdc, *cable, FPdc around next FPdc, **sc in next 3 sc, cable, sc in next 3 sc**, pc in next sc; rep from ** to ** once, FPdc around next FPdc, cable, FPdc around next FPdc, sc in next 1 (2, 4, 5, 7) sc, FPdc around next FPdc; rep from * twice more omitting last FPdc of 2nd rep, sl st in top of first FPdc to join—12 cables, 12 FPdc, 3 pc, 39 (42, 48, 51, 57) sc.

RND 2: Ch 1, FPdc around first 6 post sts, *sc in next 2 sc, sk next sc, FPdc around next 2 FPtr, sc in top of same FPtr (last FPtr that FPdc was made around, here and throughout), sc in top of next FPtr, FPdc around same FPtr (same FPtr that last sc was made in, here and throughout), FPdc around next FPtr, sk next sc, sc in next 2 sc**, sc in next pc, rep from * to ** once, FPdc around next 6 post sts, sc in next 1 (2, 4, 5, 7) sc, FPdc around next 6 post sts; rep from

* twice omitting last 6 FPdc of 2nd rep, sl st in top of first FPdc to join—60 FPdc, 42 (45, 51, 54, 60) sc.

RND 3: Ch 1, FPdc around first FPdc, *cable, FPdc around next FPdc, **sc in next sc, sk next sc, FPdc around next 2 FPdc, sc in top of same FPdc, sc in next 2 sc, sc in top of next FPdc, FPdc around same FPdc, FPdc around next FPdc, sk next sc, sc in next sc**, pc in next sc, rep from ** to ** once, FPdc around next FPdc, cable, FPdc around next FPdc, sc in next 1 (2, 4, 5, 7) sc, FPdc around next FPdc; rep from * twice omitting last FPdc of 2nd rep, sl st in top of first FPdc to join—6 cables, 36 FPdc, 3 pc, 39 (42, 48, 51, 57) sc.

RND 4: Ch 1, FPdc around first 6 post sts, *sc in next sc, FPdc around next 2 FPdc, sc in next 4 sc, FPdc around next 2 FPdc, sc in next sc**, sc in next pc; rep from * to ** once, FPdc around next 6 post sts, sc in next 1 (2, 4, 5, 7) sc, FPdc around next 6 post sts; rep from * twice omitting last 6 FPdc of 2nd rep, sl st in top of first FPdc to join—60 FPdc, 42 (45, 51, 54, 60) sc.

RND 5: Ch 1, FPdc around first FPdc, *cable, FPdc around next FPdc, **sc in next sc, sc in top of next FPdc, FPdc around same FPdc, FPdc around next FPdc, sk next sc, sc in next 2 sc, sk next sc, FPdc around next 2 FPdc, sc in top of same FPdc, sc in next sc**, pc in next sc; rep from ** to ** once, FPdc around next FPdc, cable, FPdc around next FPdc, sc in next 1 (2, 4, 5, 7) sc, FPdc around next FPdc; rep from * twice omitting last FPdc of 2nd rep, sl st in top of first FPdc to join—6 cables, 36 FPdc, 3 pc, 39 (42, 48, 51, 57) sc.

RND 6: Ch 1, FPdc around first 6 post sts, *sc in next 2 sc, sc in top of next FPdc, FPdc around same FPdc, FPdc around next FPdc, sk next 2 sc, FPdc around next 2 FPdc, sc in top of same FPdc, sc in next 2 sc**, sc in next pc; rep from * to ** once, FPdc around next 6 post sts, sc in next 1 (2, 4, 5, 7) sc, FPdc around next 6 post sts, rep from * twice omitting last 6 FPdc of 2nd rep, sl st in top of first FPdc to join—60 FPdc, 42 (45, 51, 54, 60) sc.

Rep Rnds 1–6 for patt.

Hat

Beg at crown with an adjustable ring (see Stitch Guide).

RND 1: (RS) 12 hdc in adjustable ring, sl st in first hdc to join, tighten ring—12 hdc.

RND 2: Ch 1, *FPdc (see Stitch Guide) around first hdc, working behind FPdc just made, sc in top of same hdc; rep from * in each hdc around, sl st in top of first FPdc to join—12 FPdc, 12 sc.

RND 3: Ch 1, FPdc around first FPdc, [2 sc in next sc, FPdc around next FPdc] 3 times, sc in next sc, *FPdc around next FPdc, [2 sc in next sc, FPdc around next FPdc] 3 times, sc in next sc; rep from * once, sl st in top of first FPdc to join—12 FPdc, 21 sc.

RND 4: Ch 1, 2 FPdc around first FPdc, [sc in next 2 sc, 2 FPdc around next FPdc] 3 times, sc in next sc, *2 FPdc around next FPdc, [sc in next 2 sc, 2 FPdc around next FPdc] 3 times, sc in next sc; rep from * once, sl st in top of first FPdc to join—24 FPdc, 21 sc.

RND 5: Ch 1, FPdc around each FPdc and sc in each sc around, sl st in top of first FPdc to join.

RND 6: Ch 1, FPdc around first 2 FPdc, *[2 sc in next sc, sc in next sc, FPdc around next 2 FPdc] 3 times, sc in next sc**, FPdc around next 2 FPdc; rep from * once more, then rep from * to **, sl st in top of first FPdc to join—24 FPdc, 30 sc.

RND 7: Ch 1, FPdc around first 2 FPdc, *sc in next 3 sc, FPdc around next 2 FPdc, sc in next sc, 3 sc in next sc, sc in next sc, FPdc around next 2 FPdc, sc in next 3 sc, FPdc around next 2 FPdc, sc in next sc **, FPdc around next 2 FPdc; rep from * once more, then rep from * to **, sl st in top of first FPdc to join —24 FPdc, 36 sc.

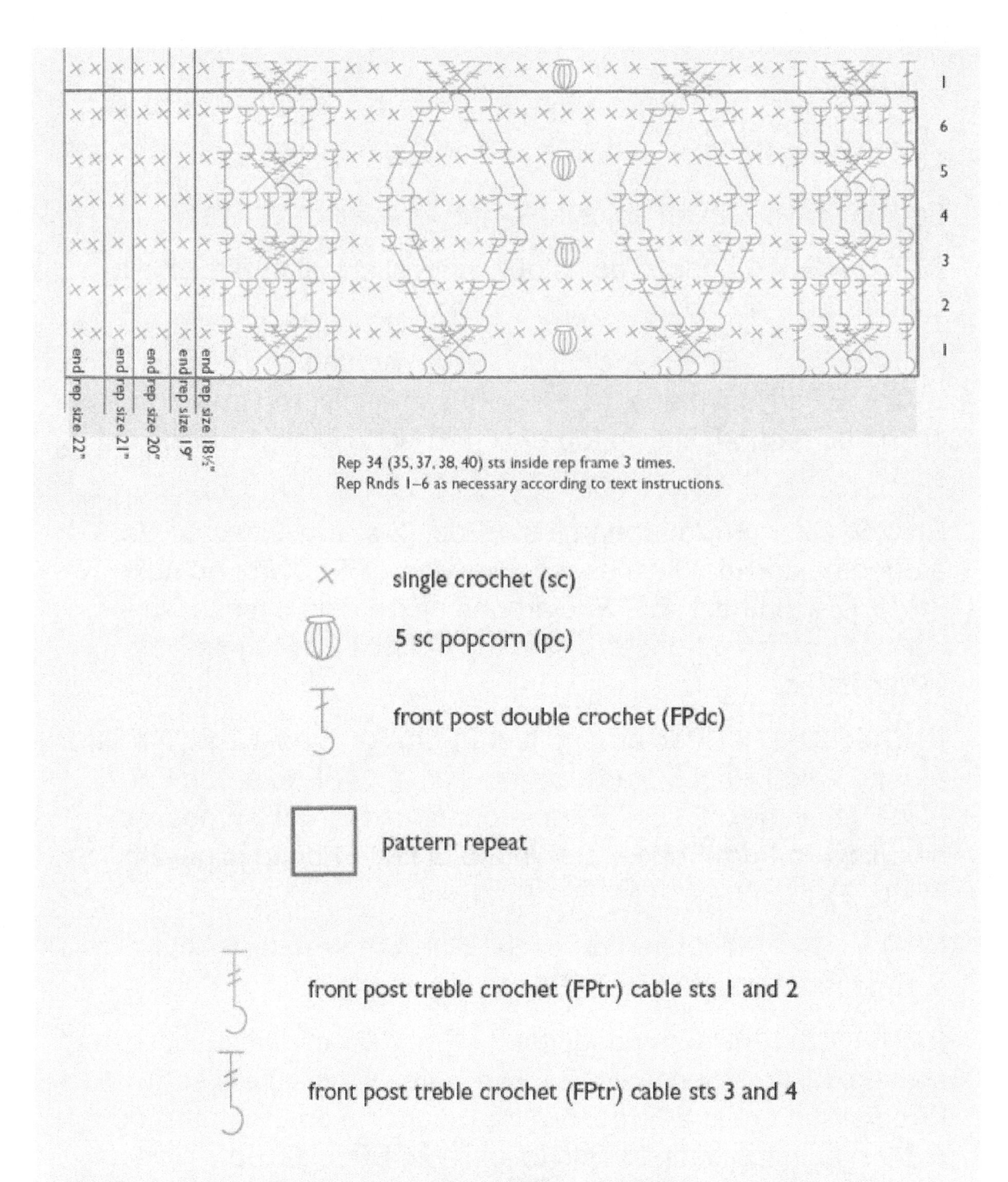

Rep 34 (35, 37, 38, 40) sts inside rep frame 3 times.
Rep Rnds 1–6 as necessary according to text instructions.

× single crochet (sc)

5 sc popcorn (pc)

front post double crochet (FPdc)

pattern repeat

front post treble crochet (FPtr) cable sts 1 and 2

front post treble crochet (FPtr) cable sts 3 and 4

RND 8: Ch 1, FPdc around first FPdc, *2 FPdc around next FPdc, sc in next 3 sc, FPdc around next FPdc, 2 FPdc around next FPdc, sc in next 2 sc, [sc in next 3 sc, FPdc around next FPdc, 2 FPdc around next FPdc] twice, sc in next sc**, FPdc around next FPdc; rep from * once more, then rep from * to **, sl st in top of first FPdc to join—36 FPdc, 36 sc.

RND 9: Ch 1, FPdc around first 3 FPdc, *sc in next 3 sc, FPdc around next 3 FPdc, 2 sc in next sc, sc in next 3 sc, 2 sc in next sc, FPdc around next 3 FPdc, sc in next 3 sc, FPdc around next 3 FPdc, sc in next sc **, FPdc around next 3 FPdc; rep from * once more, then rep from * to **, sl st in top of first FPdc to join —36 FPdc, 42 sc.

RND 10: Ch 1, FPdc around first FPdc, *2 FPdc around next FPdc, FPdc around next FPdc, sc in next 3 sc, FPdc around next FPdc, 2 FPdc around next FPdc, FPdc around next FPdc, sc in next 4 sc, [sc in next 3 sc, FPdc around next FPdc, 2 FPdc around next FPdc, FPdc around next FPdc] twice, 1 (2, 2, 2, 2) sc in next sc**, FPdc around next FPdc; rep from * once more, then rep from * to **, sl st in top of first FPdc to join—48 FPdc, 42 (45, 45, 45, 45) sc.

RND 11: Ch 1, FPdc around first FPdc, *[2 FPdc around next FPdc] twice, FPdc around next FPdc, sc in next 3 sc, FPdc around next 4 FPdc, sc in next 7 sc, FPdc around next 4 FPdc, sc in next 3 sc, FPdc around next FPdc, [2 FPdc around next FPdc] twice, FPdc around next FPdc, sc in next 1 (2, 2, 2, 2) sc**, FPdc around next FPdc; rep from * once more, then rep from * to **, sl st in top of first FPdc to join—60 FPdc, 42 (45, 45, 45, 45) sc.

Sizes 20 (21, 22)" (51 [53, 56] cm) only:

RND 12: Ch 1, FPdc around first 6 FPdc, *sc in next 3 sc, FPdc around next 4 FPdc, sc in next 4 sc, [sc in next 3 sc, FPdc around next 4 FPdc] twice, FPdc around next 2 FPdc, [2 sc in next sc] twice**, FPdc around next 6 FPdc; rep from * once more, then rep from * to **, sl st in top of first FPdc to join—60 FPdc, 51 sc.

Sizes 21 (22)" (53 [56] cm) only:

RND 13: Ch 1, FPdc around first 6 FPdc, *sc in next 3 sc, FPdc around next 4 FPdc, sc in next 4 sc, [sc in next 3 sc, FPdc around next 4 FPdc] twice, FPdc around next 2 FPdc, work 1 (2) sc in next sc, sc in next 2 sc, work 2 (3) sc in next sc**, FPdc around next 6 FPdc; rep from * once more, then rep from * to **, sl st in top of first FPdc to join—60 FPdc, 54 (60) sc.

All sizes:

Rep Rows 1–6 of main body patt (see Stitch Guide, page 82) until hat measures desired length minus ½" (1.3 cm) before brim fold, measure for length along string of popcorns. End on any rnd.

NEXT RND: Ch 1, sc in each st around, sl st flo (see Glossary) in first sc on last rnd to join, turn. Rep last rnd 2 more times—102 (105, 111, 114, 120) sc. Do not fasten off unless omitting brim.

Brim (Optional)

RND 1 (brim fold rnd): (WS) Ch 1, sc blo in each sc around; sl st in top of first sc to join—102 (105, 111, 114, 120) sc.

RNDS 2–3: Ch 1, sc around, sl st in top of first sc to join.

RNDS 4–10: Sl st in next 2 (3, 5, 6, 8) sts (maintain alignment with FPdc from hat). Work Rnds 1–6 of main body patt, then Rnd 1 once more. Work all post sts of first rnd around posts of sc.

RND 11: Ch 1, sc around, sl st blo in first sc to join—102 (105, 111, 114, 120) sc.

RND 12: Sl st blo around, sl st in first sl st to join—102 (105, 111, 114, 120) sl sts. Fasten off.

Finishing

Weave in loose ends. Fold up brim.

Back to Basics

Post *Stitches*

Post stitches are made exactly like basic stitches, with one exception. Instead of inserting your hook into one or both loops of a stitch in the previous row, insert your hook around the front or back of the stitch's post. Doing so pushes the post forward or backward, allowing you to make patterns out of the stitches in relief. Post stitches are used to create the effect of cables, ribs, piping, and any number of variations.

Double crochet is commonly used for post stitches, but any basic stitch may be substituted. You must complete at least one row or round of stitches before working post stitches.

Front Post Double Crochet *(FPdc)*

STEP 1: Yo, insert hook from front to back to front around the post of the next st in the previous row or rnd.

STEP 2: Yo and pull up lp.
You can see that the post of the stitch has already been pushed toward you.

STEP 3: [Yo, draw through 2 lps on hook] 2 times to complete the dc.

Rep Steps 1–3.

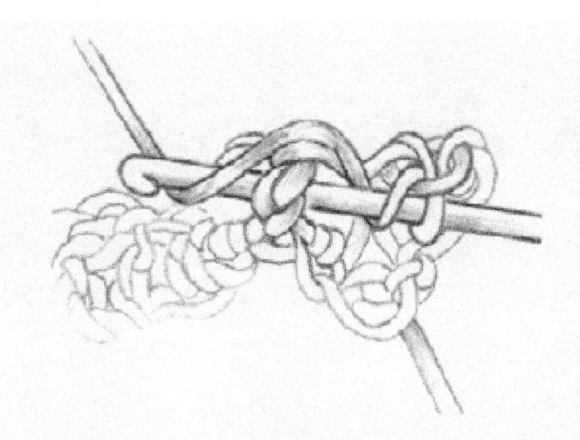

FPdc

Back Post Double Crochet *(BPdc)*

STEP 1: Yo, insert hook from back to front to back around the post of the next st in the previous row or rnd.

STEP 2: Yo and pull up lp.
You can see that the post of the stitch has already been pushed away from you.

STEP 3: [Yo, draw through 2 lps on hook] 2 times to complete the dc.

Rep Steps 1–3.

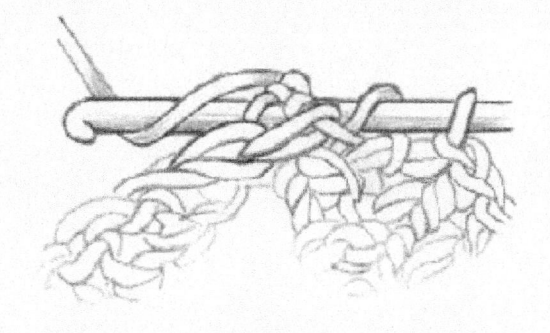

BPdc

Sólás Caomh

Irish for "tender comfort," Sólás Caomh was shaped by Jodi Euchner for a beloved baby. The engaging cable pattern provides its own tender comfort to crocheters as they shape the soft cotton-wool blanket into a future heirloom.

© Joe Hancock

Finished Size

27½" (70 cm) wide and 32" (81.5 cm) long.

Yarn

DK weight (#3 Light)

shown here: Brown Sheep Cotton Fleece (80% cotton, 20% merino wool; 215 yd [197 m]/3½ oz [100 g]; 3): #CW-840 lime light (A), 6 skeins; #CW-780 hearty merlot (B), 1 skein.

Hook

Size G/6 (4 mm). *Adjust hook size if necessary to obtain correct gauge.*

Gauge

9 sts and 5 rows = 2" (5 cm) of alternating dc, hdc rows.

Download the diagrams for this project here.

Blanket

With A, ch 123.

ROW 1: (WS) Dc in 4th ch from hook (counts as first dc) and in each ch across, turn—120 sts.

ROW 2 (CABLE-CROSS ROW): Ch 3 (counts as first dc here and throughout), dc in next 2 sts, *[sk next st, FPdc (see page

82) in next st, working behind st just made FPdc in skipped st] 3 times *; dc in next 6 sts, **[sk next 3 sts, FPtr (see page 82) in next 3 sts, working in front of sts just made FPtr in 3 skipped sts] 3 times**, dc in next 9 sts, [sk next 3 sts, FPtr in next 3 sts, working behind sts just made tr in 3 skipped sts, sk next 3 sts, tr in next 3 sts, working in front of sts just made FPtr in 3 skipped sts] 3 times, dc in next 9 sts, rep from ** to **, dc in next 6 sts, rep from * to *, dc in last 3 sts, turn.

ROW 3: Ch 2 (counts as first hdc here and throughout), hdc in next 2 sts, BPdc (see page 85) in next 6 sts, hdc in next 6 sts, BPdc in next 18 sts, hdc in next 9 sts, BPdc in next 3 sts, hdc in next 6 sts, [BPdc in next 6 sts, hdc in next 6 sts] 2 times, BPdc in next 3 sts, hdc in next 9 sts, BPdc in next 18 sts, hdc in next 6 sts, BPdc in next 6 sts, hdc in last 3 sts, turn.

ROW 4 (CABLE-CROSS ROW): Ch 3, dc in next 2 sts, *FPdc in next st, [sk next st, FPdc in next st, working in front of st just made FPdc in skipped st] 2 times, FPdc in next st*, dc in next 6 sts, **FPdc in next 3 sts [sk next 3 sts, FPtr in next 3 sts, working behind sts just made FPtr in 3 skipped sts] 2 times, FPdc in next 3 sts**, dc in next 9 sts, FPdc in next 3 sts, dc in next 6 sts, [sk next 3 sts, FPtr in next 3 sts, working behind sts just made FPtr in 3 skipped sts, dc in next 6 sts] 2 times, FPdc in next 3 sts, dc in next 9 sts, rep from ** to **, dc in next 6 sts, rep from * to *, dc in last 3 sts, turn.

ROW 5: Rep Row 3.

ROW 6 (CABLE-CROSS ROW): Ch 3, dc in next 2 sts, *[sk next st, FPdc in next st, working behind st just made FPdc in skipped st] 3 times*, dc in next 6 sts, **[sk next 3 sts, FPtr in next 3 sts, working in front of sts just made FPtr in 3 skipped sts] 3 times**, dc in next 9 sts, [sk next 3 sts, tr in next 3 sts, working in front of sts just made FPtr in 3 skipped sts, sk next 3 sts, FPtr in next 3 sts, working behind sts just made tr in 3 skipped sts] 3 times, dc in next 9 sts, rep from ** to **, dc in next 6 sts, rep from * to *, dc in last 3 sts, turn.

ROW 7: Ch 2, hdc in next 2 sts, BPdc in next 6 sts, hdc in next 6 sts, BPdc in next 18 sts, hdc in next 12 sts, [BPdc in next 6 sts, hdc in next 6 sts] 2 times, BPdc in next 6 sts, hdc in next 12 sts, BPdc in next 18 sts, hdc in next 6 sts, BPdc in next 6 sts, hdc in last 3 sts, turn.

ROW 8 (CABLE-CROSS ROW): Ch 3, dc in next 2 sts, *FPdc in next st, [sk next st, FPdc in next st, working in front of st just made FPdc in skipped st] 2 times, FPdc in next st*, dc in next 6 sts, **FPdc in next 3 sts, [sk next 3 sts, FPtr in next 3 sts, working behind sts just made FPtr in 3 skipped sts] 2 times, FPdc in next 3 sts**, dc in next 12 sts, [sk next 3 sts, FPtr in next 3 sts, working in front of sts just made FPtr in 3 skipped sts, dc in next 6 sts] 2 times, sk next 3 sts, FPtr in next 3 sts, working in front of sts just made FPtr in 3 skipped sts, dc in next 12 sts, rep from ** to **, dc in next 6 sts, rep from * to *, dc in last 3 sts, turn.

ROW 9: Rep Row 7.

Rep Rows 2–9 ten more times. Do not fasten off.

Border

RND 1: Ch 1, hdc evenly around blanket, working 2 hdc in each dc row-end, 1 hdc in each hdc row-end, and 3 hdc in each corner, changing to B in last st, sl st in beg hdc to join, do not turn.

RND 2: Ch 2, *[BPdc in next st, FPdc in next st] to corner st, (FPdc, hdc, FPdc) in corner st; rep from * around, sl st in first st to join, do not turn.

RND 3: Ch 1, sc in each st around working 3 sc in each corner.

Fasten off, weave in loose ends, and block to measurements.

Jodi Euchner, a mechanic by day, crochets and knits with her three daughters. See more of her work at shamelesstwist.com.

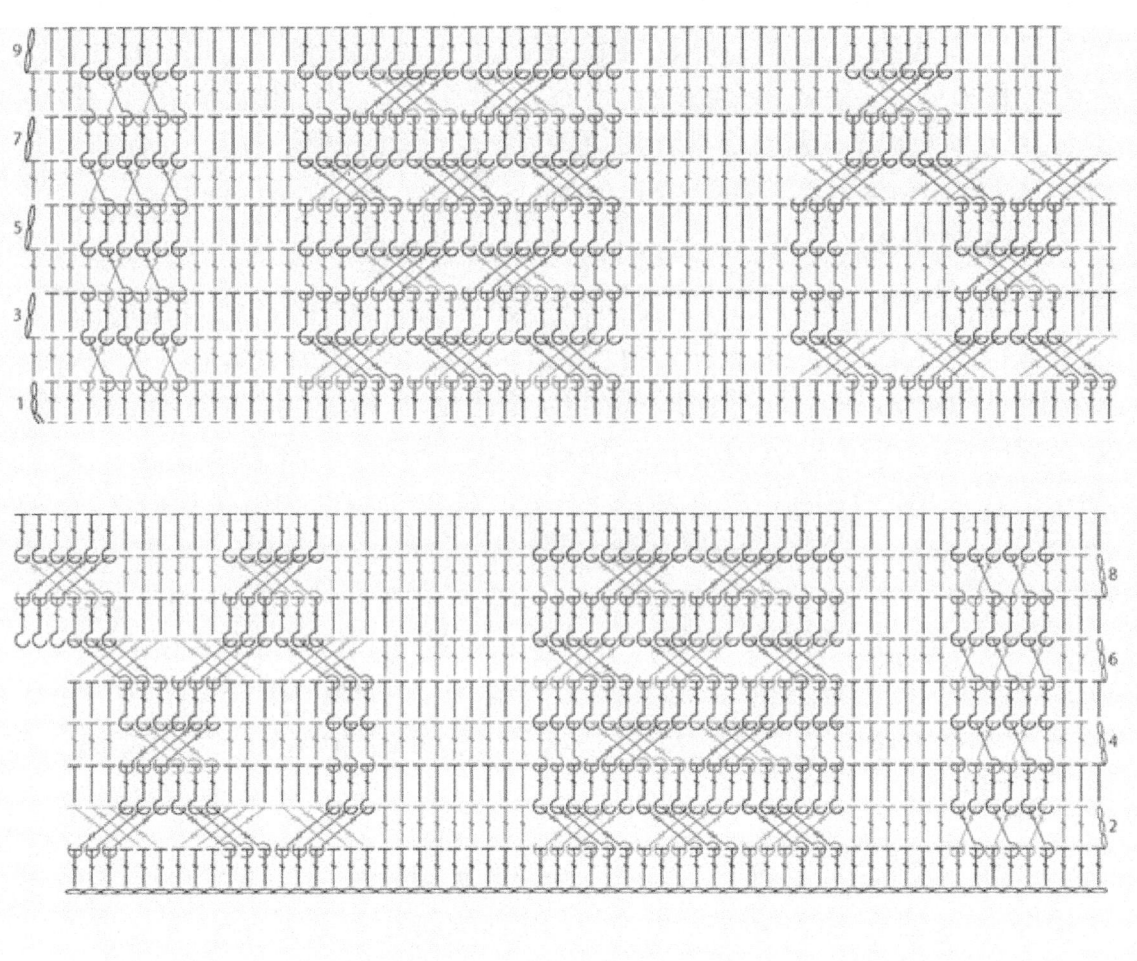

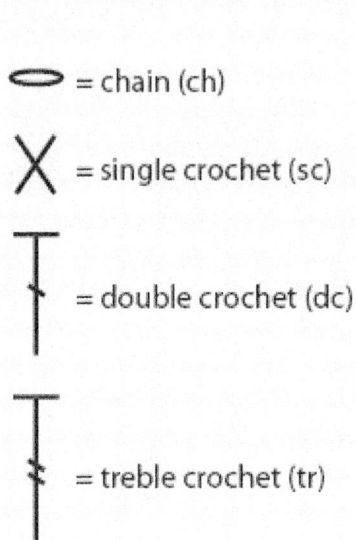

◯ = chain (ch)

✗ = single crochet (sc)

╤ = double crochet (dc)

╤ = treble crochet (tr)

= front post double crochet (FPdc)

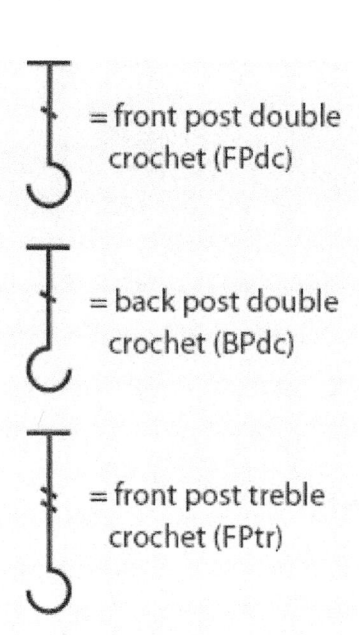

= back post double crochet (BPdc)

= front post treble crochet (FPtr)

Kathryn in Beauly Dress and Hat

Inspired by her namesake niece, designer Kathy Merrick was reminded of the colors of the Highlands around Beauly, Scotland, in spring when making this toddler's dress. The smart bonnet can be worn with the striped edge flat or folded back.

Pamela Bethel

Finished Size

Dress: 22 (24, 26, 28)" (56 [61, 66, 71] cm) chest circumference; 13½ (14¼, 16¼, 17)" (34 [36, 41, 43] cm) length from shoulder for ages 6–9 months (12 months, 18 months, 24 months). Garment is very loose fitting. Garment shown is 26" (66 cm).

Hat: 8 (8¼)" (20.5 [21] cm) from center back to front; 6½ (6½)"

(16.5 [16.5] cm) from top of head to back of neck to fit ages 6–12 months (12–24 months). Hat shown measures 8" (20.5 cm).

Yarn

Sportweight (#2 Fine)

shown here: Rowan 4-ply Cotton (100% cotton; 186 yd [178 m]/1¾ oz [50 g]; 2): #131 fresh (MC), 2 (2, 3, 3) balls; #146 violetta (A); #142 mandarine (B); #121 ripple (C); #112 opaque (D); #137 cooking apple (E); #130 ardour (F), 1 ball each. Yarns distributed by Westminster Fibers.

note: This yarn has been discontinued. Suggested substitution: Brown Sheep Cotton Fine.

Hook

Size E/9 (3.5 mm). *Adjust hook size if necessary to obtain the correct gauge.*

Notions

Three ½" (1.3 cm) buttons.

Gauge

18 sts and 16 rows = 4" (10 cm) in hdc.

Notes

- On inc rows for dress yoke, do not inc in first and last st. For inc Rows 3 and 7 only, do not work in tch of previous row, the last hdc of the row is the last st.
- Dress and bonnet are worked entirely in hdc. Dress is worked from the top down.

Stitch Guide

Hdc3tog: [Yo, insert hook in next st, yo and pull up a lp, yo, draw through 2 lps on hook] 3 times, yo and draw through all lps on hook.

Dress

With A, ch 46 (50, 54, 58).

ROW 1: Hdc in 3rd ch from hook and in each ch across, turn—45 (49, 53, 57) hdc.

ROW 2: Change to C, ch 2 (counts as hdc here and throughout), hdc in each hdc across, turn.

ROW 3 (inc row): Ch 2, hdc in first hdc, 2 hdc in each hdc to last hdc, hdc in last hdc, turn—87 (95, 103, 111) hdc.

ROW 4: Change to MC, ch 2, hdc in each hdc across, turn.

ROW 5: Change to B, ch 2, hdc in each hdc across, turn.

Sizes 26 (28)" (66 [71] cm) only:

NEXT ROW: Rep Row 5.

All sizes:

ROW 6 (6, 7, 7): Change to F, ch 2, hdc in each hdc across, turn.

ROW 7 (7, 8, 8) (INC ROW): Rep Row 3—171 (187, 203, 219) hdc.

ROWS 8–9 (9, 10, 10): Change to D, ch 2, hdc in each hdc across, turn.

ROW 10 (10, 11, 11): Change to A, ch 2, hdc in each hdc across, turn.

ROW 11 (11, 12, 12): Change to E, ch 2, hdc in each hdc across, turn.

Sizes 26 (28)" (66 [71] cm) only:

NEXT ROW: With E, ch 2, hdc across, turn.

All sizes:

ROWS 12–13 (13, 15, 15): Change to B, ch 2, hdc in each hdc across, turn.

ROW 14 (14, 16, 16): Change to MC, ch 2, hdc in each hdc across, turn.

ROW 15 (15, 17, 17) (INC ROW): Change to C, hdc in each of next 0 (3, 1, 4) hdc, 2 hdc in next hdc, *hdc in each of next 4 hdc, 2 hdc in next hdc; rep from * to last 0 (3, 1, 4) hdc, hdc in each of rem st(s)—206 (224, 244, 262) hdc. Fasten off.

Divide for front, back, sleeves as foll:

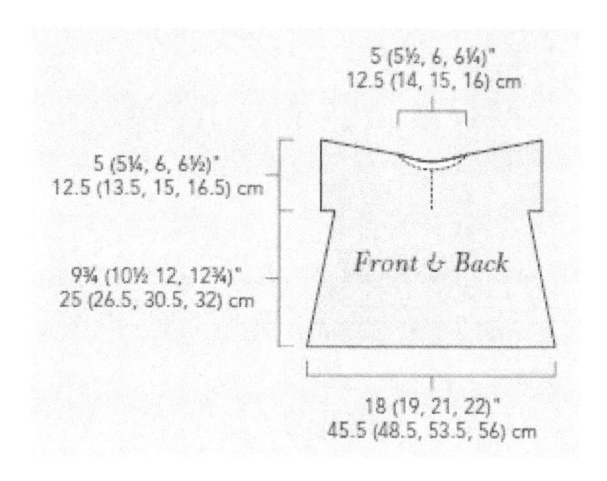

Diagram: Front & Back
- 5 (5½, 6, 6¼)" / 12.5 (14, 15, 16) cm
- 5 (5¼, 6, 6½)" / 12.5 (13.5, 15, 16.5) cm
- 9¾ (10½, 12, 12¾)" / 25 (26.5, 30.5, 32) cm
- 18 (19, 21, 22)" / 45.5 (48.5, 53.5, 56) cm

Right sleeve

ROW 1: (RS) Change to MC, ch 5 (5, 6, 6) for underarm, sk next 35 (37, 41, 43) sts for right back, sl st in next st, ch 2, hdc in each of next 32 (37, 40, 44) hdc for right sleeve, ch 7 (7, 8, 8) for underarm, turn.

ROW 2: Hdc in 3rd ch from hook and in each ch and hdc across turn—42 (47, 52, 56) hdc.

ROWS 3–6 (7, 8, 9): Ch 2, hdc in each hdc across, turn.

ROW 7 (8, 9, 10): Change to A, ch 2, hdc in each hdc across. Fasten off.

Left sleeve

ROW 1: (RS) With RS facing, beg at front edge of right sleeve, join MC with sl st, ch 5 (5, 6, 6) for underarm, sk next 71 (75, 82, 87) hdc for front, sl st in next st, ch 2 hdc in each of next 32 (37, 40, 44) hdc for left sleeve, ch 7 (7, 8, 8) for underarm, turn.

ROWS 2–7 (8, 9, 10): Work as for right sleeve.

Back

ROW 1: With RS facing, join MC with sl st in 5th (5th, 6th, 6th) left-sleeve-underarm st, hdc in each ch across underarm, hdc2tog (see Glossary) over side edge of first sleeve row and first st of left back, hdc in each of next 33 (37, 40, 43) hdc to end of row; *join with right back:* hdc in each of next 34 (36, 40, 42) hdc across right back to join back of yoke, hdc2tog over last st from right back and side edge of first sleeve row—81 (85, 94, 99) hdc.

WORK EVEN until piece measures 3¼ (3¾, 4¼, 4¾)" (8 [9.5 11, 12] cm) from underarm. With D, work 2 rows even. With C, work 2 rows even. With F, work 1 row even. With E, work 1 (1, 2, 2) row(s) even. With B, work 1 (1, 2, 2) row(s) even. With A, work 2 rows even. With D, work 1 row even. With F, work 2 rows even. With MC, work 1 row even. With C, work 1 row even. With B, work 2 rows even. With E, work 2 rows even. With F, work 1 row even. With B, work 1 row even. With C, work 1 row even. With MC, work 4 (5, 6, 7) rows even. With A, work 1 row even. Fasten off and weave in loose ends.

Front

ROW 1: With RS facing, join MC with sl st in 5th (5th, 6th, 6th) right sleeve underarm st, hdc2tog over side edge of the first sleeve row and first st of front, hdc in each of next 69 (73, 80, 85) hdc, hdc2tog over last st from front and side edge of first sleeve row—81 (85, 94, 99) hdc.

Work remainder of front as for back.

Finishing

Sew side and sleeve seams. With RS facing, join MC with sl st to neck edge of right-back neck opening, work 17 (17, 18, 18) hdc down right side of opening, work hdc3tog (see Stitch Guide, page 92) over 1 st from right back, 1 st from center of opening, and 1 st from left back, work 17 (17, 18, 18) hdc up left of side opening, turn—35 (35, 37, 37) hdc.

BUTTONHOLE ROW: Ch 3 (counts as hdc, ch 1), sk next hdc, hdc in next 14, (14, 15, 15) sts, hdc3tog as in last row worked, hdc in each of next 16 (16, 17, 17) sts up right side of opening, turn—32 (32, 34, 34) hdc, 1 ch-1 sp.

NEXT ROW: Ch 2, hdc in next 14 (14, 15, 15) hdc, hdc3tog as est, hdc in next 13 (13, 14, 14) hdc, hdc in ch-1 sp hdc in last st —31 (31, 33, 33) hdc. Sew button opposite buttonhole.

Bonnet

NOTE: *Bonnet is worked in a spiral with WS facing, without joining rnds. With A, ch 3.*

RND 1: 7 hdc in 3rd ch from hook, place marker (pm) in last st.

NOTE: *Move marker up with each rnd to indicate where to change colors—8 hdc.*

RND 2: Change to C, 2 hdc in each hdc around to m—16 hdc.

RND 3: Hdc in each hdc around to m.

RND 4: Change to MC, 2 hdc in each hdc around to m—32 hdc.

RND 5: Change to B, hdc in each hdc around to m.

RNDS 6–7: Change to F, hdc in each hdc around to m.

RND 8: Change to D, hdc in each hdc around to m.

RND 9: Change to E, 2 hdc in each hdc around to m—64 hdc.

RND 10: Hdc in each hdc around to m.

RND 11: Change to A, hdc in each hdc around to m.

RND 12: Change to E, hdc in each hdc around to m.

RND 13: Change to B, hdc in each hdc around to m.

RND 14: *2 hdc in next st, hdc in each of next 3 (2) sts; rep from * to last 0 (1) hdc, hdc in last hdc—80 (85) hdc. Fasten off.

Join MC with sl st in 12th (13th) st from end of last rnd. Work 56 (59) hdc, turn leaving rem sts unworked. Work 11 (12) more rows even. Work 1 row each in C, F, D, B, E, A. Fasten off and weave in loose ends.

Chin Strap

With A, ch 51 (53).

ROW 1: Hdc in 3rd ch from hook and in each ch across, turn—50 (52) hdc.

ROW 2: Change to MC, ch 3 (counts as first hdc), hdc in each hdc across, turn.

ROW 3 (buttonhole row): Change to B, ch 3, hdc in next hdc, ch 1, sk next hdc, hdc in each hdc to last 3 hdc, ch 1, sk next hdc, hdc in last hdc, turn.

ROW 4: Change to D, ch 3, hdc in each hdc across, turn.

ROW 5: Change to F, ch 3, hdc in each hdc across. Fasten off.

Sew buttons to hat at each end of 4th (5th) row of MC band.

Back to Basics

Changing *Colors*

Both of the techniques described below apply to changing to a new color of yarn or to new yarn if the current ball has run out.

To seamlessly change yarn in the middle of a row or round:

STEP 1: With the working yarn, make the next stitch until only one step remains to complete it (e.g., for double crochet: yo, insert hook in next st and pull up lp, yo and draw through 2 lps on hook; for sc2tog: [insert hook in next st and pull up lp] 2 times).

STEP 2: Drop the working yarn and let it fall to the back of your work, yarn over with the new yarn and draw through the remaining loops on your hook to complete the stitch **(Figure 1)**.

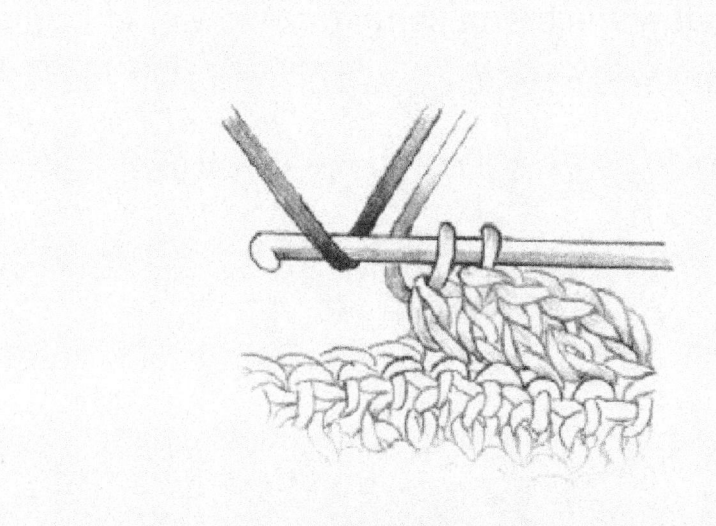

Figure 1

STEP 3: Continue with the new yarn (**Figure 2**).

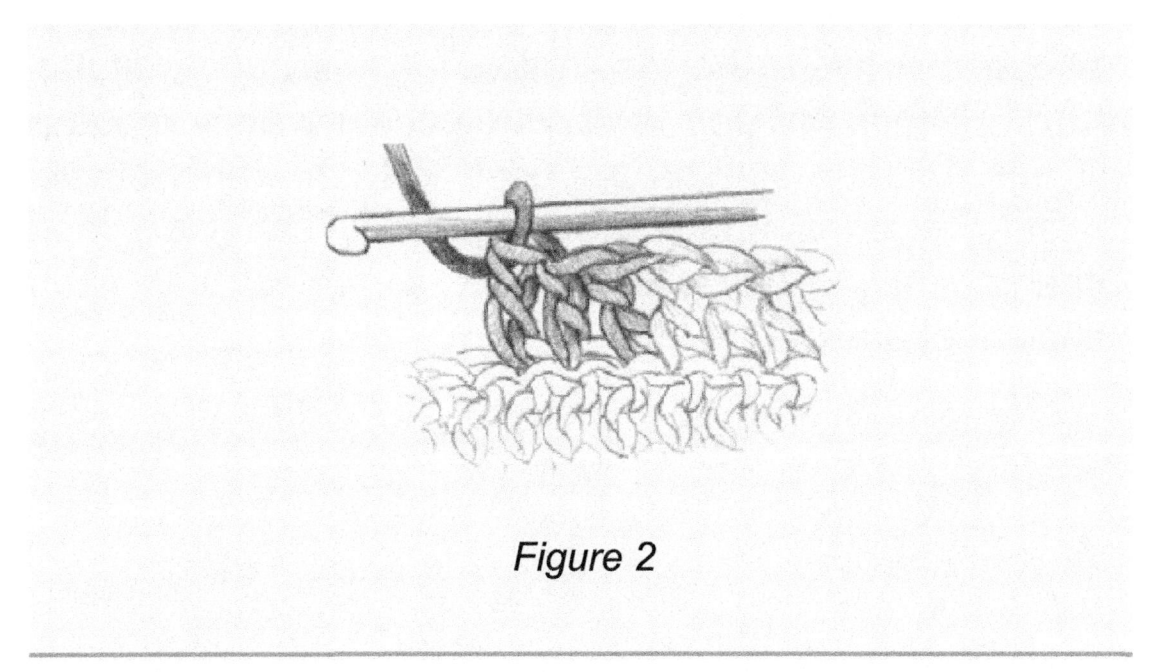

Figure 2

For a video tutorial on changing colors, visit crochetme.com.

To change yarn at the end of a row, follow Steps 1–3 for the last stitch of the row. Make your turning chain with the new yarn.

To change yarn at the end of a round when you are joining each round with a slip stitch in the first stitch:

Complete the last stitch of the round with the working yarn.

Drop the working yarn and let it fall to the back of your work, insert your hook in the first stitch of the round. Yarn over with the new yarn and draw it through both the stitch and the loop on your hook to make a slip stitch.

Make your beginning chain with the new yarn.

If you are doing stranded colorwork, do not cut the first yarn but keep it handy for the next time you need it. If you are done using the first yarn, be sure to leave a tail long enough to weave in.

Sir Stephen the Bunny

Antique toys were the inspiration for this cuddly stuffed rabbit. Each body part is crocheted separately in basic stitches. Vintage buttons are used to both embellish and to join the arms and legs so the doll can be posed. Organic cotton yarn makes this a perfect gift for a recipient of any age.

Pamela Bethel

Finished Size

About 16" (40.5 cm) tall with legs extended.

Yarn

Worsted weight (#4 Medium)

shown here: Blue Sky Alpacas Organic Cotton (100% cotton; 150 yd [137 m]/3½ oz [100 g]; 4): #83 sage (MC), 2 skeins; #80 bone (A) and #82 nut (B), 1 skein each.

Hook

Sizes G/6 (4 mm) and I/9 (5.5 mm). *Adjust hook size if necessary to obtain the correct gauge.*

Notions

Fiberfill; yarn needle; two ½" (1.3 cm) shank buttons; four ⅞" (2.2 cm) 2-hole buttons; three ½" (1.3 cm) buttons; DMC pearl cotton size #5, color #223; 1 yd (1 m) of ¾" (2 cm) wide ribbon.

Gauge

Rabbit: 15 sts and 7 rows = 4" (10 cm) in dc with smaller hook. Vest: 12 sts and 9 rows = 4" (10 cm) in dc/ sc patt with larger hook.

Notes

+ If the toy is intended for a child three years old or younger, embroider features and sew pieces tog securely; do not use buttons or other embellishments that might pose a choking hazard.

+ Head, body, arms, and legs are worked separately in rnds without turning. When fastening off each piece, leave a long tail for sewing.

Head

With smaller hook and MC, ch 4, sl st in first ch to form ring.

RND 1: Ch 3 (counts as dc here and throughout), 11 dc in ring, sl st in top of beg ch-3 to join—12 sts.

RND 2: Ch 3, 2 dc in each st around, dc in base of beg ch-3, sl st in top of beg ch-3 to join—24 sts.

RND 3: Ch 3, *dc in next st, 2 dc in next st; rep from * around, ending with dc in base of beg ch-3, sl st in top of beg ch-3 to join—36 sts.

RND 4: Ch 3, *dc in each of next 2 dc, 2 dc in next st; rep from * around, ending with dc in base of beg ch-3, sl st in top of beg ch-3 to join—48 sts.

RND 5: Ch 3, dc in each st around, sl st in top of beg ch-3 to join.

RND 6: Ch 3, dc in each of first 20 sts, 2 dc in each of next 6 sts for nose, dc in each of last 21 sts, sl st in top of beg ch-3 to join—54 sts.

RND 7: Ch 3, dc in each of first 20 sts, [dc2tog (see Glossary) over next 2 sts] 6 times, dc in each of last 21 sts, sl st in top of beg ch-3 to join—48 sts.

RND 8: Ch 3, dc in next st, dc2tog over next 2 sts, *dc in each of next 2 sts, dc2tog over next 2 sts; rep from * around, sl st in top of beg ch-3 to join—36 sts.

RND 9: Ch 3, *dc2tog over next 2 sts, dc in next st; rep from * to last 2 sts, dc2tog over last 2 sts, sl st in top of beg ch-3 to join—24 sts.

RND 10: Ch 3, *dc2tog over next 2 sts; rep from * to last st, yo, insert hook in next st, yo and pull up a lp, yo and draw through 2 lps on hook (2 lps rem on hook), insert hook in top of beg ch-3, yo and draw through ch and both lps on hook—12 sts. Fasten off and set aside (see Notes).

Body

With smaller hook and MC ch 4, sl st in first ch to form ring.

RNDS 1–4: Rep Rnds 1–4 as for head—48 sts.

RNDS 5–12: Ch 3, dc in each st around, sl st in top of beg ch-3 to join.

RND 13: Ch 3, dc in next st, dc2tog over next 2 sts, *dc in each of next 2 sts, dc2tog over next 2 sts; rep from * around, sl st in top of beg ch-3 to join—36 sts.

RND 14: Rep Rnd 5.

RND 15: Ch 3, dc2tog over next 2 sts, *dc in next st, dc-2tog over next 2 sts; rep from * around, sl st in top of beg ch-3 to join—24 sts.

RND 16: Ch 3, *dc2tog over next 2 sts; rep from * to last st, yo, insert hook in next st, yo and pull up a lp, yo and draw through 2 lps on hook (2 lps rem on hook), insert hook in top of beg ch-3, yo and draw through ch and both lps on hook—12 sts. Fasten off and set aside.

Arms *(make 2)*

With smaller hook and A, ch 4, sl st in first ch to form ring.

RND 1: Ch 3, 11 dc in ring, sl st in top of beg ch-3 to join—12 sts.

RND 2: Ch 3, 2 dc in next st and in each st around, dc in base of beg ch-3; changing to MC, sl st in top of beg ch-3 to join—24 sts.

RNDS 3–7: With MC, ch 3, dc in each st around, sl st in top of beg ch-3 to join.

RND 8: Ch 3, dc2tog over next 2 sts, dc in each of next 8 sts, [dc2tog over next 2 sts] 2 times, dc in each of next 8 sts, yo, insert hook in next st, yo and pull up a lp, yo and draw through 2 lps on hook (2 lps rem on hook), insert hook in top of beg ch-3, yo and draw through ch and both lps on hook, sl st in top of beg ch-3 to join—20 sts.

RND 9: Ch 3, dc2tog over next 2 sts, dc in each of next 6 sts, [dc2tog over next 2 sts] 2 times, dc in each of next 5 sts, yo, insert hook in next st, yo and pull up a lp, yo and draw through 2 lps on hook (2 lps rem on hook), insert hook in top of beg ch-3, yo and draw through ch and both lps on hook—16 sts. Fasten off. Stuff and use yarn needle and tail to sew closed. Set aside.

Legs *(make 2)*

With smaller hook and MC, ch 4, sl st in first ch to form ring.

RNDS 1–7: Rep Rnds 1–7 as for arms—24 sts.

RND 8: Ch 3, dc in each of next 8 sts, 3 dc in each of next 6 sts, dc in each of last 9 sts, sl st in top of beg ch-3 to join—36 sts.

RND 9: Ch 3, dc in each st around, sl st in top of beg ch-3 to join. Fasten off. Stuff but do not sew closed. Set aside.

Soles *(make 2)*

With smaller hook and A, ch 4, sl st in first ch to form ring.

RND 1: Ch 3, 11 dc in ring, sl st in top of beg ch-3 to join—12 sts.

RND 2: Ch 3, 2 dc in each st around, dc in base of beg ch-3, sl st in top of beg ch-3 to join—24 sts.

ROW 3: Ch 3, dc in each of next 7 sts, turn leaving rem sts unworked—8 sts rem.

ROW 4: Ch 3, dc2tog over next 2 sts, dc in each of next 2 sts, dc2tog over next 2 sts, dc in last st—6 sts. Fasten off.

Using yarn needle and tail from sole, sew a sole on bottom of each leg to close.

Ears *(make 2)*

With smaller hook and MC, ch 18.

ROW 1: (RS) Sc in bottom ridge lp of 2nd ch from hook and in bottom ridge lp of each ch across, turn—17 sts.

ROW 2: (WS) Ch 1, sc in each of first 17 sts, 3 sc in side of last sc of Row 1, turn work 180°, sc in both lps of each ch of foundation ch, turn—37 sts.

ROW 3: Ch 1, sc in each of first 18 sts, 3 sc in next st, sc in each of last 18 sts, turn—39 sts.

ROW 4: Ch 1, sc in each of first 19 sts, 3 sc in next st, sc in each of last 19 sts, turn—41 sts.

ROW 5: Ch 1, sc in each of first 20 sts, 3 sc in next st, sc in each of last 20 sts—43 sts.

Fasten off. Fold ear in half lengthwise with RS tog and whipstitch (see page 122) from straight short end of ear along long edge for 2" (5 cm).

Vest

With larger hook and B, ch 46.

ROW 1: (WS) Sc in 2nd ch from hook and in each ch across, turn—45 sts.

ROW 2: (RS) Ch 3 (counts as dc), sk first st, dc in each st across, turn.

ROW 3: Ch 1, sc in each st across, turn.

ROWS 4–5: Rep Rows 2–3.

Right front

ROW 6: Ch 3, dc2tog over next 2 sts, dc in each of next 2 sts, dc2tog over next 2 sts, dc in next st, turn leaving rem sts unworked—6 sts.

ROW 7: Ch 1, sc in each st across, turn.

ROW 8: Ch 3, [dc2tog over next 2 sts] 2 times, dc in last st, turn—4 sts.

ROW 9: Rep Row 7—4 sts.

ROW 10: Ch 3, dc2tog over next 2 sts, dc in last st—3 sts. Fasten off.

Back

ROW 1: With RS facing, sk 8 sts of Row 5 and join yarn with sl st in 9th st, ch 3, dc2tog over next 2 sts, dc in each of next 7 sts, dc2tog over next 2 sts, dc in next st, turn—11 sts.

ROW 2: Ch 1, sc in each st across, turn—11 sts.

ROW 3: Ch 3, dc2tog over next 3 sts, dc in each of next 5 sts, dc2tog over next 2 sts, dc in last st, turn—9 sts.

ROW 4: Rep Row 2.

ROW 5: Ch 3, dc in each st across.

Fasten off.

Left front

ROW 1: With RS facing, sk 8 sts of Row 5 of vest base and join yarn with sl st in 9th st, ch 3, dc2tog over next 2 sts, dc in next 2 sts, dc2tog over next 2 sts, dc in last st, turn—6 sts.

Rep Rows 7–10 of right front. Fasten off. With yarn needle and B, sew shoulders. Join B with sl st at left underarm, sc evenly around armhole. Rep for right armhole. Sc evenly around outside edge of vest. Sew three ½" (1.3 cm) buttons on right front.

Finishing

Stuff body and head. Using pearl cotton, pass yarn needle from left side of body near neck edge through to right side and through first arm, through 1 hole of 2-hole button, back through other hole of button, back through arm, back through right side of body, and back through left side of body. Cont through left arm and first hole, then 2nd hole of 2-hole button and back through left arm. You will have the 2 ends of the cord between the left arm and left side of body. Pull tightly to shape body and tie a secure knot. Attach the legs in the same way. On head, sew shank buttons on either side of nose with pearl cotton, pulling the ends tog from inside of head to shape the face. Embroider nose and mouth with pearl cotton. Sew ears to either side of head, tilting them back at an angle. Sew head to body, adding a little more stuffing as you go so the head stands firmly. Weave in loose ends. Put the vest on the bunny and tie ribbon in a bow around his neck.

Donna Childs loves to come up with her own crochet designs, especially stuffed animals, and still uses the same crochet hooks she bought for herself when she was ten years old.

Beyond the Basics

The Adjustable Ring
by DONNA HULKA

One of the most popular articles on CrochetMe.com is Donna Hulka's tutorial on *The Magic Adjustable Ring,* a way to crochet in the round without the pesky hole in the middle of your work. Adding this simple technique to your arsenal will make you feel like a crochet superhero.

Figure 1

Leaving a 6" (15 cm) tail, make a ring by placing the tail end of yarn behind the working yarn.

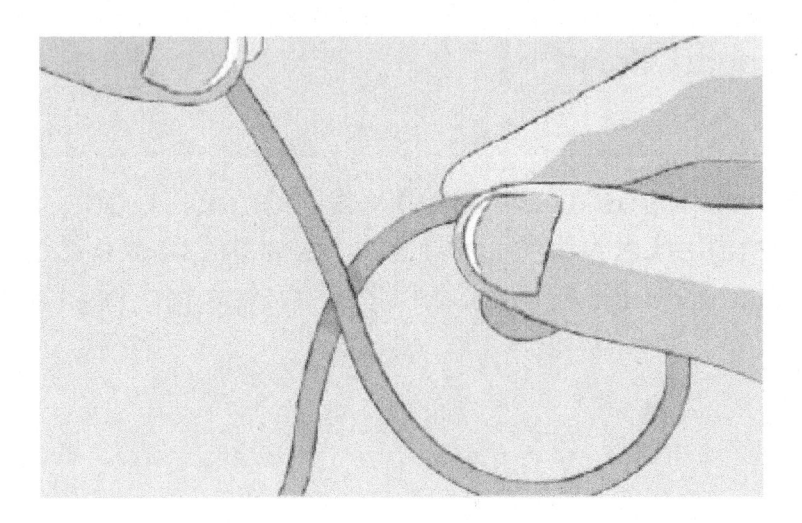

Figure 2

Insert your hook from front to back through the center of the ring, yo with the working yarn, and pull up a lp. Ch 1 (this assumes you'll be making sc sts. Ch the appropriate number if you'll be making hdc, dc, etc.).

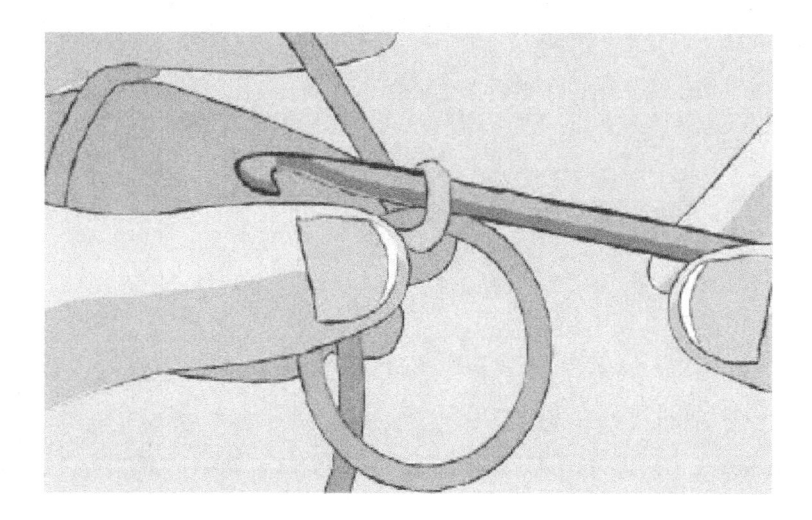

Figure 3

Continuing to hold the ring closed with your nondominant hand, work several sc sts into the ring, covering the tail.

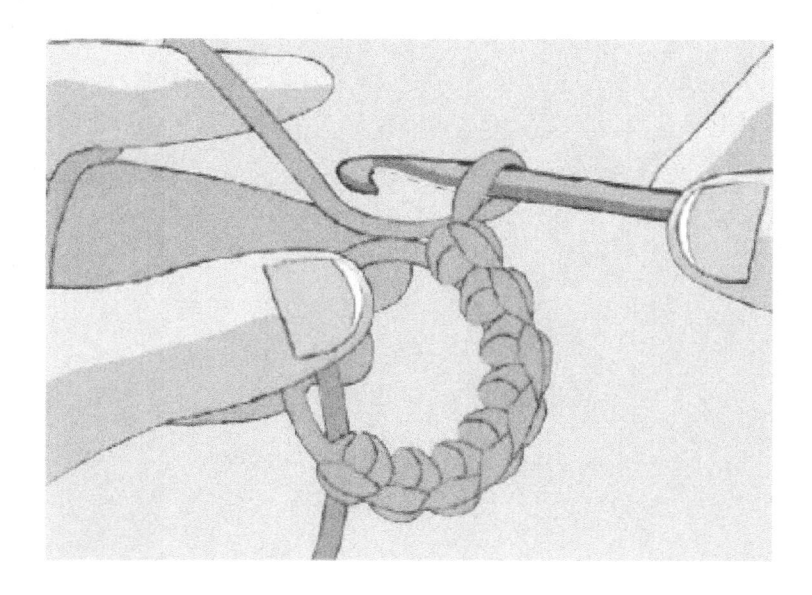

Figure 4

Pull the yarn tail to tighten the ring. Presto! No hole in the center of your work. Continue to work in the round as usual.

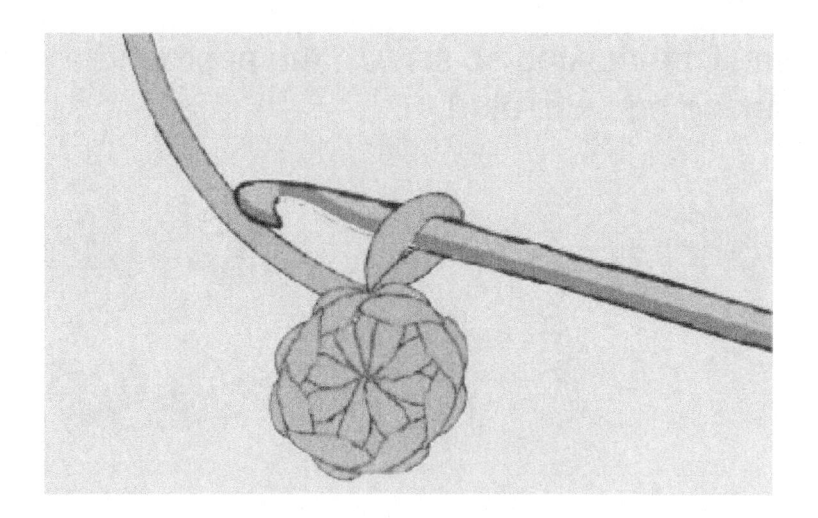

Donna Hulka's crochet patterns have been featured in many books, including *Crochet Me* (Interweave). See more of Donna's work at yarntomato.com.

Babette Blanket

Inspired by the work of designers Kaffe Fassett and Liza Prior Lucy, this blanket offers a journey in color for the crocheter. The modules are all based on the same motif pattern; they vary only in the number of rounds worked. Crocheted in superwash wool, this blanket is sure to become a modern heirloom.

© Chris Hartlove

Finished Size

43" (109 cm) wide and 40" (101.5 cm) long.

Yarn

Sockweight (#1 Superfine)

shown here: Koigu Wool Designs KPM (100% merino wool; 175 yd [160 m]/1 3/4 oz [50 g]; (1)): #2424 taupe (A), 3 skeins; #2343 sage green (B), #2229 tomato red (C), and #2326 French blue (D), 2 skeins each; #2339 vicious green (E), #2236 purple-grey (F), #1239 golden brown (G), #2370 melon (H), #1040 deep blue-green (J), #2332 citron (K), #1500 turquoise (L), #2260 bright lilac (M), #2151 baby blue (N), #1005 robin's egg (O), #2233 rose (P), #1150 bright pink (R), and #2128 dusty lavender (S), 1 skein each.

Hook

Sizes E/4 (3.5mm) and C/2 (2.75mm). *Adjust hook sizes if necessary to obtain the correct gauge.*

Notions

Tapestry needle.

Gauge

A two-round square = 1 3/4" (4.5 cm) using larger hook.

Download the diagrams for this project here.

Notes

- There are six sizes of squares, each made in the same way. The sizes only vary by numbers of rounds worked: 2, 4, 6, 8, 10, or 12 rounds.

- Work over tails as you go along to save hours of finishing.

- Make squares in colors as desired or follow color charts as given on pages 104–105 to make the blanket as pictured.

- Change colors every round for two-round squares. For larger squares, use one color for two or more rounds.
- Make 50 two-round squares, 49 four-round squares, 16 six-round squares, 7 eight-round squares, 2 ten-round squares, and 2 twelve-round squares.

Two-Round Square

RND 1: Using larger hook, ch 4 (counts as ch 1, dc), (dc, [ch 2, 3 dc] 3 times, ch 2, dc) all in 4th ch from hook, join with sl st in 3rd ch of beg ch-4. Do not turn.

RND 2: Ch 3, dc in next dc, *(2 dc, ch 2, 2 dc) in ch-2 sp, dc in each of next 3 dc**, rep from * to ** twice more; (2 dc, ch 2, 2 dc) in last ch-2 sp, ending dc in next dc, join with sl st in top of beg ch-3.

Fasten off.

TWO-ROUND SQUARES

	Rnd 1	Rnd 2
2-1	R	A
2-2	H	G
2-3	K	F
2-4	L	M
2-5	C	H
2-6	C	G
2-7	N	H
2-8	A	R
2-9	O	L
2-10	E	B
2-11	F	C
2-12	K	J
2-13	P	S
2-14	K	O
2-15	L	G
2-16	K	R
2-17	B	D
2-18	C	A
2-19	O	E
2-20	C	H
2-21	L	A
2-22	D	R
2-23	C	L
2-24	S	B
2-25	J	O
2-26	M	C
2-27	E	P
2-28	O	G
2-29	D	K
2-30	B	L
2-31	A	D
2-32	G	B
2-33	P	S
2-34	D	K
2-35	G	R
2-36	E	N
2-37	O	L
2-38	H	M
2-39	D	H
2-40	P	J
2-41	K	G
2-42	H	F
2-43	D	B
2-44	N	M
2-45	R	H
2-46	E	A
2-47	D	N
2-48	G	K
2-49	O	M
2-50	L	E

Four-Round Square

RNDS 1 AND 2: Rep Rnds 1 and 2 of two-round square.

RND 3: Ch 3, dc in each of next 3 dc, *(2 dc, ch 2, 2 dc) in ch-2 sp, dc in each of next 7 dc**, rep from * to ** twice more, (2 dc, ch 2, 2 dc) in last ch-2 sp, ending dc in each of next 3 dc, join with sl st in top of beg ch-3.

RND 4: Ch 3, dc in each of next 5 dc,*(2 dc, ch 2, 2 dc) in ch-2 sp, dc in each of next 11 dc**, rep from * to ** twice more, (2 dc, ch 2, 2 dc) in last ch-2 sp, ending dc in each of next 5 dc, join with sl st in top of beg ch-3.

Fasten off.

FOUR-ROUND SQUARES

	Rnd 1	Rnd 2	Rnd 3	Rnd 4
4-1	O	O	O	P
4-2	M	E	J	J
4-3	D	D	C	C
4-4	H	H	J	R
4-5	L	L	L	B
4-6	M	M	G	G
4-7	S	S	J	J
4-8	K	A	A	H
4-9	O	O	S	S
4-10	G	G	G	E
4-11	M	F	J	J
4-12	D	D	H	B
4-13	R	B	H	C
4-14	J	A	A	K
4-15	E	L	S	P
4-16	N	N	M	M
4-17	K	J	J	G
4-18	H	F	F	F
4-19	B	B	C	C
4-20	P	P	K	K
4-21	E	L	A	H
4-22	D	D	O	F
4-23	N	N	K	K
4-24	G	S	S	R
4-25	H	E	A	G
4-26	N	N	P	P
4-27	M	H	H	H
4-28	K	K	S	S
4-29	O	O	N	N
4-30	A	A	C	C
4-31	O	B	B	B
4-32	C	C	D	S
4-33	G	E	A	N
4-34	R	B	B	O
4-35	K	K	L	L
4-36	A	R	R	N
4-37	O	S	S	E
4-38	C	C	A	A
4-39	E	F	F	R
4-40	H	H	J	J
4-41	M	M	K	L
4-42	J	J	J	S
4-43	G	G	P	K
4-44	F	M	M	M
4-45	H	J	N	P
4-46	O	O	K	K
4-47	N	N	G	G
4-48	J	C	C	C
4-49	A	A	P	B

SIX-ROUND SQUARES

	Rnd 1	Rnd 2	Rnd 3	Rnd 4	Rnd 5	Rnd 6
6-1	E	A	A	N	N	N
6-2	C	C	K	K	F	F
6-3	G	G	G	F	F	F
6-4	R	R	K	A	A	A
6-5	C	C	C	B	D	D
6-6	E	E	N	N	R	D
6-7	H	H	B	L	G	G
6-8	K	O	O	O	J	M
6-9	J	J	J	K	B	B
6-10	S	S	G	C	C	E
6-11	L	L	A	A	A	J
6-12	M	C	C	E	D	D
6-13	C	H	H	K	D	D
6-14	G	G	E	L	L	R
6-15	M	B	B	B	E	J
6-16	C	C	S	S	H	H

EIGHT-ROUND SQUARES

	Rnd 1	Rnd 2	Rnd 3	Rnd 4	Rnd 5	Rnd 6	Rnd 7	Rnd 8
8-1	N	N	P	P	P	B	C	N
8-2	A	B	P	P	S	G	C	C
8-3	M	M	B	B	C	L	A	A
8-4	G	J	J	H	K	F	F	F
8-5	G	G	P	J	N	N	B	H
8-6	F	F	F	K	K	A	A	O
8-7	L	L	B	B	R	G	P	L

TWELVE- AND TEN-ROUND SQUARES

	Rnd 1	Rnd 2	Rnd 3	Rnd 4	Rnd 5	Rnd 6	Rnd 7	Rnd 8	Rnd 9	Rnd 10	Rnd 11	Rnd 12
12-1	F	N	N	C	A	M	M	J	H	A	A	F
12-2	R	R	R	N	H	H	B	G	G	B	P	P
10-1	B	B	B	D	D	K	N	N	B	S		
10-2	D	D	D	A	A	R	H	H	S	D		

COLOR TABLE KEY

- A Taupe
- B Sage green
- C Tomato red
- D French blue
- E Vicious green
- F Purple-grey
- G Golden brown
- H Melon
- J Deep blue-green
- K Citron
- L Turquoise
- M Bright lilac
- N Baby blue
- O Robin's egg blue
- P Rose
- R Bright pink
- S Dusty lavender

Each square is represented by 2 numbers; i.e., 4-1 identifies one individual motif.

Subsequent rounds of larger squares

Ch 3, dc in each dc across to next ch-2 sp, *(2 dc, ch 2, 2 dc) in ch-2 sp, dc in each dc to next ch-2 sp**, rep from * to ** twice more, (2 dc, ch 2, 2 dc) in last ch-2 sp, ending dc in each dc to end of rnd, join with sl st in top of beg ch-3. Fasten off.

Finishing

Follow assembly diagram on page 106 first joining squares to form units as numbered and then joining units in numerical order. Sew squares together using a tapestry needle and color A, matching edges, and working stitch to stitch.

Outer border

With smaller hook and D, attach yarn to one side of blanket, ch 3, dc in each edge st of blanket, working (2 dc, ch 2, 2 dc) in each corner ch-2 sp. Fasten off D, attach A. Work 2 rnds in A, and then 1 rnd in C working in same manner as Round 1. Fasten off. Block.

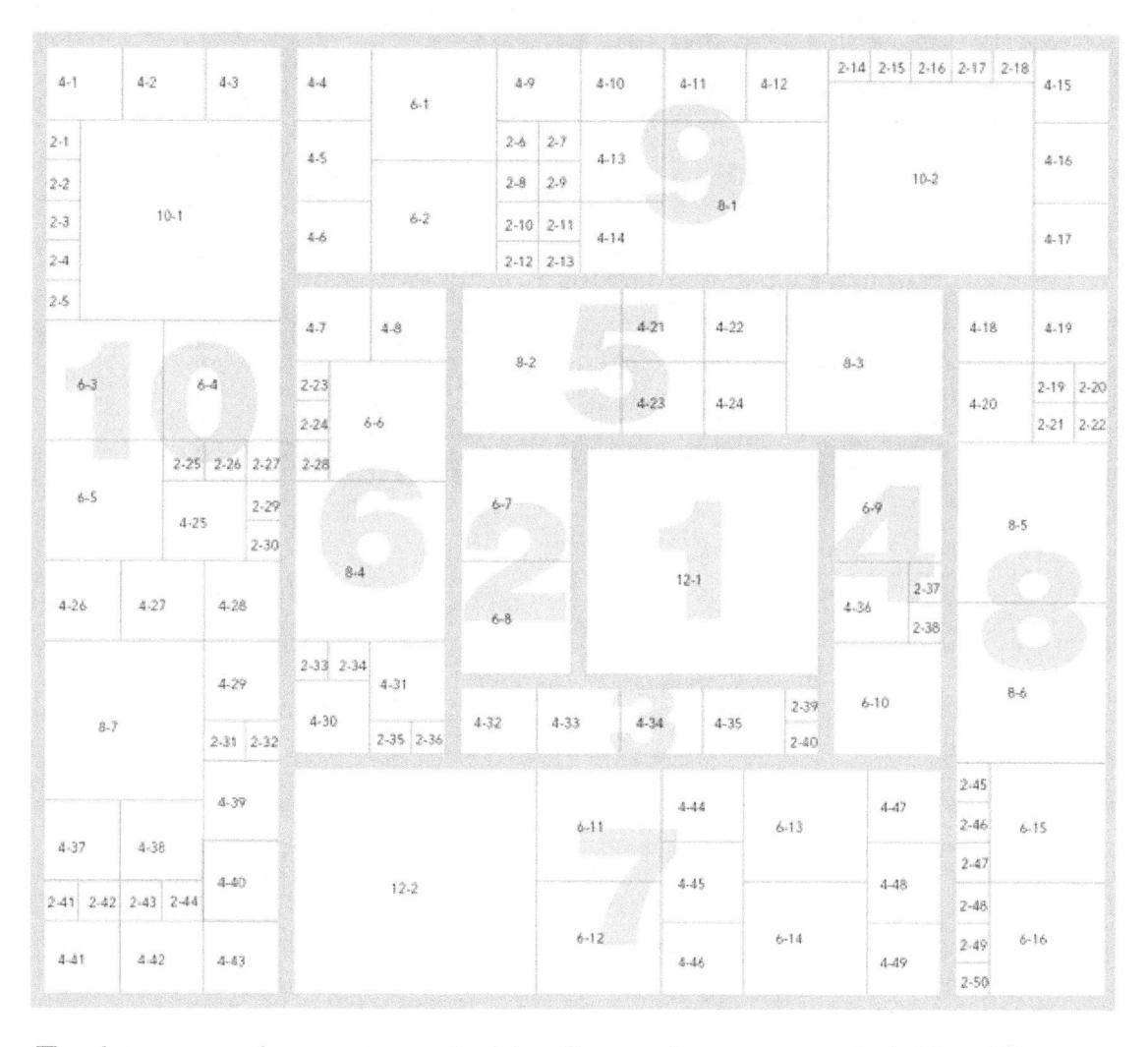

Each square is represented by 2 numbers; e.g., 4-1 identifies one individual motif.

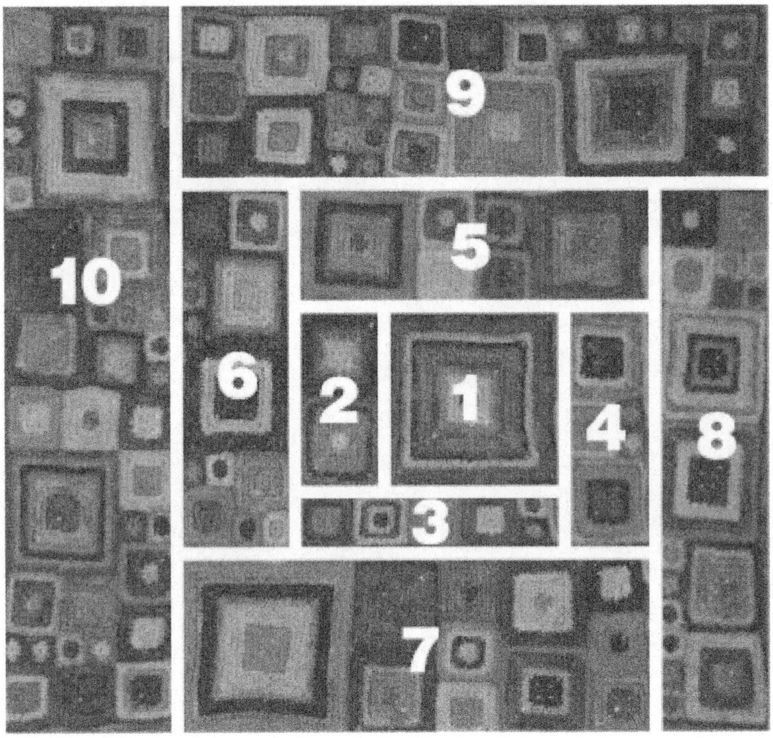
9
5
10
6
2
1
4
8
3
7

Beyond the Basics

Sewing *Stitches*

With all projects, use a fine sewing needle and sewing thread that matches the crocheted work. The goal is to create a strong enough stitch for the task without showing the stitches on the front side. When sewing fabric to crochet work, sew through the fabric and through the yarn on the crocheted loops closest to the fabric. Check the front frequently to make sure stitches don't show. Here are key stitches for sewing fabric and crochet work:

Backstitch: This is a sturdy stitch, suitable for seams and sewing through several layers of fabric.

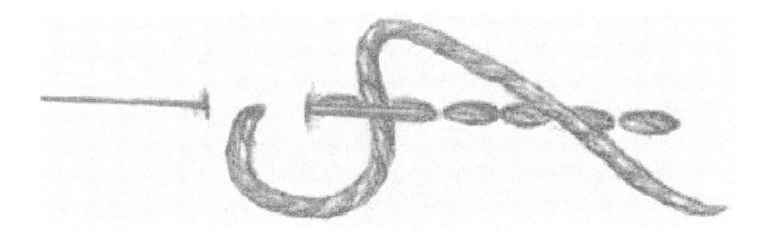

Backstitch

Whipstitch: This is a good basic stitch for sewing almost anything together. Once you find the right stitch length, it is speedy to work. The strength of the join and amount of "show" of the stitch depends on how large and deep you go with the needle. Too loose and things can catch in the thread loops, too tight and the fabric will pucker. Aim for the Goldilocks just-right stitch.

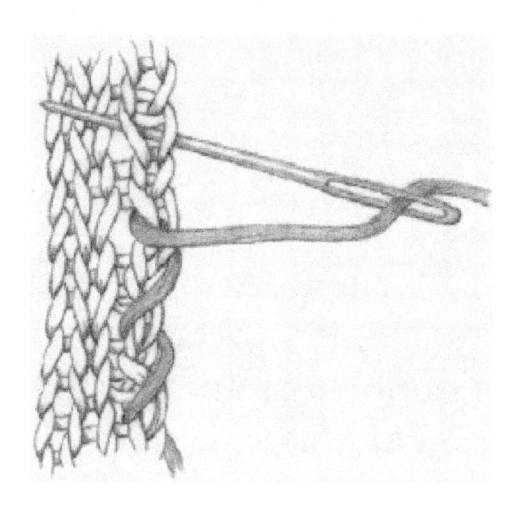

Whipstitch

Blindstitch: This demure stitch is perfect for hems and necklines when you don't want the stitch to show. Unlike the whipstitch, which shows on the outside, the length of this stitch is hidden in the fold. You pick up a few threads of the fabric, then insert the needle back in the fold. The front of the garment will show just a tiny vertical stitch.

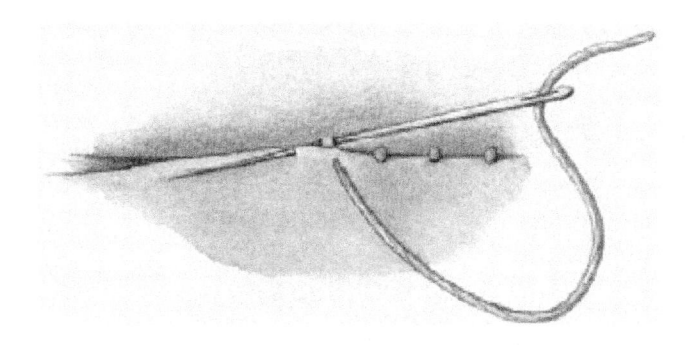

Blindstitch

Running or basting stitch: Often this is a temporary stitch, used to secure two pieces of fabric so they don't slide apart while working the real stitch. Basting stitches are usually removed after the sewing is complete. However, in some projects, this stitch is used to gather a single layer of fabric, and it is not removed after sewing (if you remove it, the gathers will fall out).

Running or basting stitch

Boho Blocks Cardigan

If you're a fan of motifs, this sophisticated cardigan is the project for you. Worked entirely in granny squares that are slip-stitched together, the jacket has a boxy look that makes it ideal for casual weekend wear. For a contemporary edge, Valentina Devine worked it in jewel tones and, by holding two strands of a variegated yarn together, she achieved a rich marled effect. And for the moms out there, Valentina also designed a matching child's pullover; the pattern for the Child's Boho Blocks Pullover can be found online at crochetme.com.

© Chris Hartlove

Finished Size

28 (40, 56)" (71 [101.5, 142] cm) bust circumference when buttoned. Cardigan shown measures 40" (101.5 cm).

Yarn

Fingering weight (#0 Lace)

shown here: Lorna's Laces Helen's Lace (50% silk, 50% wool; 1,250 yd [1,143 m]/4 oz [114 g]; 0): mother lode (A), 2 (2, 3) skeins; Douglas fir (B) and camouflage (C), 1 skein each.

Hook

Size E/4 (3.5 mm). *Adjust hook size if necessary to obtain correct gauge.*

Notions

5 (5, 6) ⅞" (2.2 cm) diameter shank buttons; tapestry needle.

Gauge

Each motif = 3½" (9 cm) square with 2 strands of yarn held tog.

Notes

- Garment is assembled from squares that are crocheted together.
- Hold two strands of yarn together throughout.

Basic Motif

With 2 strands of yarn held tog, ch 4 and join with sl st to form ring.

RND 1: (RS) Ch 3 (counts as dc), work 15 dc into ring, sl st in top of beg ch-3 to join—16 dc.

RND 2: Ch 5 (counts as dc, ch 2), sk first dc, *dc in next dc, ch 2; rep from * around, sl st in 3rd ch of beg ch-5 to join.

RND 3: Sl st across to first ch-2 sp, ch 3 (counts as dc), 2 dc in same ch-2 sp, *ch 1, sk next dc, 3 dc in next ch-2 sp; rep from *, ending ch 1, sl st in top of beg ch-3 to join.

RND 4: Sl st across to first ch-sp, [ch 3, sk 3 dc, sc in next ch-sp] twice, (ch 6, sk 3 dc) for corner, sc in next ch-sp, *[ch 3, sk 3 dc, sc in next ch-sp] 3 times, (ch 6, sk 3 dc) for corner, sc in next ch-sp; rep from * twice more, ch 3, sl st in beg sc to join.

RND 5: Sl st across to first ch-sp, ch 3 (counts as dc), 2 dc in same ch-sp, sk next sc, 3 dc in next ch-sp, *sk next sc, (3 dc, ch 2, 3 dc) in corner ch-lp, [sk next sc, 3 dc in next ch-sp] 3 times; rep from * twice more, sk next sc, (3 dc, ch 2, 3 dc) in corner ch-lp, sk next sc, 3 dc in next ch-sp, sl st in top of beg ch-3 to join.

Fasten off.

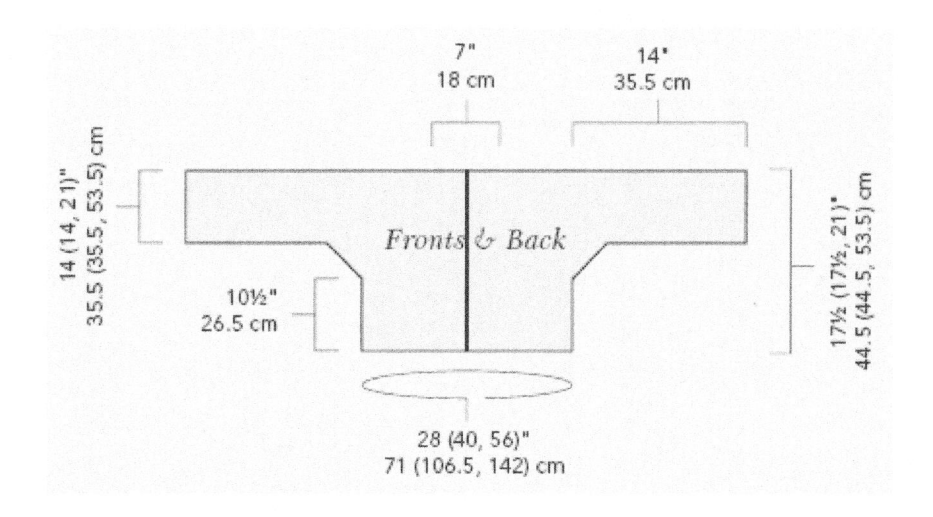

Cardigan

Make 8 (12, 16) motifs each with B and C. Make 58 (70, 114) motifs with A. Arrange B motifs into a strip of 8 (12, 16). With RS facing, sl st in each st of both squares at sides to secure tog. Rep with C squares to make 1 strip. In same manner, arrange 4 (6, 8) A squares into a strip and sl st tog. Rep to make 3 (3, 4) A strips for back. Arrange and secure 2 (3, 4) A squares into a strip for front. Make 6 (6, 8) front strips from A. With RS facing, sl st C strip to one long edge of B strip, lining up corners. To keep corners lying flat, work a ch 1 at corner of each motif. Sl st 3 (3, 4) A back strips tog. Sl st 3 (3, 4) A front strips tog for left front. Rep to join rem A front strips tog for right front. Lining up squares, sl st front strips and back strips to B/C strips. Leave front and back A strips separate for armholes. Secure 1 (2, 3) pair(s) of squares tog at shoulders, leaving center 2 squares unattached for neckline. Cardigan is 4 (6, 8) squares across the back, 2 (3, 4) across each front and 5 (5, 6) squares down from shoulder.

BASIC MOTIF

- chain (ch)
- slip st (sl st)
- × single crochet (sc)
- ┬ double crochet (dc)

Sleeves

Sl st 4 (4, 6) A squares tog into a strip. Make 4 strips for each sleeve. Sl st 4 strips tog along long edges for sleeve. Fold 1 square in half diagonally for underarm gusset. Sl st 1 side of gusset square to last motif at one end of sleeve. Sl st adjacent side of gusset square to first motif at same edge of sleeve. Gusset square fits diagonally into end of sleeve and closes sleeve. Sl st rem motifs of sleeve tog for sleeve seam. Sl st edge of sleeve with gusset to front and back armhole edges. Rep for opposite sleeve.

Finishing

Turn right side out. With RS facing, join C at lower edge of right front and sc evenly up right front, around neckline and down left front, changing colors to match motifs. Work 1 row of reverse sc. Fasten off.

Bottom ruffle

With RS facing and C, sc evenly along bottom edge of jacket. Turn.

NEXT ROW: Sl st in first st, *ch 30, sl st into same st, sc in next st; rep from * across lower edge of cardigan.

Sleeve ruffle

With RS facing and A, sc evenly along bottom edge of sleeve. Turn.

NEXT ROW: Sl st in first st, *ch 20, sl st into same st, sc in next st; rep from * across lower edge of sleeve. Sew buttons on left front, placed opposite top corners of motifs. Corner spaces will be used as buttonholes. With yarn threaded on a tapestry needle, weave in loose ends.

Valentina Devine, born in Moscow and raised in Berlin, crochets and knits one-of-a-kind garments and wall hangings.

Ocean Pearls Cardigan

Polka-dot bobbles add playful interest to this simple cardigan. The cotton-viscose blend yarn gives it a nice sheen and beautiful drape, perfect for cool summer days and evenings.

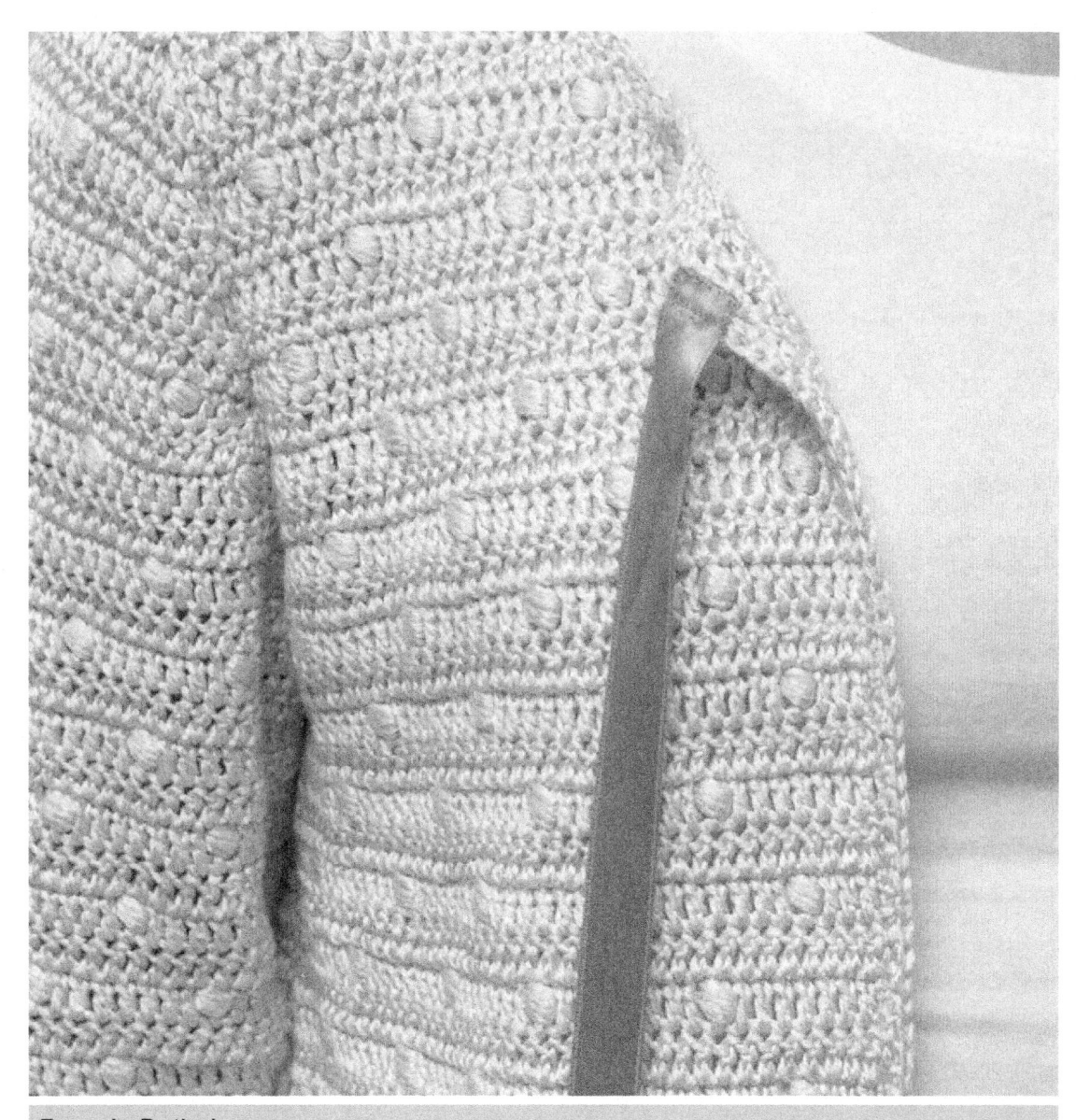

Pamela Bethel

Finished Size

33¼ (36½, 40, 43½, 50)" (84.5 [93, 101.5, 110.5, 127] cm) bust circumference. Garment shown measures 36½" (93 cm); 0–1" (0–2.5 cm) of ease is suggested.

Yarn

Sportweight (#2 Fine)

shown here: GGH Mystik (54% cotton, 46% viscose; 120 yd [110 m]/1¾ oz [50 g]; (2)): #75, 9 (10, 12, 13, 15) skeins. Yarn distributed by Muench Yarns.

Hook

Size G/6 (4 mm). *Adjust hook size if necessary to obtain the correct gauge.*

Notions

Yarn needle; 1 yard (1 m) of ½" (1.3 cm) wide ribbon.

Gauge

19 sts and 10 rows = 4" (10 cm) in dc.

Notes

- Tch counts as dc; sk first dc in each row. At beg of row, when instructed to mb or dc "in next X sts," sk first st, mb in next st or dc in next X sts.
- On dec rows, sl sts worked at beg of row do not count toward st count. When working even in patt, do not work bobble at beg or end of row if there are fewer than 3 sts bet bobble and edge of work, unless otherwise noted.

Stitch Guide

Make bobble (mb): Yo, insert hook in next st and pull up a lp, yo and draw through 2 lps on hook (2 lps rem on hook), *yo, insert hook bet st just made and last st, pull up a lp; rep from * 3 more times; yo, draw through all 10 lps on hook.

Back

Ch 81 (89, 97, 105, 121).

ROW 1: (RS) Dc in 4th ch from hook, dc in next ch, *mb (see Stitch Guide), dc in next 3 ch; rep from * across, turn—79 (87, 95, 103, 119) sts including tch.

ROW 2: Ch 3 (counts as first dc here and throughout), *mb (see Notes), dc in next 3 sts; rep from * to last 2 sts, mb, dc in next st, turn.

ROW 3: Ch 3, dc in next 2 sts, *mb, dc in next 7 sts; rep from * to last 4 sts, mb, dc in last 3 sts, turn.

ROW 4: Ch 3, dc across, turn.

ROW 5: Ch 3, dc in next 6 sts, *mb, dc in next 7 sts; rep from * to end, turn.

ROW 6: Rep Row 4.

Rep Rows 3–6 for patt until work measures 12 (12, 12¾, 12¾, 13½)" (30.5 [30.5, 32, 32, 34.5] cm). Cont in patt as foll:

Shape armholes

ROW 1: (RS) Sk first st, sl st in next 2 (2, 3, 3, 4) sts, sc in next st, work in patt to last 4 (4, 5, 5, 6) sts, sc in next st, turn leaving rem sts unworked—73 (81, 87, 95, 109) sts.

ROW 2: Sk first st, sl st in next 1 (1, 2, 2, 3) st(s), sc in next st, work in patt to last 3 (3, 4, 4, 5) sts, sc in next st, turn—69 (77,

81, 89, 101) sts.

ROW 3: Sk first st, sl st in next 1 (1, 1, 2, 3) st(s), sc in next st, work in patt to last 3 (3, 3, 4, 5) sts, sc in next st, turn—65 (73, 77, 83, 93) sts.

Sizes 36½ (40, 43½, 50)" (93 [101.5, 110.5, 127] cm) only:

ROW 4: Sk first st, sl st in next 1 (1, 1, 2) st(s), sc in next st, work in patt to last 3 (3, 3, 4) sts, sc in next st, turn leaving rem sts unworked—69 (73, 79, 87) sts.

Sizes 43½ (50)" (110.5 [127] cm) only:

ROW 5: Sk first st, sl st in next st, sc in next st, work in patt to last 3 sts, sc in next st, turn—75 (83) sts.

Size 50" (127 cm) only:

Rep Row 5—79 sts.

All sizes:

NEXT ROW: Ch 3, dc2tog (see Glossary), work in patt to last 2 sts, dc2tog, turn—63 (67, 71, 73, 77) sts. Rep this row 2 (2, 3, 2, 2) more times—59 (63, 65, 69, 73) sts. Work even in patt until armhole measures 7¼ (7½, 8, 8¼, 9)" (18.5 [19, 20.5, 21, 23] cm). Fasten off.

Right Front

Ch 42 (46, 50, 54, 62).

ROW 1: (RS) Dc in 4th ch from hook and in next 2 ch, *mb, dc in next 3 ch; rep from * to end, turn—40 (44, 48, 52, 60) sts including tch.

ROW 2: Ch 3 (counts as first dc here and throughout), dc in next 4 sts, *mb, dc in next 3 sts; rep from * to last 3 sts, mb, dc in next 2 sts, turn.

ROW 3: Ch 3, dc in next 3 sts, *mb, dc in next 7 sts; rep from * to last 4 (8, 4, 8, 8) sts, mb, dc to end, turn.

ROW 4: Ch 3, dc across, turn.

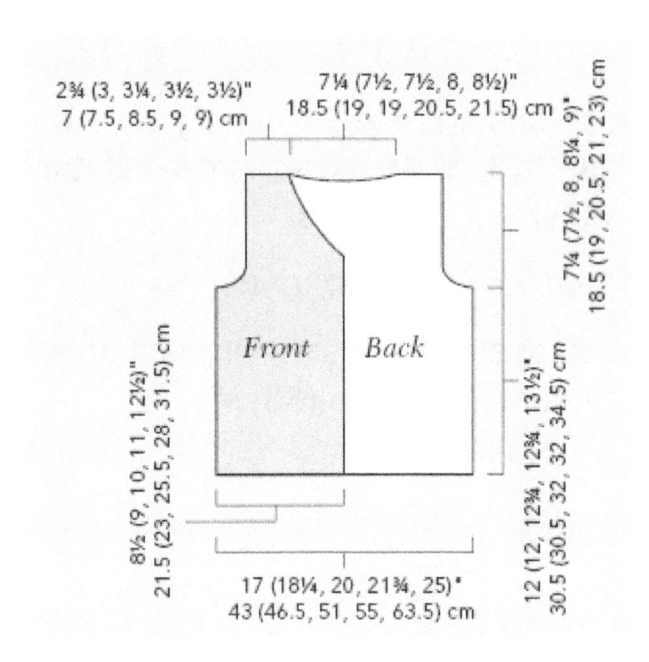

2¾ (3, 3¼, 3½, 3½)"
7 (7.5, 8.5, 9, 9) cm

7¼ (7½, 7½, 8, 8½)"
18.5 (19, 19, 20.5, 21.5) cm

7¼ (7½, 8, 8¼, 9)"
18.5 (19, 20.5, 21, 23) cm

Front   Back

8½ (9, 10, 11, 12½)"
21.5 (23, 25.5, 28, 31.5) cm

12 (12, 12¾, 12¾, 13½)"
30.5 (30.5, 32, 32, 34.5) cm

17 (18¼, 20, 21¾, 25)"
43 (46.5, 51, 55, 63.5) cm

ROW 5: Ch 3, dc in next 7 sts, *mb, dc in next 7 sts; rep from * to last 8 (4, 8, 4, 4) sts, mb, dc to end, turn.

ROW 6: Rep Row 4.

Rep Rows 3–6 for patt until work measures 12 (12, 12¾, 12¾, 13½)" (30.5 [30.5, 32, 32, 34.5] cm). Cont in patt as foll:

Sleeve

5 (5¾, 6, 6½, 7)"
12.5 (14.5, 15, 16.5, 18) cm

12 (12, 13, 13, 13½)"
30.5 (30.5, 33, 33, 34.5) cm

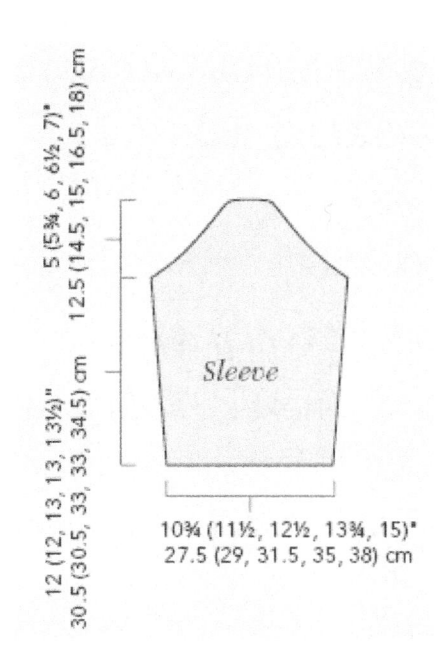

10¾ (11½, 12½, 13¾, 15)"
27.5 (29, 31.5, 35, 38) cm

Shape armholes

ROW 1: (RS) Ch 3, work in patt to last 4 (4, 5, 5, 6) sts, sc in next st, turn leaving rem sts unworked—37 (41, 44, 48, 55) sts.

ROW 2: Sk first st, sl st in next 1 (1, 2, 2, 3) st(s), sc in next st, work in patt across, turn—35 (39, 41, 45, 51) sts.

ROW 3: Ch 3, work in patt to last 3 (3, 3, 4, 5) sts, sc in next st, turn leaving rem sts unworked—33 (37, 39, 42, 47) sts.

Size 33¼" only:

ROW 4: Ch 3, dc2tog, dc across, turn—32 sts.

ROW 5: Ch 3, work in patt to last 2 sts, dc2tog, turn—31 sts.

ROW 6: Rep Row 4—30 sts.

ROW 7: Work even in patt.

Sizes 36½ (40)" (93 [101.5] cm) only:

ROW 4: Sk first st, sl st in next st, sc in next st, work in patt across, turn—35 (37) sts.

ROW 5: Ch 3, work in patt to last 2 sts, dc2tog, turn—34 (36) sts.

ROW 6: Ch 3, dc2tog, work in patt across, turn—33 (35) sts.

ROW 7: Rep Row 5—32 (34) sts.

Size 40" (101.5 cm) only:

Rep Row 6—33 sts.

Sizes 43½ (50)" (110.5 [127] cm) only:

ROW 4: Sk first st, sl st in next st, sc in next 1 (2) st(s), work in patt across, turn—40 (44) sts.

ROW 5: Ch 3, work in patt to last 3 sts, sc in next st, turn leaving rem sts unworked—38 (42) sts.

Size 43½" (110.5 cm) only:

ROW 6: Ch 3, dc2tog, work in patt across, turn—37 sts.

ROW 7: Ch 3, work in patt to last 2 sts, dc2tog, turn—36 sts.

ROW 8: Rep Row 6—35 sts.

ROW 9: Work even in patt.

Size 50" (127 cm) only:

ROW 6: Sk first st, sl st in next st, sc in next st, work in patt across, turn—40 sts.

ROW 7: Ch 3, work in patt to last 2 sts, dc2tog, turn—39 sts.

ROW 8: Ch 3, dc2tog, work in patt across, turn—38 sts.

ROW 9: Rep Row 7—37 sts.

ROWS 10–11: Work even in patt.

All sizes:

Cont in est patt as foll:

Shape neckline

Size 33¼" (84.5 cm) only:

ROW 1: (WS) Ch 3, work in patt to last 6 sts, sc in next st, turn leaving rem sts unworked—25 sts.

ROW 2: Sk first st, sl st in next 2 sts, sc in next st, work in patt across, turn—22 sts.

ROW 3: Ch 3, work in patt to last 3 sts, sc in next st, turn leaving rem sts unworked—20 sts.

ROW 4: Sk first st, sl st in next st, sc in next st, work in patt across, turn—18 sts.

ROW 5: Rep Row 3—16 sts.

ROW 6: Ch 3, dc2tog, work in patt across, turn—15 sts.

ROW 7: Work even in patt, turn.

Rep Rows 6–7 two more times—13 sts. Fasten off.

Size 40" (101.5 cm) only:

ROW 1: (RS) Sk first st, sl st in next 4 sts, sc in next st, work in patt across, turn—28 sts.

ROW 2: Ch 3, work in patt to last 4 sts, sc in next st, turn leaving rem sts unworked—25 sts.

ROW 3: Sk first st, sl st in next st, sc in next st, work in patt across, turn—23 sts.

ROW 4: Ch 3, work in patt to last 3 sts, sc in next st, turn leaving rem sts unworked—21 sts.

ROW 5: Sk first st, sl st in next st, sc in next st, work in patt across, turn—19 sts.

ROW 6: Ch 3, work in patt to last 2 sts, dc2tog, turn—18 sts.

ROW 7: Ch 3, dc2tog, work in patt across, turn—17 sts.

ROW 8: Work even in patt, turn.

Rep Rows 7–8 two more times—15 sts.

Sizes 36½ (43½, 50)" (93 [110.5, 127] cm) only:

ROW 1: (WS) Ch 3, work in patt to last 6 (7, 8) sts, sc in next st, turn leaving rem sts unworked—27 (29, 30) sts.

ROW 2: Sk first st, sl st in each of next 2 sts, sc in next st, work in patt across, turn—24 (26, 27) sts.

ROW 3: Ch 3, work in patt to last 3 sts, sc in next st, turn leaving rem sts unworked—22 (24, 25) sts.

ROW 4: Sk first st, sl st in next st, sc in next st, work in patt across, turn—20 (22, 23) sts.

ROW 5: Rep Row 3—18 (20, 21) sts.

ROW 6: Ch 3, dc2tog, work in patt across, turn—17 (19, 20) sts.

ROW 7: Ch 3, work in patt to last 2 sts, dc2tog, turn—16 (18, 19) sts.

ROW 8: Work even in patt, turn.

Rep Rows 7–8 two more times—14 (16, 17) sts. Fasten off.

Left Front

Ch 42 (46, 50, 54, 62).

ROW 1: (RS) Dc in 4th ch from hook, dc in next ch, *mb, dc in next 3 ch; rep from * to last ch, dc in last ch, turn—40 (44, 48, 52, 60) sts including tch.

ROW 2: Ch 3 (counts as dc here and throughout), dc in next st, *mb, dc in next 3 sts; rep from * to last 2 sts, dc in last 2 sts, turn.

ROW 3: Ch 3, dc in next 2 (6, 2, 6, 6) sts, *mb, dc in next 7 sts; rep from * to last 5 sts, mb, dc in each st across, turn.

ROW 4: Ch 3, dc across, turn.

ROW 5: Ch 3, dc in next 6 (2, 6, 2, 2) sts, *mb, dc in next 7 sts; rep from * to last st, dc in last st, turn.

ROW 6: Ch 3, dc across, turn.

Rep Rows 3–6 for patt until work measures 12 (12, 12¾, 12¾, 13½)" (30.5 [30.5, 32, 32, 34.5] cm). Cont in patt as foll:

Shape armholes

ROW 1: (RS) Sk first st, sl st in next 2 (2, 3, 3, 4) sts, sc in next st, cont in patt across, turn—37 (41, 44, 48, 55) sts.

ROW 2: Ch 3, work in patt to last 3 (3, 4, 4, 5) sts, sc in next st, turn leaving rem sts unworked—35 (39, 41, 45, 51) sts.

ROW 3: Sk first st, sl st in next 1 (1, 1, 2, 3) st(s), sc in next st, work in patt across, turn—33 (37, 39, 42, 47) sts.

ROW 4: Ch 3, work in patt to last 2 sts, dc2tog, turn—32 sts.

ROW 5: Ch 3, dc2tog, work in patt across, turn—31 sts.

ROW 6: Rep Row 4—30 sts.

ROW 7: Work even in patt.

Sizes 36½ (40)" (93 [101.5] cm) only:

ROW 4: Ch 3, work in patt to last 3 sts, sc in last st, turn leaving rem sts unworked—35 (37) sts.

ROW 5: Ch 3, dc2tog, work in patt across, turn—34 (36) sts.

ROW 6: Ch 3, work in patt to last 2 sts, dc2tog, turn—33 (35) sts.

ROW 7: Rep Row 5—32 (34) sts.

Size 40" (101.5 cm) only:

Rep Row 6—33 sts.

Sizes 43½ (50)" (110.5 [127] cm) only:

ROW 4: Ch 3, work in patt to last 3 (4) sts, sc in next st, turn leaving rem sts unworked—40 (44) sts.

ROW 5: Sk first st, sl st in next st, sc in next st, work in patt to end, turn—38 (42) sts.

Size 43½" (110.5 cm) only:

ROW 6: Ch 3, work in patt to last 2 sts, dc2tog, turn—37 sts.

ROW 7: Ch 3, dc2tog, work in patt across, turn—36 sts.

ROW 8: Rep Row 6—35 sts.

ROW 9: Work even in patt.

Size 50" (127 cm) only:

ROW 6: Ch 3, work in patt to last 3 sts, sc in next st, turn leaving rem sts unworked—40 sts.

ROW 7: Ch 3, dc2tog, work in patt across, turn—39 sts.

ROW 8: Ch 3, work in patt to last 2 sts, dc2tog, turn—38 sts.

ROW 9: Rep Row 7—37 sts.

ROWS 10–11: Work even in patt.

All sizes:

Cont in patt as foll:

Shape neckline

Size 33¼" (84.5 cm) only:

ROW 1: (WS) Sk first st, sl st in next 4 sts, sc in next st, work in patt across, turn—25 sts.

ROW 2: Ch 3, work in patt to last 4 sts, sc in next st, turn leaving rem sts unworked—22 sts.

ROW 3: Sk first st, sl st in next st, sc in next st, work in patt across, turn—20 sts.

ROW 4: Ch 3, work in patt to last 3 sts, sc in next st, turn leaving rem sts unworked—18 sts.

ROW 5: Rep Row 3—16 sts.

ROW 6: Ch 3, work in patt to last 2 sts, dc2tog, turn—15 sts.

ROW 7: Ch 3, work in patt across, turn.

Rep Rows 6–7 two more times—13 sts. Fasten off.

Size 40" (101.5 cm) only:

ROW 1: (RS) Ch 3, work in patt to last 6 sts, sc in next st, turn leaving rem sts unworked—28 sts.

ROW 2: Sk first st, sl st in next 2 sts, sc in next st, work in patt across, turn—25 sts.

ROW 3: Ch 3, work in patt to last 3 sts, sc in next st, turn leaving rem sts unworked—23 sts.

ROW 4: Sk first st, sl st in next st, sc in next st, work in patt across, turn—21 sts.

ROW 5: Ch 3, work in patt to last 3 sts, sc in next st, turn leaving rem sts unworked—19 sts.

ROW 6: Ch 3, dc2tog, work in patt across, turn—18 sts.

ROW 7: Ch 3, work in patt to last 2 sts, dc2tog, turn—17 sts.

ROW 8: Work even in patt, turn.

Rep Rows 7–8 two more times—15 sts. Fasten off.

Sizes 36½ (43½, 50)" (93 [110.5, 127] cm) only:

ROW 1: (WS) Sk first st, sl st in next 4 (5, 6) sts, sc in next st, work in patt across, turn—27 (29, 30) sts.

ROW 2: Ch 3, work in patt to last 4 sts, sc in next st, turn leaving rem sts unworked—24 (26, 27) sts.

ROW 3: Sk first st, sl st in next st, sc in next st, work in patt across, turn—22 (24, 25) sts.

ROW 4: Ch 3, work in patt to last 3 sts, sc in next st, turn leaving rem sts unworked—20 (22, 23) sts.

ROW 5: Sk first st, sl st in next st, sc in next st, work in patt across, turn—18 (20, 21) sts.

ROW 6: Ch 3, work in patt to last 2 sts, dc2tog, turn—17 (19, 20) sts.

ROW 7: Ch 3, dc2tog, work in patt across, turn—16 (18, 19)

ROW 8: Work even in patt, turn.

Rep Rows 7–8 two more times—14 (16, 17) sts. Fasten off.

Sleeves *(make 2)*

Ch 53 (57, 61, 67, 73).

ROW 1: (RS) Dc in 4th ch from hook, dc in next 3 (1, 3, 2, 1) ch, *mb, dc in next 3 ch; rep from * to last 2 (4, 2, 5, 4) ch, mb, dc in last 1 (3, 1, 4, 3) ch, turn—51 (55, 59, 65, 71) sts including tch.

ROW 2: Ch 3 (counts as dc here and throughout), dc in next 2 (0, 2, 1, 0) st(s), *mb, dc in next 3 sts; rep from * to last 4 (6, 4, 3, 6) sts, mb, dc in rem sts, turn.

ROW 3: Ch 3, dc in next 4 (2, 4, 3, 2) sts, *mb, dc in next 7 sts; rep from * to last 6 (4, 6, 5, 4) sts, mb, dc to end, turn.

ROW 4: Ch 3, dc across, turn.

ROW 5: Ch 3, dc in next 8 (6, 8, 7, 6) sts, *mb, dc in next 7 sts; rep from * to last 2 (8, 2, 9, 8) sts, mb, dc to end, turn.

INC ROW: (RS) Ch 3, dc in first st, work in patt to last st, 2 dc in last st, turn—53 (57, 61, 67, 73) sts. Work 5 rows even in patt. Rep Inc row—55 (59, 63, 69, 75) sts. Work 3 rows even in patt. Rep last 4 rows 3 more times—61 (65, 69, 75, 81) sts. Work even in patt until work measures 12 (12, 13, 13, 13½)". Cont in patt as foll:

Shape sleeve cap

ROW 1: (RS) Sk first st, sl st in next 2 (2, 3, 3, 4) sts, work in patt to last 4 (4, 5, 5, 6) sts, sc in next st, turn leaving rem sts unworked—55 (59, 61, 67, 71) sts.

ROW 2: Sk first st, sl st in next 2 sts, sc in next st, work in patt to last 4 sts, sc in next st, turn leaving rem sts un-worked—49 (53, 55, 61, 65) sts.

ROW 3: Rep Row 2—43 (47, 49, 55, 59) sts.

ROWS 4–5: Sk first st, sl st in next st, sc in next st, work in patt to last 3 sts, sc in next st, turn leaving rem sts un-worked—35 (39, 41, 47, 51) sts.

ROW 6: Ch 3, dc2tog, work in patt to last 2 sts, dc2tog, turn—33 (37, 39, 45, 49) sts.

Rep Row 6 four (five, six, six, seven) more times—25 (27, 27, 33, 35) sts. Rep Row 4 two (one, one, one, one) time(s)—17 (23, 23, 29, 31) sts. Rep Row 2 one (two, two, three, three) time(s)—11 (11, 11, 11, 13) sts. Fasten off.

Finishing

Block all pieces to measurements. Sew shoulder seams and side seams. Sew sleeves into armholes. Sew sleeve seams. Weave in loose ends.

Center-front and neckline edging

With RS facing, join yarn at lower corner of right front, ch 1, 2 sc in each row end along right-front edge, 3 sc in corner, 1 sc in each dc and 2 sc in each row-end around neckline, 3 sc in corner, 2 sc in each row end along left-front edge. Fasten off. Cut ribbon in half, use sewing thread to sew each half to one inside front edge just below neckline, as shown in photo.

Beyond the Basics

Garment Construction: Seaming
by ANNETTE PETAVY

Seaming: many crocheters simply dread it. Some motifs can be crocheted together as you go, and some crocheted garments are specifically designed to keep seaming to a strict minimum. However, for most crochet patterns involving more than one piece, seaming is necessary. The right seaming technique, skillfully executed, can make all the difference in your project, taking it from amateurish to outstanding.

You can use one of several seaming techniques to assemble your crocheted pieces. As you'll see, the different techniques are appropriate for different projects. And personal preference definitely plays a role: Experiment with the various kinds of seams to see which one suits both your taste and your project.

A NOTE ABOUT NOTIONS: Most seaming is done with a large-eye, blunt needle (e.g., a tapestry needle) and the same yarn used in the project. Whatever needle you use must have an eye large enough to accommodate the yarn.

A NOTE ABOUT YARNS: Seaming with the yarn you used in the project ensures that the seams blend in with the overall color and texture of your project. However, if the project yarn is thick or fuzzy, the seams may be too bulky. If the project yarn is too fragile (e.g., a single-spun yarn), it might not stand up to seaming without breaking. In either of these circumstances, you can use a thin smooth yarn in a matching color. Try to use a yarn with a similar fiber content. You'll want to be sure the seaming yarn is colorfast and can be washed in the same way as the yarn used in your project.

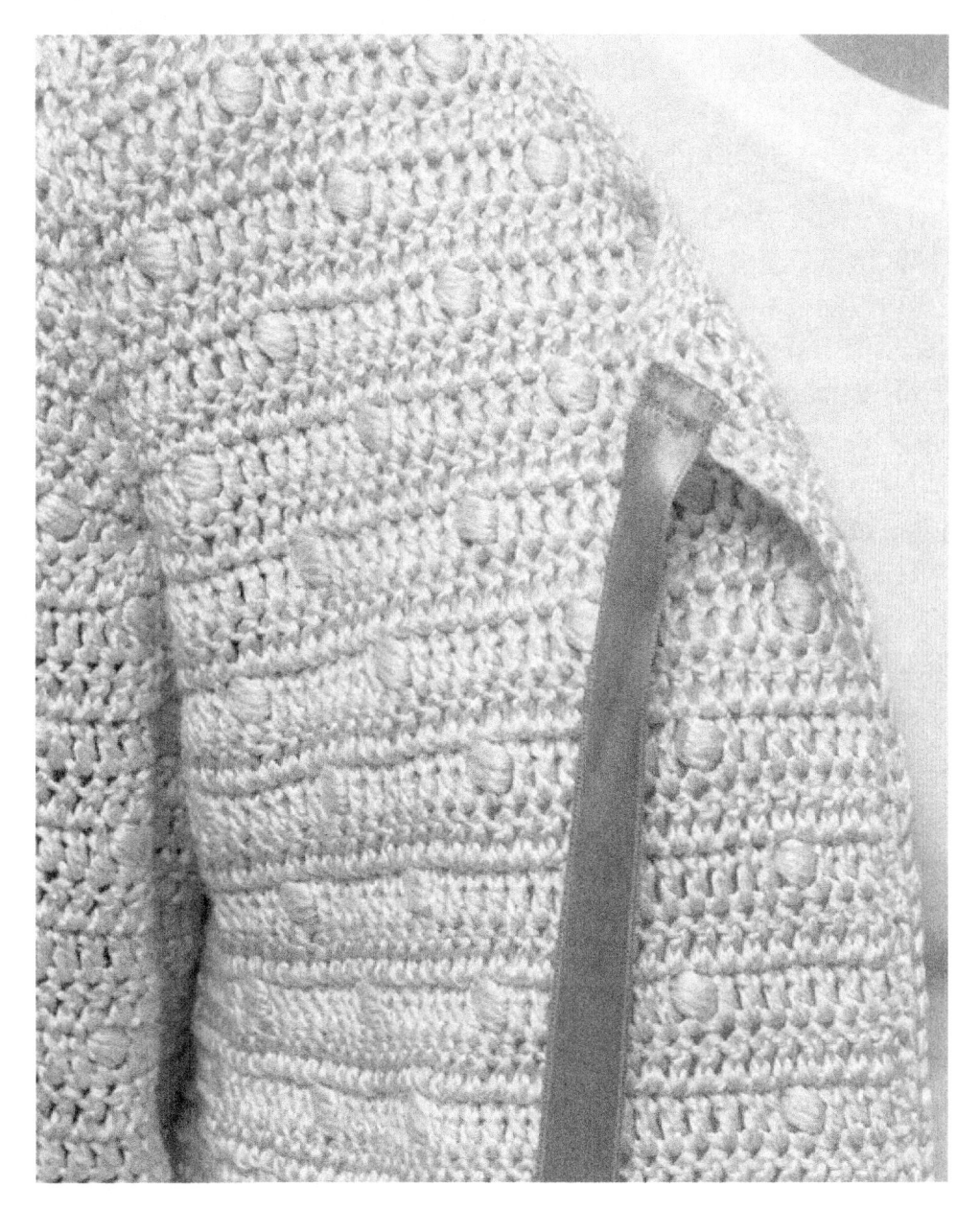

Detail of Ocean Pearls Cardigan, page 112.

Preparing for Good Seams

You start preparing for seaming at the very moment you begin your project. The quality of your seams will depend on the quality of the edges of your fabric. Try to make your edges as neat and consistent as possible.

Be sure to block your crocheted pieces before you start seaming. Blocking will help set the shape of your pieces and can even out edges and stitches, which can help with the seaming. You can also slightly adjust the finished pieces to make them more uniform so they fit together nicely for seaming.

When your pieces are finished, make sure the pieces you're going to seam together are the same size where they meet. Don't just measure them with a measuring tape; check the pieces against one another. The edges of pieces crocheted at very different gauges or of very different dimensions won't match well enough to be seamed together neatly. If you do find that your gauge is slightly inconsistent, however, it's more important to match numbers of rows or stitches than to have the exact same measurement within a fraction of an inch. You'll find seaming much easier if the size of the pieces and the gauge are consistent.

Study the edges of the finished pieces to determine where you will place the seam. Generally, you place a seam one stitch from the edge of each piece. One stitch, then, will be hidden in the seam. If you've turned your rows counting the turning chain as a stitch, then in every second row, the seam will run between the turning chain and the first real stitch of the row. If you've turned your rows without counting the turning chain as a stitch, the seam will always run inside the first real stitch of the row.

If your project is made in a very bulky yarn, you may want to work the seam in the center of the first stitch of each row to avoid a seam that is too thick. Also, if the stitches are particularly tall, you may want to work through rather than between the stitches.

I generally recommend securing the end of the seaming yarn at the beginning of the seam, working two to three stitches in the same spot. If you prefer, you can leave a tail of yarn to be woven in after the seam is finished. The latter approach is especially useful if you are seaming with a yarn other than the one you used in the project because you can hide all the yarn tails in the finished seams.

Seaming Techniques

I describe five types of seams—woven, backstitch, whipstitch, single-crochet, and slip stitch—each of which will be right for certain projects. Woven seams are especially useful for matching crocheted elements, such as rows. Backstitch seams are sturdy and can withstand pulling. Whipstitch seams have the advantage of being simple, but they're bulky. Single-crochet seams are entirely crocheted, but they, too, are bulky. Slip-stitch seams, also crocheted, are sturdy, but you must closely control stitch tension.

Woven Seams

A woven seam is the crocheter's equivalent of the knitter's mattress stitch. The seam is worked with the right sides of the pieces facing you. This makes the woven seam particularly useful in situations where you want to match rows, stitches, or stripes.

Place the pieces you're assembling side by side on a flat surface in front of you, right sides facing you. The edges to be seamed should line up row by row or stitch by stitch.

STEP 1: Secure the seaming yarn on the wrong side of piece A at the start of the seam. Pass the needle through to the right side at the bottom of the first stitch.

STEP 2: Put the needle through the bottom of the first stitch of piece B and pass it up to the right side again at the top of the stitch (or in the stitch above, if you're working in single crochet).

STEP 3: Put the needle through the bottom of the first stitch of piece A, exactly where you previously passed the needle to the right side, and bring the needle to the right side at the top of the stitch.

STEP 4: Put the needle through piece B, where you previously passed the needle to the right side, and bring the needle to the right side at the top of the stitch.

STEP 5: Put the needle through piece A, where you previously passed the needle to the right side, and bring the needle through to the right side at the top of the stitch in the next row.

Repeat Steps 4 and 5, gently tightening the seam as you go, being careful not to distort the fabric. Allow the rows to line up but don't make the seam tighter than the edges themselves. The edges will roll to the wrong side of the work. Secure the end of the seaming yarn.

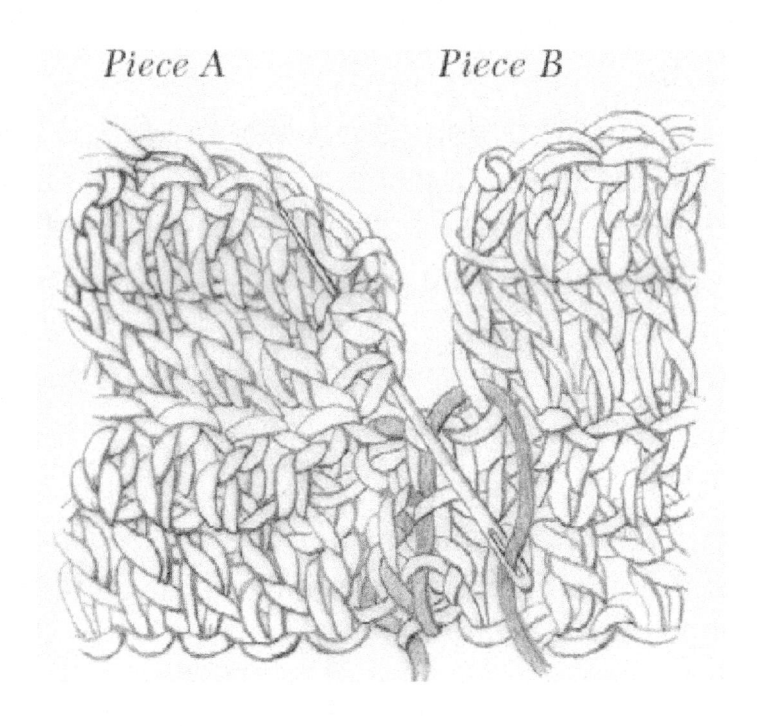

Woven seam applied "row to row"

This technique can also be used for seaming stitch to stitch. To do so, pass your needle through to the right side at the first stitch of piece A (through both loops at the top of the stitch), put it through the first stitch of piece B and pass it up to the right side again at the second stitch of piece B. Continue seaming in the same weaving fashion as described above, catching a new stitch every time you pass your needle through the fabric.

Backstitch Seams

Backstitch seams are very sturdy and are especially suitable for seams that will be exposed to pulling and tugging, such as the shoulder seams of a garment or the seams of a crocheted bag. Backstitch seams are useful when you assemble pieces "row to stitch." They're also valuable for joining pieces of a different nature, such as one crocheted piece and one knitted piece. And backstitch seams work well if the pieces you're assembling have uneven edges, but the seam needs to be straight. However, backstitch seaming isn't suitable if you want the seam to be stretchy.

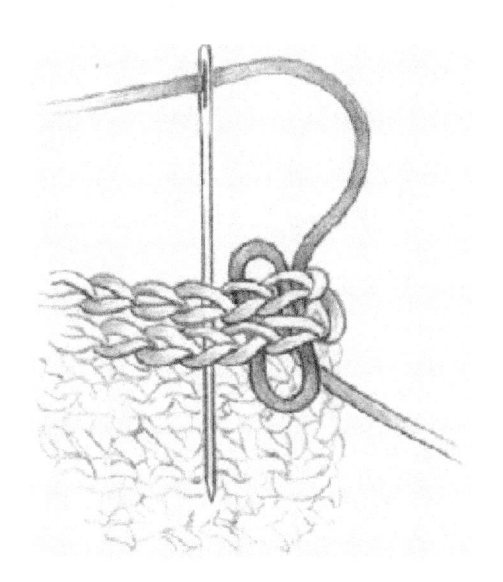

Backstitch seam applied stitch to stitch

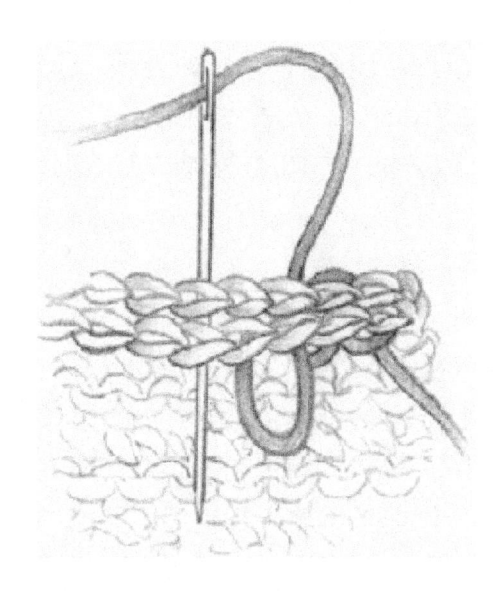

Step 3 of backstitch seam

For this seam, bring the right sides of the pieces together. Hold the pieces in your hand with the two edges facing you and piece A closest to you. Work from right to left.

STEP 1: Secure the seaming yarn on the wrong side of piece A at the start of the seam. Pass the needle through both pieces, from front to back in the first stitch. Then pass the needle through the first stitch to the left, back to front.

STEP 2: Pass the needle through from front to back, at the same spot worked front to back in Step 1. Then pass the needle through from back to front in the second stitch to the left.

STEP 3: Pass the needle through from front to back in the first stitch to the right at the same spot where the needle came through back to front in the previous stitch. Then pass the needle through from back to front in the second stitch to the left.

Repeat Step 3 to complete the seam. Secure the end of the seaming yarn.

Whipstitch Seams

A whipstitch seam, which is simple and almost intuitive to execute, is a good seam for beginners. However, whipstitch seams are relatively bulky. Be careful if your yarn is heavy or if you're assembling a close-fitting garment. In those cases, it might be worthwhile to use a woven or backstitch seam. In the example (above), the whipstitch seam is worked from the wrong side of the pieces to create a seam that will be invisible from the right side. Place the pieces with right sides together. Hold the pieces in your hand with the two edges facing you.

STEP 1: Secure the seaming yarn on the wrong side of one piece, at the start of the seam. Pass the needle through the pieces from back to front at the start of the seam. This creates a small stitch to begin the seam.

STEP 2: A little farther to the left, pass the needle through the pieces, again from back to front.

Repeat Step 2 to complete the seam. Secure the end of the seaming yarn.

You can also work the whipstitch seam on the right side to create a visible seam that becomes part of the project's overall design.

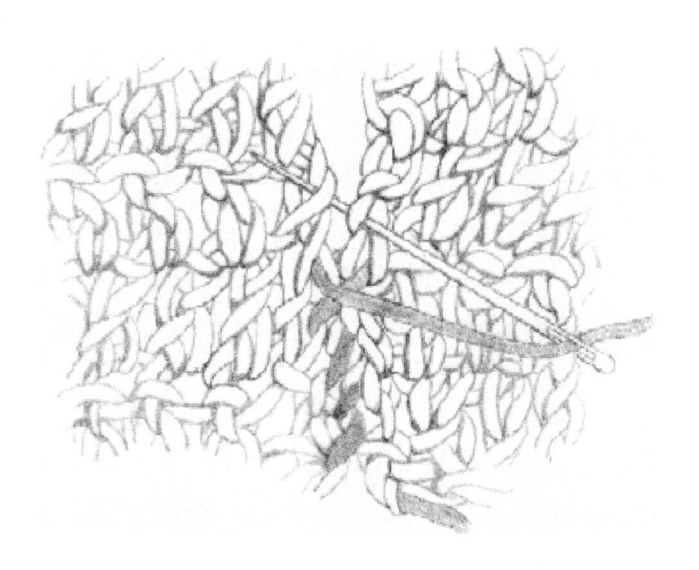

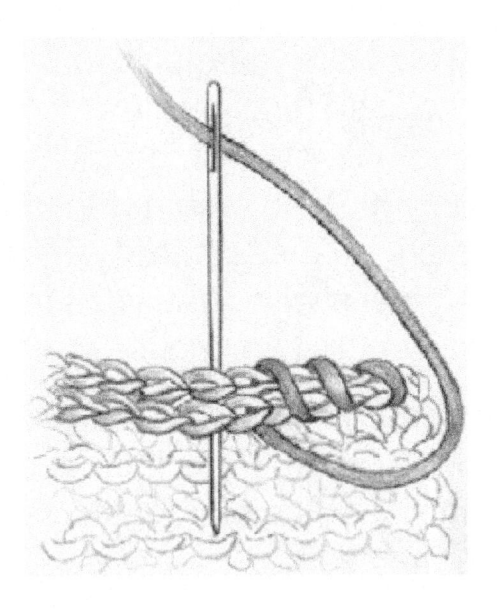

Whipstitch is a very simple, though bulky, seam.
Top: Whipstitch worked row to row.
Bottom: Whipstitch worked stitch to stitch.

Single-Crochet Seams

A single-crochet seam is entirely crocheted, which makes it easy to work and appealing to many crocheters. However, be sure to take into account that the seam will be bulky. You can use that quality to your advantage as a design element—perhaps by working single-crochet seams on the right side of your pieces in a contrasting color.

Place the pieces together with the wrong or right sides facing depending on whether you want your seam to be hidden on the wrong side or show on the right side of your work. Hold the pieces in your hand with the two edges facing you.

Insert the hook through both pieces at the beginning of the seam and pull up a loop, chain one. Work a row of single crochet by inserting your hook through both pieces at the same time. Complete the seam and secure the end of the seaming yarn.

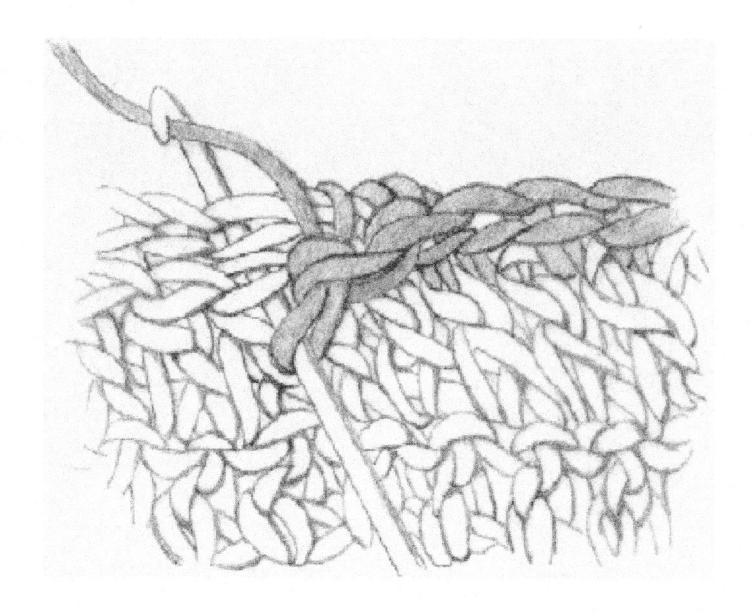

To seam with single crochet, make stitches as usual, but insert the hook through both pieces of fabric at the same time.

Slip-Stitch Seams

The slip stitch creates a neat and sturdy crocheted seam. However, you must control the tension of your stitches. If they're worked too tightly, the seam will pull in and be somewhat inflexible. As you might guess, this seam isn't well suited to lacy fabrics.

Begin by placing the pieces with right sides together. Hold the pieces in your hand with the two edges facing you.

Attach the yarn by inserting your hook through both pieces at the beginning of the seam, pulling up a loop, and chaining one. Work slip stitches, inserting your hook through both pieces at the same time, from front to back, and pulling up the yarn from behind. Complete the seam and secure the seaming yarn.

Detail of Luna Sweater, page 58.

Seaming Without Dread

Now that you've reviewed the instructions for these five seaming techniques, I hope you'll feel able to choose an appropriate technique for each of your projects and execute that seam with confidence. Good seaming will give your crochet projects the well-made finish they deserve.

Sera Lace Top

Every woman can use one fabulous lacy top in her wardrobe. When you wear lace over a solid color, the eye focuses on the lace, not on what's beneath, which is magically figure-flattering. This pullover is roomy and stretchy, with a wide neckline; long, flared sleeves; and picot trim. Flaring gently to mid-hip, it's perfect for an evening of elegance or a day of feeling pretty.

Kathryn Martin

Finished Size

36 (40, 44, 48, 52, 56)" (91.5 [101.5, 112, 122, 132, 142] cm) bust circumference. Sweater shown measures 36" (91.5 cm).

Yarn

Sportweight (#2 Fine)

shown here: Filatura Di Crosa Sera (84% wool, 11% viscose, 5% polyamide; 147 yd [135 m]/1¾ oz [50 g]; **2**): #40 silver grey, 5 (6, 6, 7, 7, 8) balls. Yarn distributed by Tahki Stacy Charles.

Hook

Size G/7 (4.5 mm). *Adjust hook size if necessary to obtain the correct gauge.*

Notions

Removable stitch markers (m).

Gauge

13 fsc = 4" (10 cm); (shell, sc, ch 5, sc) 2 times in patt and 8 rows = 4" (10 cm).

Notes

- This fabric grows when worn, particularly the sleeves. Keep this in mind before deciding to lengthen.
- Top is made from the neck down in joined rounds worked back and forth. Incs in patt are made at each of four "corners" and shape the raglan-style shoulders of the yoke. Mark the ch-sp or st at each corner and move markers (m) up as you go.

Stitch Guide

Shell (sh): 5 dc in same st or sp.

Picot-sh: (3 dc, ch 3, sl st in top of dc just made, 2 dc) in same st.

Shell Trellis Patt (worked in joined rnds):

RND 1: (WS) Ch 1, sc in first ch-sp, *ch 5, sc in 3rd dc of next sh, ch 5, sc in next ch-5 sp; rep from * around, omitting last sc, and ending with sl st in first sc, turn.

RND 2: (RS) Ch 3, 2 dc in same sc, *sc in next ch-5 sp, ch 5, sk next sc, sc in next ch-5 sp, sh in next sc; rep from * around, omitting last sh on final rep, and ending with 2 dc in same sc as beg, sl st in top of beg ch, turn.

RND 3: Ch 1, sc in same dc, ch 5, sc in next ch-5 sp, *ch 5, sc in 3rd dc of next sh, ch 5, sc in next ch-5 sp; rep from * around, ending with ch 2, dc in first sc, turn.

RND 4: Ch 1, sc in first ch-sp, sh in next sc, sc in next ch-5 sp, *ch 5, sk next sc, sc in next ch-5 sp, sh in next sc, sc in next ch-5 sp; rep from * around, ending with ch 2, sk next sc, dc in first sc, turn.

Rep Rnds 1–4 for patt.

9 (9, 9, 10, 10, 11)"
23 (23, 23, 25.5, 25.5, 28) cm

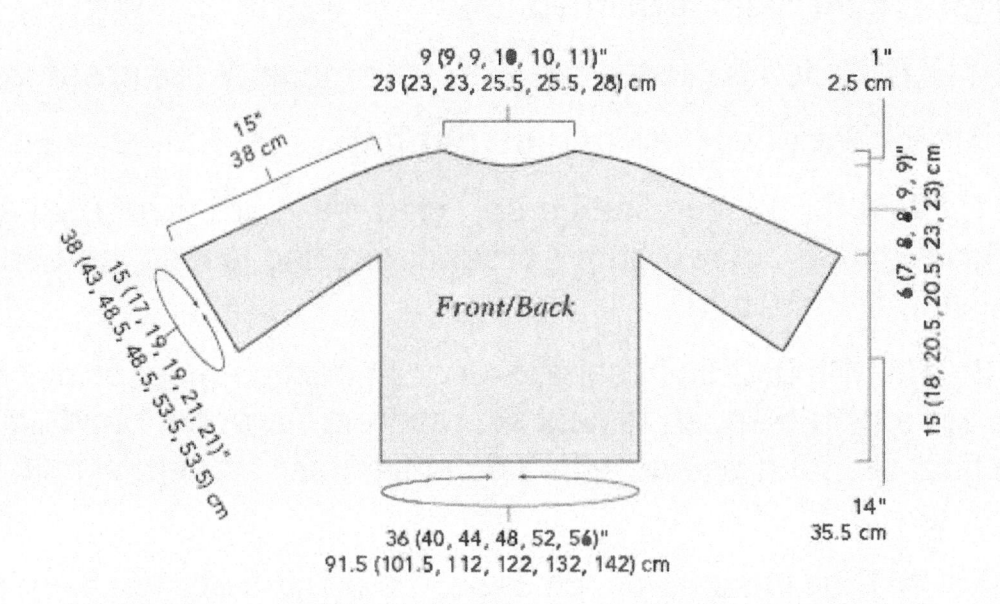

1"
2.5 cm

15"
38 cm

6 (7, 8, 8, 9, 9)"
15 (18, 20.5, 20.5, 23, 23) cm

15 (17, 19, 19, 21, 21)"
38 (43, 48.5, 48.5, 53.5, 53.5) cm

Front/Back

15 (18, 20.5, 20.5, 23, 23) cm

14"
35.5 cm

36 (40, 44, 48, 52, 56)"
91.5 (101.5, 112, 122, 132, 142) cm

- ⭕ Chain (ch)
- ● Slip st (sl st)
- ✕ Single crochet (sc)
- ⊤ Double crochet (dc)
- 5-dc shell
- Ch-3 picot

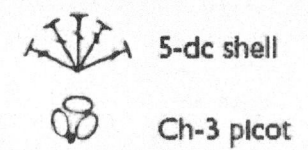

PICOT-SHELL TRIM

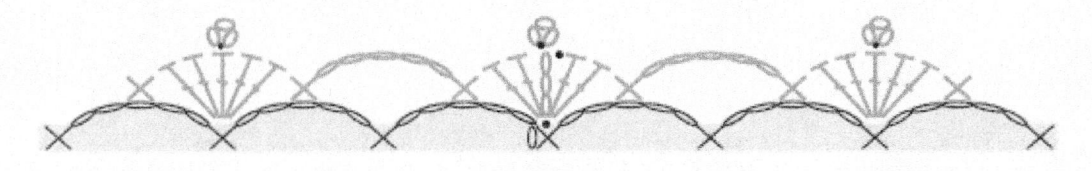

LOWER-BODY SHELL TRELLIS

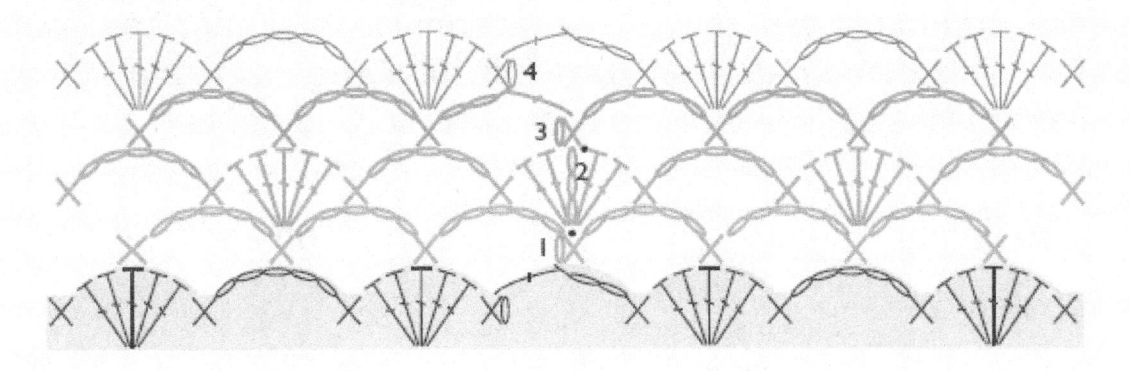

Upper Body

Fsc (see Glossary) 72 (72, 72, 80, 80, 80), sl st in beg fsc to form ring, being careful not to twist sts. Set up 12 (12, 12, 14, 14, 16) reps with incs as foll. (Sizes 48 (52, 56)" (122 [132, 142] cm) have "cheat" sts at center-front and -back neck.)

Sizes 36 (40, 44)" (91.5 [101.5, 112] cm) only:

RND 1: (RS) Ch 3, 4 dc in same fsc, *[sk next fsc, sc in next fsc, ch 5, sk next fsc, sc in next fsc, sk next fsc, sh in next fsc]** 4 times, (ch 2, sh) in same fsc for corner, rep from * to ** 2 times*, (ch 2, sh) in same fsc for corner; rep from * to *, placing last sh in same fsc as beg, ch 1, sc in top of beg ch, turn—16 sh.

Sizes 48 (52)" (122 [132] cm) only:

RND 1: (RS) Ch 3, 4 dc in same fsc, *[sk next fsc, sc in next fsc, ch 5, sk next fsc, sc in next fsc, sk next fsc, sh in next fsc]** 2 times, sc in next fsc, ch 5, sk next fsc, sc in next fsc, sh in next fsc; rep from * to ** 2 times, (ch 2, sh) in same fsc for corner; rep from * to ** 2 times*, (ch 2, sh) in same fsc for corner; rep from * to *, placing last sh in same fsc as beg, ch 1, sc in top of beg ch, turn—18 sh.

Size 56" (142 cm) only:

RND 1: (RS) Ch 3, 4 dc in same fsc, *sk next fsc, sc in next fsc, ch 5, sk next fsc, sc in next fsc, sk next fsc, sh in next fsc**, [sc in next fsc, ch 5, sk next fsc, sc in next fsc, sh in next fsc] 4 times, rep from * to **, (ch 2, sh) in same fsc for corner, rep from * to ** 2 times*, (ch 2, sh) in same fsc for corner; rep from * to *, placing last sh in same fsc as beg, ch 1, sc in top of beg ch, turn—20 sh.

Place corner marker at each ch-2 sp. Move m up each rnd.

All sizes:

RND 2: (WS) Ch 1, sc in first ch-sp, ch 5, sc in 3rd dc of next sh, *[ch 5, sc in next ch-5 sp, ch 5, sc in 3rd dc of next sh]**; rep from * to ** to next corner ch-2 sp, ch 5, sc in corner ch-2 sp, ch 5, sc in 3rd dc of next sh*; rep from * to * 2 times; rep from * to ** to end, ch 5, sl st in beg sc, turn.

RND 3 (inc rnd): Ch 3, 4 dc in first sc, *[sc in next ch-5 sp, ch 5, sk next sc, sc in next ch-5 sp, sh in next sc] to next corner, placing last sh in next corner sc**, (ch 2, sh) in same corner sc*; rep from * to * 2 times; rep from * to ** once, place last sh in same corner sc as beg, ch 1, sc in top of beg ch, turn—20 (20, 20, 22, 22, 24) sh.

Size 36" (91.5 cm) only:

RNDS 4–8: Rep Rnds 2–3 two times, then Rnd 2 once more—28 sh.

Size 40" (101.5 cm) only:

RNDS 4–10: Rep Rnds 2–3 three times, then Rnd 2 once more—32 sh.

Sizes 44 (48)" (112 [122] cm) only:

RNDS 4–12: Rep Rnds 2–3 four times, then Rnd 2 once more—36 (38) sh.

Sizes 52 (56)" (132 [142] cm) only:

RNDS 4–14: Rep Rnds 2–3 five times, then Rnd 2 once more—42 (44) sh.

All sizes:

Work Rnds 2–4 of est patt once more. Moving toward armhole, join front and back at underarms as foll:

JOINING RND: (WS) Ch 1, sc in first ch-sp, *ch 1, fsc 7 for underarm, sk 6 (7, 8, 8, 9, 9) sh of armhole, sc in next corner ch-5 sp, [ch 5, sc in 3rd dc of next sh, ch 5, sc in next ch-5 sp] across*, placing last sc in next corner ch-5 sp; rep from * to *, omitting last sc on final rep, sl st in beg sc.

Lower Body

Fill in patt over underarms, work even on 18 (20, 22, 24, 26, 28) sh as foll:

RND 1: (RS) Ch 3, 2 dc in same sc, *[sc in next ch-5 sp, ch 5, sk next sc, sc in next ch-5 sp, sh in next sc] to next underarm, placing sh in sc before fsc at underarm, sk next fsc, sc in next fsc, ch 5, sk next 3 fsc, sc in next fsc, sk rem fsc, sh in next sc; rep from *, omitting last sh, 2 dc in same sc as beg, sl st in top of beg ch, turn—18 (20, 22, 24, 26, 28) sh.

RNDS 2–24: Work sh trellis patt (see Stitch Guide) Rnds 3–4, then Patt Rnds 1–4 five times, then work Rnd 1 once more.

NOTE: *For shorter top, omit 2 rnds (1" [2.5 cm]) or work to desired length, end by working sh trellis patt Rnd 1 or 3. For longer top, add 2 rnds (1" [2.5 cm]) or work to desired length, end by working patt Rnd 1 or 3.*

Beg lower-edge trim

(RS) Work same as sh trellis patt Rnd 2 except replace each sh with a picot-sh (see Stitch Guide), end with 2 dc in same sc as beg, sl st in top of beg ch, ch 3, sl st in top of same beg ch. Fasten off. If you altered the length and ended by working a Patt Rnd 3, then work trim same as patt Rnd 4, substituting picot sh for each sh, end with ch 5, sl st in beg sc. Fasten off.

Sleeves

With WS facing, join yarn with sl st in 4th base ch of fsc at center of underarm.

RND 1: Ch 1, sc in same base ch, ch 5, sk rem 3 base ch, sc in next corner ch-5 sp (same as joined at underarm), [ch 5, sc in 2nd dc of next sh, ch 5, sc in next ch-5 sp] 6 (7, 8, 8, 9, 9) times, placing sc in next corner ch-5 sp at join, ch 2, dc in beg sc, turn.

RNDS 2–27: Work sh trellis patt Rnd 4, then patt Rnds 1–4 six times, then patt Rnd 1 once more.

NEXT RND: Work picot trim around, sl st in beg sc. Fasten off.

Finishing

If your neck base ch has stretched, or if you prefer a slightly closer neckline, crochet the edging more firmly. Otherwise, work to gauge. With RS facing, join yarn with sl st in any fsc of neck, ch 1, sc in same fsc, sc in each fsc around, sl st in beg sc—72 (72, 72, 80, 80, 80) sc. Fasten off. Weave in loose ends; block to measurements.

Doris Chan, a professional member of the Crochet Guild of America, is author of several crochet books. You can follow her at dorischancrochet.com.

Beyond the Basics

Shoring up *on Shells*
by DORIS CHAN

Shells are the showgirls of the crochet world, with an "Oh, wow!" factor created with visual impact, contrasting texture, dimensionality, openness, and movement. Shells and sister stitches V, fan, cluster, and bobble are not exact terms but names given to describe discrete multiple-stitch figures. They do not mean the same thing in every pattern. The basic stitches used to create one of these elements (double crochet, triple crochet, chain, and so on), as well as the number of basic stitches in a figure and how the figure is employed in an overall stitch pattern, are infinitely variable and are defined by the pattern's author. So a shell may have three stitches or twenty stitches—it depends on the pattern.

Basically, a shell is a figure comprising multiple stitches (or spokes) that all start in the same place, with each spoke finished separately. **Swatch A** (page 130) contains, from bottom to top, 5-dc shells, (2 dc, ch 2, 2 dc) shells, and (4 dc, ch 1, dc) tilted shells.

A shell with two spokes, often with a chain space in the middle, is a V st. A fan is an amped-up shell that spreads out more than a basic shell. There may be chain spaces between the spokes, or the spokes may be made not in one single stitch but in one bigger hole, like a chain space, or there may be so many spokes, nine or more, that the figure really fans out. Sometimes a basic shell is topped by an amplifying row of stitches separated by a chain, as in **Swatch B** (page 130). At the top is a crescent fan. At bottom is a peacock fan.

With clusters and bobbles, the multiple stitches are finished as one. Although the two names may be used interchangeably, technically the spokes of a cluster are started in different places, creating a figure that appears as the inverted image of a shell. For a bobble, the spokes all start in the same place and finish as one. A bobble made with three or more half double crochet stitches finished as one is known as a *puff.* **Swatch C** (page 130) shows alternating rows of shells with, from bottom to top, clusters, bobbles, and puffs.

The three-dimensionality of these figures makes them natural decorative elements, key players in trims, edgings, and ornamental doodads. By varying the height and number of basic tall stitches in a shell, you can sculpt the petals of a flower.

When you dissect fancy stitch patterns, you'll find that many of the scary ones are just shells and combinations of the above figures with some chain spaces thrown in for holes. The easiest patterns to read are the stitch patterns where the shells are in line, with shells stacked on shells, often with a one-or two-row repeat. Swatches A, B, and C all feature in-line shells or fans.

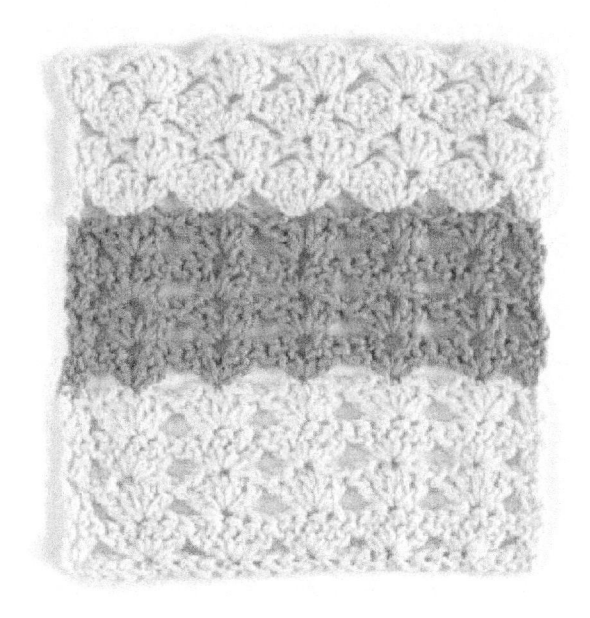

Swatch A Shells

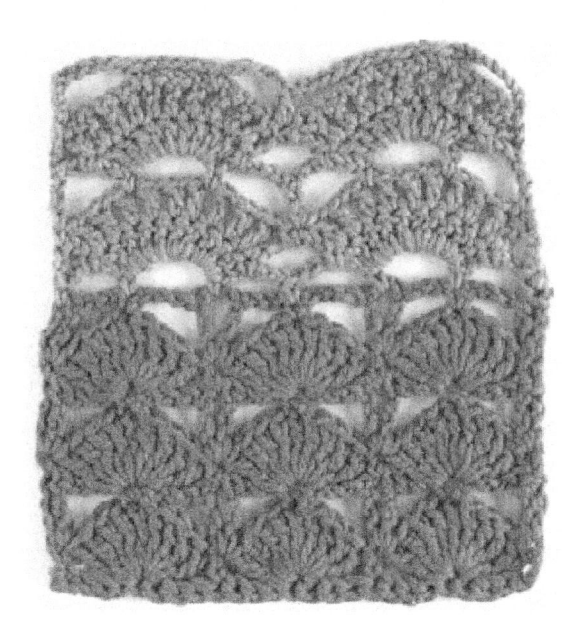

Swatch B Fans

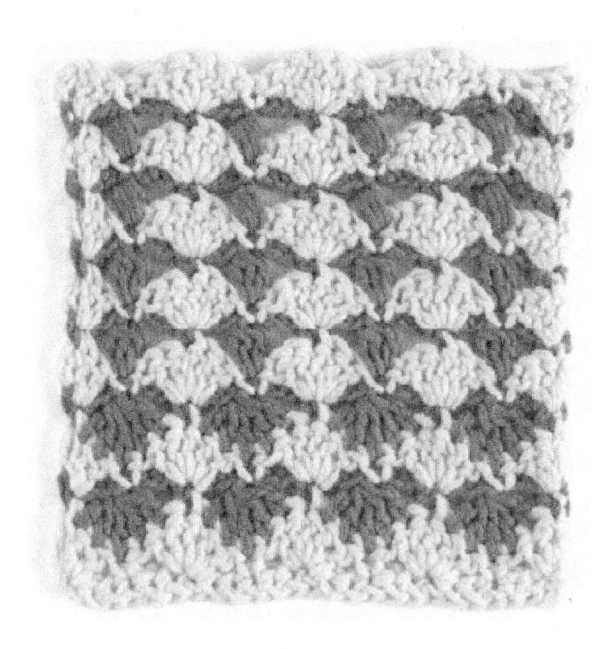

Swatch C Clusters

More intricate patterning happens when shells are staggered or shifted, requiring two or more rows to complete the stitch pattern. **Swatch D** illustrates three stitch patterns that feature staggered shells or fans.

Swatch D Staggered Patterns

Shells are indispensable as shapers. Each shell is actually an increase, since you plant all the feet in one spot but end up with many heads. It takes the following rows of crochet to keep this expansion in check. However, the tendency of shell fabric to spread can be used to great advantage when designing garments from the top down. Worked this way, the last shells are set free, unfettered, allowing the bottom edge to flare for built-in hip shaping.

In fact, you shape with shells every time you make the corners of a granny square **(Swatch E)**. And shells and clusters work in tandem to turn solid fabric into the familiar ripple pattern **(Swatch F)**.

Swatch E Granny Square

Swatch F Ripple Stitch

Another way to make increases or decreases is to change the number of shells in the row. This needs to be done gradually and carefully if you wish to maintain the progression and integrity of the repeating stitch pattern as you go, while avoiding excessive rippling or puckering. There are as many approaches to shaping shells as there are shells, and the method varies so much from designer to designer that it is beyond the scope of this article to describe the process. But what I can say with conviction is that the more shell patterns and designs you create, the better you'll understand how this shaping works. **Swatch G** begins with three pattern repeats and increases to four; this is sometimes called cone stitch.

Swatch G Interior Shaping

To be worked evenly at the ends of rows, some stitch patterns have wonky bits at the edges, extra stitches, or partial shells. Because of this complexity, counting becomes a headache. Obviously you would not count individual basic stitches as you would in solid-stitch rows. If the count is given in shells, you count whole, completed shells. But if the count is given in repeats, you are responsible for knowing what individual stitches constitute a stitch-pattern repeat. This refers to the group of stitches that make up a complete piece of pattern, the group that is worked over and over across a row. In Swatch D, some rows have two shells, some have three, but the swatch is three stitch-pattern repeats wide throughout.

Seafoam Vest

This loose-fitting, deep-V-neck vest has a unique construction that will flatter a wide variety of figures. Wear it layered over a long-sleeved tee or collared shirt on chilly days or with an ultra-long tank top on warmer days.

Kathryn Martin

Finished Size

32 (35, 39, 42, 46)" (81.5 [89, 99, 106.5, 117] cm) bust circumference. Vest shown measures 39" (99 cm).

Yarn

Worsted weight (#4 Medium)

shown here: Rowan Summer Tweed (70% silk, 30% cotton; 118 yd [108 m]/1¾ oz [50 g]; (4)): #513 dew (pale green), 5 (5, 6, 7, 8) skeins. Yarn distributed by Westminster Fibers.

Hook

Size G/6 (4 mm). *Adjust hook size if necessary to obtain the correct gauge.*

Notions

Yarn needle; removable stitch markers (m).

Gauge

13 sts and 16 rows = 4" (10 cm) in sc; 14 sts and 6½ rows = 4" (10 cm) in dc-flo patt.

Note

✛ The body of this vest is made flat in one piece to the armholes. From the armholes, each upper part (right-front shoulder panel, left-front shoulder panel, and back shoulder panel) is worked separately.

Stitch Guide

Dc2tog flo decrease: Working through front lps only, yo, insert hook in next st, draw up a lp (3 lps on hook), yo, draw through first 2 lps on hook, yo, insert hook in next st, draw up a lp (4 lps on hook), yo, draw through first 2 lps on hook, yo, draw through 3 lps on hook.

Vest

NOTE: *The waistband is worked in a spiral, without joining rnds. To avoid losing count, place a marker in first st of rnd. Move m up for each rnd.*

Waistband

Ch 100 (108, 116, 128, 140); sl st in first ch to form ring, being careful not to twist chain.

RND 1: Sc in each st around—100 (108, 116, 128, 140) sc.

Rep last rnd 7 (7, 8, 8, 8) more times.

ROW 1: Sc in each of next 15 (16, 17, 19, 21) sts, sc in back lp only (blo) of next st, ch 2 (counts as dc), dc blo in each of next 19 (21, 23, 25, 27) sts, dc in each of next 80 (86, 92, 102, 112) sts, dc in front lp only (flo) of each of next 20 (22, 24, 26, 28) sts (these are the same sts as the 20 (22, 24, 26, 28) dc blo sts—this beg the overlap of the right and left fronts), turn—120 (130, 140, 154, 168) dc.

NOTE: *The remainder of vest is worked in dc flo.*

ROW 2: Ch 2 (counts as dc), sk first dc, dc flo in each dc to last dc, turn, leaving turning chain (tch) unworked—119 (129, 139, 153, 167) dc.

Rep Row 2 for 18 (20, 22, 24, 26) more rows, ending with a WS row—101 (109, 117, 129, 141) dc.

ROW 1: (RS) Ch 2 (counts as dc here and throughout), sk first dc, dc flo in each of next 14 (15, 16, 18, 20) sts, turn—15 (16, 17, 19, 21) sts.

ROW 2: Ch 2, sk first dc, dc flo in next st, dc2tog flo (see Stitch Guide) over next 2 sts, dc flo in next st, dc2tog flo over next 2 sts, dc flo in each st to last dc, turn, leaving tch unworked—12 (13, 14, 16, 18) sts.

ROW 3: Ch 2, sk first dc, dc flo in each st to last dc, turn, leaving tch unworked—11 (12, 13, 15, 17) sts.

ROW 4: Rep Row 3—10 (11, 12, 14, 16) sts.

ROW 5: Ch 2, sk first dc, dc flo in each st to last dc, dc in top of tch, turn—10 (11, 12, 14, 16) sts.

Rep Row 5 for 8 (8, 9, 9, 10) more rows. Fasten off.

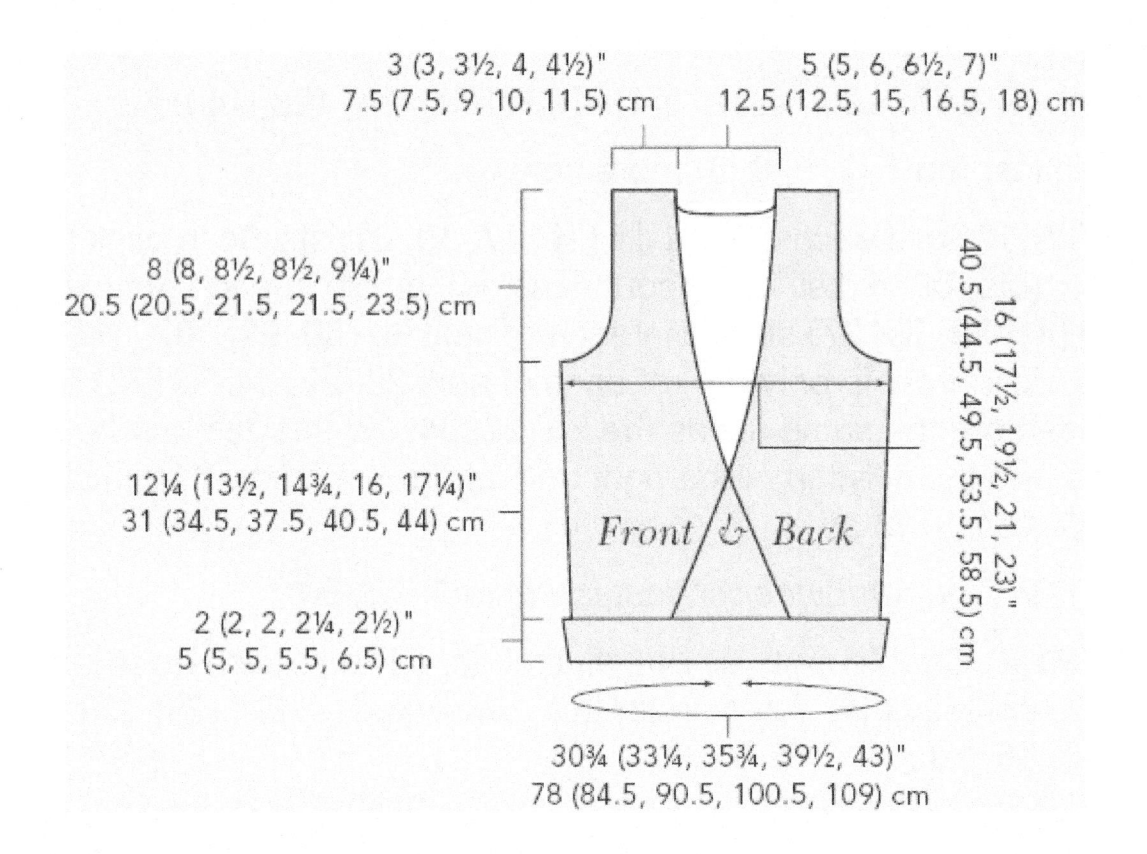

ROW 1: With RS facing, join yarn with sl st to 16th (17th, 18th, 20th, 22nd) st from neck edge of left front and, working toward

neck edge, ch 2 (counts as dc here and throughout), sk first dc, dc flo in each of next 14 (15, 16, 18, 20) sts, turn, leaving tch unworked—15 (16, 17, 19, 21) sts.

ROW 2: (WS) Ch 2, sk first dc, dc flo in each of next 8 (9, 10, 12, 14) sts, dc2tog flo over next 2 sts, dc flo in next st, dc2tog flo over next 2 sts, turn, leaving tch unworked—12 (13, 14, 16, 18) sts.

ROW 3: Ch 2, sk first dc, dc flo in each st to last dc, turn, leaving tch unworked—11 (12, 13, 15, 17) sts.

ROW 4: Rep Row 3—10 (11, 12, 14, 16) sts.

ROW 5: Ch 2, dc flo in each st to last dc, dc in top of tch, turn—10 (11, 12, 14, 16) sts.

Rep Row 5 for 8 (8, 9, 9, 10) more rows.

ROW 1: With RS facing, sk 12 (13, 14, 15, 16) sts of underarm from armhole edge of right-front shoulder panel, join yarn with sl st to 12th (13th, 14th, 15th, 16th) st, ch 2 (counts as dc here and throughout), sk first dc, dc flo in each of next 48 (52, 56, 62, 68) sts, turn—49 (53, 57, 63, 69) sts.

ROW 2: Ch 2, sk first dc, dc flo in next st, dc2tog flo over next 2 sts, dc flo in next st, dc2tog flo over next 2 sts, dc flo in each of next 36 (40, 44, 50, 56) sts, dc2tog flo over next 2 sts, dc flo in next st, dc2tog flo over next 2 sts, turn, leaving tch unworked—44 (48, 52, 58, 64) sts.

ROW 3: Ch 2, sk first dc, dc flo in each st to last dc, turn, leaving tch unworked—43 sts (47, 51, 57, 63) sts.

Rep Row 3 for 7 more rows—36 (40, 44, 50, 56) sts.

ROW 4: Ch 2, sk first dc, dc flo in each st across, dc in top of tch, turn.

Fasten off.

Finishing

With RS tog, seam shoulders. Finish vest by working a row of sc along edges of armholes, neck, and front panels, working 1 sc in each st across and work 2 sc in the side of each dc row. Fasten off. Weave in loose ends.

Chloe Nightingale lives in Scotland, where all her crocheted goodies come in handy in the winter. You can find her blog at reallycrabbycrafter.blogspot.com.

Larger Than Life Bag

Always a showstopper, this oversized bag is ready to haul yarn, books, and projects, and it can be a dramatic exhibit of your personality and skill. Lined with matching fabric, the bag features the Willow Block from *200 Crochet Blocks for Blankets, Throws, and Afghans* by Jan Eaton (Interweave, 2004).

Kathryn Martin

Finished Size

22" (56 cm) wide, 4" (10 cm) deep, and 14" (35.5 cm) high, not including strap.

Yarn

DK weight (#3 Light)

shown here: Koigu Kersti Merino Crepe (100% wool; 114 yd [104 m]/ 1¾ oz [50 g]; 3): #K1220 rusty red (MC), 3 skeins. 1 skein of each for contrast colors: #K1515 blue, #K0000 off-white, #K1520 lime green, #K2370 apricot, #K2260 purple, #K1141 pink, #K1125 rose.

Hook

Size H/8 (5 mm). *Adjust hook size if necessary to obtain the correct gauge.*

Notions

Yarn needle; 1⅛ yd (1 m) of 45" (114 cm) wide fabric for lining; matching thread and 18" (46 cm) zipper; sharp handsewing needle.

Gauge

Finished block measures 6½" (16.5 cm) square. 16 sc = 4" (10 cm).

Notes

+ When assembling the bag, you will need to choose a right side and a wrong side of your work.
+ Each block motif consists of three colors: Color A for the center, Color B for the middle, and Color C for the outside. Choose any color combination you like for each block, changing colors on Rnds 3 and 6.

Block

(see block diagram)

Make 12 blocks total—6 for each side of bag. With A, ch 4. Sl st in first ch to form ring.

RND 1: Ch 3 (counts as dc), 15 dc into ring, sl st in 3rd ch of beg ch-3 to join—16 dc.

RND 2: Ch 4 (counts as dc, ch 1), *dc in next dc, ch 1; rep from * 15 times, sl st in 3rd ch of beg ch-4 to join. Fasten off.

RND 3: Join B to any dc from previous rnd with sl st, ch 3 (counts as dc), *2 dc in next ch-1 sp, dc in next dc; rep from * 15 times, sl st in 3rd ch of beg ch-3 to join—48 dc.

RND 4: Ch 1, sc in sl st, *ch 5, sl st in 5th ch from hook, sk 2 dc, sc in next dc, ch 2, sk 2 dc, sc in next dc, ch 3, sk 2 dc, sc in next dc, ch 2, sk 2 dc**, sc in next dc*; rep from * to * 2 times, then rep from * to ** 1 time, sl st in beg sc to join.

RND 5: Sl st in next ch-5 sp, ch 3 (counts as dc), (4 dc, ch 3, 5 dc) in same sp, *sc in the next ch-2 sp, 5 dc in next ch-3 sp, sc in next ch-2 sp**, (5 dc, ch 3, 5 dc) in next ch-5 sp*; rep from * to * 2 times, then rep from * to ** 1 time, sl st in 3rd ch of beg ch-3 to join. Fasten off.

RND 6: Join C to any corner ch-3 sp with sl st, ch 1, (sc, ch 3, sc) in same ch sp, *ch 5, dc in next sc, ch 3, sk 2 dc, sc in next dc, ch 3, sk 2 dc, dc in next sc, ch 5**, (sc, ch 3, sc) in next ch-3 sp*; rep from * to * 2 times, then rep from * to ** 1 time, sl st in beg sc to join.

RND 7: Sl st in ch-3 sp, ch 3 (counts as dc), (2 dc, ch 2, 3 dc) in same ch-3 sp, *5 dc in next ch-5 sp, 3 dc in next ch-3 sp, 3 dc in next ch-3 sp, 5 dc in next ch-5 sp**, (3 dc, ch 2, 3 dc) in next ch-3 sp*; rep from * to * 2 times, then rep from * to ** 1 time, sl st in 3rd ch of beg ch-3 to join. Fasten off.

BLOCK DIAGRAM

- ⌒ chain (ch)
- • slip st (sl st)
- ✕ single crochet (sc)
- ╈ double crochet (dc)

Panel assembly

With RS tog, use matching yarn and a yarn needle to whipstitch (see page 122) through the closest lp of each st on each block.

Create 2 separate panels of 6 blocks each.

Border

RND 1: Sc around all panel edges, working (sc, ch 2, sc) in each corner and dec in each ch sp where the blocks are joined by: sc in ch sp, sc2tog working in same ch sp, and then in next ch sp.

RND 2: Sc around all edges working (sc, ch 2, sc) in each corner.

Side and Bottom Band

With MC, ch 15.

ROW 1: Sc in 2nd ch and each ch across, turn.

ROW 2: Ch 1, sc in each st across, turn.

NOTE: *To create a more solid fabric, the turning chain (tch) will not function as a dc. Be careful not to work into the tch, this will create unintended incs.*

ROW 3: Ch 2, dc in each st across, turn.

ROW 4: Ch 1, sc in each st across, turn.

ROW 5: Rep Row 2.

ROW 6: Rep Row 3.

ROW 7: Rep Row 4.

ROWS 8–137: Rep Rows 5–7 forty-three times.

Band border

With MC, work 1 sc into the side of each sc row and 2 sc into the side of each dc row—182 sc total.

Seam band to panels

Hold WS tog and work sl st into the outside lp of the sc of each piece to seam the pieces tog, cont sl st seam along the side, 2 sc into the ch sp at corner, seam along the bottom, 2 sc into the ch sp at the corner, sl st seam along the side. Fasten off and weave in ends.

Lining and Finishing

Cut a 36" × 26¼" (91.5 × 67 cm) rectangle across the width of the lining fabric. Press folds as shown in **Figure 1**.

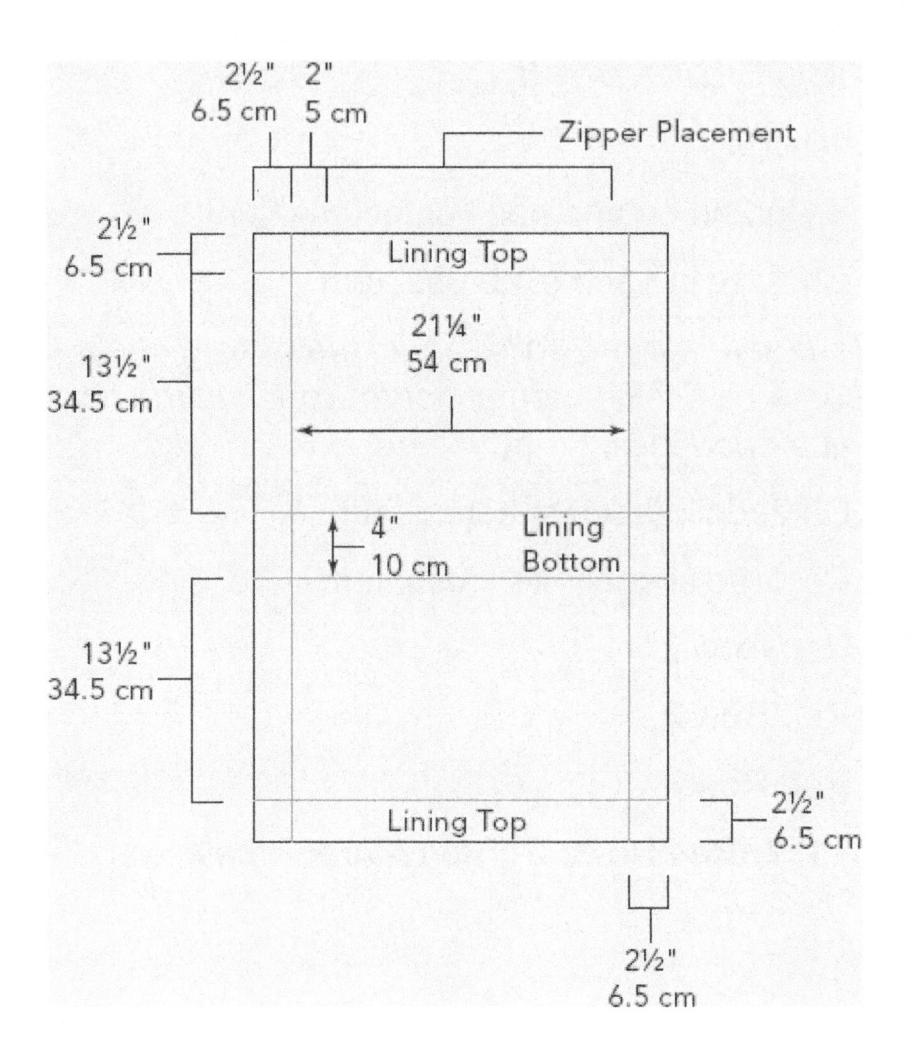

Figure 1

Fold the fabric in half, widthwise, with RS tog and align the short edges (the top of the bag). Beginning at one edge, stitch for 4¾" (12 cm), change to a basting stitch for the next 17" (43 cm) (zipper opening), then change back to a regular stitch for the rest of the seam. Press the seam open and center the zipper face down over the seam allowances within the basted area. Stitch the zipper in place and remove the basting stitches. Stitch the remaining side edges together using a ½" (1.3 cm) seam allowance. Press all seams open.

Straps

Cut two 4½" × 40" (11.5 × 101.5 cm) fabric strips. Fold strips in half lengthwise with RS tog and stitch the long edges using a ¼" (6 mm) seam allowance. Turn RS out, center the seam, and press flat. Rep for the second strap. Pin a strap to each side of the bag lining about 4" (10 cm) in from the side seam and 2" (5 cm) from the zipper and stitch in place **(Figure 2)**. Box the lining's upper and lower corners as foll: Turn lining WS out. At one lower corner, fold the side seam down flat against the bottom of the bag, creating a point. Stitch 2" (5 cm) from the point, forming a triangle **(Figure 3)**. Repeat for the remaining three corners. Sew lining into bag, whipstitching (see page 122) into middle of (not around) crochet stitches along the top of the bag.

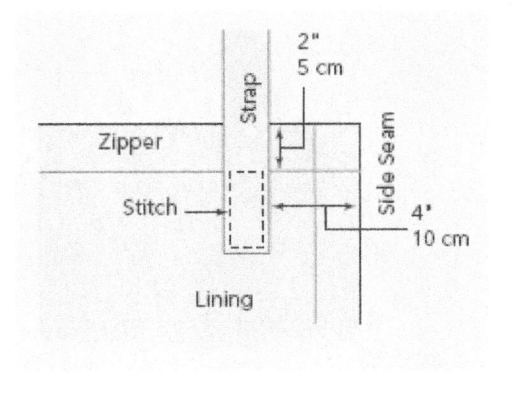

Figure 2

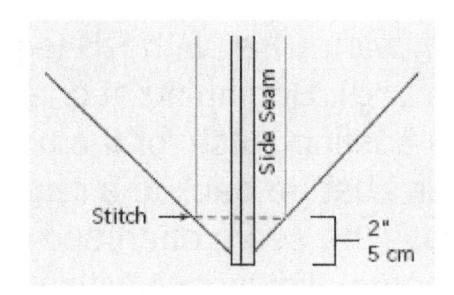

Figure 3

Cecily Keim, crochet designer, blogs at suchsweethands.blogspot.com.

Diamonds Silk Scarf

Two silk yarns are tapestry crocheted to create the diamond motif on this luxurious scarf with excellent drape. One yarn is carried while the other is crocheted. It is possible to make a variety of sizes with the same motif simply by increasing or decreasing the size of the base chain. The increases at the ends of the scarf form a pattern as they build one upon the other.

Kathryn Martin

Finished Size

9" (23 cm) wide by 64" (162.5 cm) long.

Yarn

Sockweight (#1 Superfine)

shown here: Halcyon Gemstone Silk 2/12 (100% silk; 610 yd [558 m]/3½ oz [99 g]; 1): #103 ruby (A), 1 skein.

DK weight (#3 Light)

shown here: Halcyon Gemstone Silk Bouclé (100% silk; 324 yd [296 m]/3½ oz [99 g]; 3): #106 rose gold (B), 1 skein.

Hook

Size I/9 (5.5 mm). *Adjust hook size if necessary to obtain the correct gauge.*

Notions

Stitch marker (m).

Gauge

16 sc and 20 rows = 4" (10 cm).

Notes

- Inc or dec foundation ch in multiples of 8 ch to make a longer or shorter scarf. Scarf is worked in the rnd as a spiral, beg at center. Place marker (pm) in last st to indicate end of rnd; move m up with each rnd.

- One strand each of A and B is carried beg with Rnd 2; only 1 color is worked at a time while the other is carried. To carry unused yarn, lay it across top of next st and work over it with active yarn. Switch colors when 2 lps rem on hook; yo with new color and draw it through both lps to complete st.

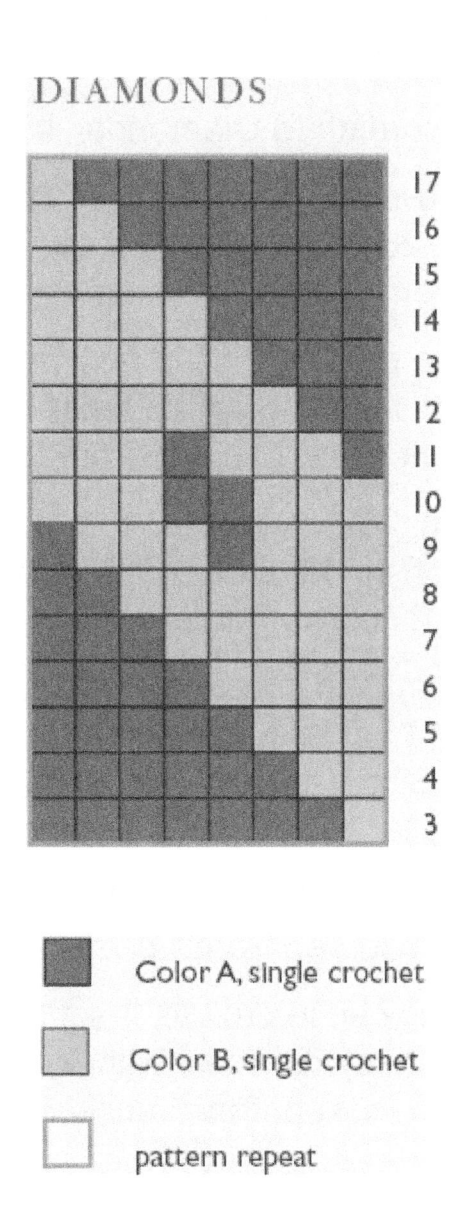

DIAMONDS

■ Color A, single crochet
□ Color B, single crochet
□ pattern repeat

Scarf

With A and leaving a 10" tail, loosely ch 230.

RND 1: Sc in 2nd ch from hook and in next 228 ch, 3 sc in last ch—231 sc. Rotate the chain 180° and cont to sc across the bottom ridge of the ch, carrying the "tail" across the tops of the sts until it runs out, 2 sc in last st, place marker (pm) in last st, do not join—460 sts.

RND 2: Beg to carry B across top of sts, *with A, 2 sc in each of first 2 sts, 226 sc, 2 sc in each of next 2 sts; rep from * once—468 sts.

Work Rnds 3–17 according to Diamonds chart, inc as foll:

RND 3: *With A, 2 sc in next st, 1 sc, 2 sc in next st, 2 sc, [with B, 1 sc, with A, 7 sc] 28 times, with A, 2 sc, 2 sc in next st, 1 sc, 2 sc in next st; rep from * once—476 sts.

RND 4: *With A, sc in next st, 2 sc in next st, 1 sc, 2 sc in next st, 3 sc, [with B, 2 sc, with A, 6 sc] 28 times, with A, 3 sc, 2 sc in next st, 1 sc, 2 sc in next st, 1 sc; rep from * once—484 sts.

RND 5: *With A, 2 sc, 2 sc in next st, 1 sc, 2 sc in next st, 4 sc, [with B, 3 sc, with A, 5 sc] 28 times, with A, 4 sc, 2 sc in next st, 1 sc, 2 sc in next st, 2 sc; rep from * once—492 sts.

RND 6: * With A, 3 sc, 2 sc in next st, 1 sc, 2 sc in next st, 5 sc, [with B, 4 sc, with A, 4 sc] 28 times, with A, 5 sc, 2 sc in next st, 1 sc, 2 sc in next st, 3 sc; rep from *once—500 sts.

RND 7: *With A, 4 sc, 2 sc in next st, 1 sc, 2 sc in next st, 6 sc, [with B, 5 sc, with A, 3 sc] 28 times, with A, 6 sc, 2 sc in next st, 1 sc, 2 sc in next st, 4 sc; rep from * once—508 sts.

RND 8: *With A, 5 sc, 2 sc in next st, 1 sc, 2 sc in next st, 7 sc, [with B, 6 sc, with A, 2 sc] 28 times, with A, 7 sc, 2 sc in next st, 1 sc, 2 sc in next st, 5 sc; rep from * once—516 sts.

RND 9: *With A, 6 sc, 2 sc in next st, 1 sc, 2 sc in next st, 8 sc, [with B, 3 sc, with A, 1 sc, with B, 3 sc, with A, 1 sc] 28 times, with A, 8 sc, 2 sc in next st, 1 sc, 2 sc in next st, 6 sc; rep from * once—524 sts.

RND 10: *With A, 7 sc, 2 sc in next st, 1 sc, 2 sc in next st, 9 sc, [with B, 3 sc, with A, 2 sc, with B, 3 sc] 28 times, with A, 9 sc, 2 sc in next st, 1 sc, 2 sc in next st, 7 sc; rep from * once—532 sts.

RND 11: *With A, 8 sc, 2 sc in next st, 1 sc, 2 sc in next st, 10 sc, [with A, 1 sc, with B, 3 sc, with A, 1 sc, with B, 3 sc] 28 times, with A, 10 sc, 2 sc in next st, 1 sc, 2 sc in next st, 8 sc; rep from * once—540 sts.

RND 12: *With A, 9 sc, 2 sc in next st, 1 sc, 2 sc in next st, 11 sc, [with A, 2 sc, with B, 6 sc] 28 times, with A, 11 sc, 2 sc in next st, 1 sc, 2 sc in next st, 9 sc; rep from * once—548 sts.

RND 13: *With A, 10 sc, 2 sc in next st, 1 sc, 2 sc in next st, 12 sc, [with A, 3 sc, with B, 5 sc] 28 times, with A, 12 sc, 2 sc in next st, 1 sc, 2 sc in next st, 10 sc; rep from * once—556 sts.

RND 14: *With A, 11 sc, 2 sc in next st, 1 sc, 2 sc in next st, 13 sc, [with A, 4 sc, with B, 4 sc] 28 times, with A, 13 sc, 2 sc in next st, 1 sc, 2 sc in next st, 11 sc; rep from * once—564 sts.

RND 15: *With A, 12 sc, 2 sc in next st, 1 sc, 2 sc in next st, 14 sc, [with A, 5 sc, with B, 3 sc] 28 times, with A, 14 sc, 2 sc in next st, 1 sc, 2 sc in next st, 12 sc; rep from * once—572 sts.

RND 16: *With A, 13 sc, 2 sc in next st, 1 sc, 2 sc in next st, 15 sc, [with A, 6 sc, with B, 2 sc] 28 times, with A, 15 sc, 2 sc in next st, 1 sc, 2 sc in next st, 13 sc; rep from * once—580 sts.

RND 17: *With A, 14 sc, 2 sc in next st, 1 sc, 2 sc in next st, 16 sc, [with A, 7 sc, with B, 1 sc] 28 times, with A, 16 sc, 2 sc in next st, 1 sc, 2 sc in next st, 14 sc; rep from * once—588 sts.

RND 18: *Carry B, with A, 15 sc, 2 sc in next st, 1 sc, 2 sc in next st, 258 sc, 2 sc in next st, 1 sc, 2 sc in next st, 15 sc; rep from * once—596 sts.

RND 19: *Carry B, with A, 16 sc, 2 sc in next st, 1 sc, 2 sc in next st, 260 sc, 2 sc in next st, 1 sc, 2 sc in next st, 16 sc; rep from * once—604 sts.

RND 20: *Carry B, with A, 17 sc, 2 sc in next st, 1 sc, 2 sc in next st, 262 sc, 2 sc in next st, 1 sc, 2 sc in next st, 17 sc; rep from * once—612 sts.

RND 21: *Carry B, with A, 18 sc, 2 sc in next st, 1 sc, 2 sc in next st, 264 sc, 2 sc in next st, 1 sc, 2 sc in next st, 18 sc; rep from * once—620 sts.

RND 22: Working with both A and B held tog, 620 sc, sl st in next st. Fasten off both yarns.

Finishing

Weave in loose ends. Block scarf.

Carol Ventura, art historian at Tennessee Technological University, documents craftspeople from around the world. See more of her work and learn about tapestry crochet at tapestrycrochet.com.

Lace Dress

Lily Chin, the fastest crocheter in the world and one of the craft's most innovative designers, has made a graceful lace dress that's sure to please both steadfast traditionalists and up-to-the-minute trendsetters. Intricate as it looks, the dress is composed of basic crochet stitches: chain, single and double crochet, and slip stitch. The bodice is worked in a solid crocheted fabric, while a variety of lace patterns circles the skirt in horizontal bands. "Each pattern has an inherent logic," says Lily. "Once you've established the pattern, it's easy to keep track of where you are."

© Chris Hartlove

Finished Size

34 (36, 38, 40, 42)" (86.5 [91.5, 96.5, 101.5, 106.5] cm) bust circumference. Dress shown measures 34" (86.5 cm).

Yarn

DK weight (#3 Light)

shown here: Lang Golf (100% mercerized cotton; 136 yd [125 m]/50 g; 3): #24 pearl grey, 13 (14, 15, 17, 18) balls. Yarn distributed by Berroco.

note: This yarn has been discontinued. Suggested substitution: Cotton Classic Lite or Patons Grace.

Hook

Sizes D/3 (3.25 mm) and F/5 (3.75 mm). *Adjust hook size if necessary to obtain the correct gauge.*

Notions

Tapestry needle.

Gauge

1 shell st = 1" (2.5 cm), 12 shell rows = 4" (10 cm) on smaller hook; 12 st-rep of first diamond pattern = 2" (5 cm) blocked, stretched lengthwise.

Stitch Guide

Lace Shell Stitch: Sc in center-dc of next lace shell, *ch 2, skip 2 dc, dc in next sc, ch 2, skip 2 dc, sc in next st (center-dc of next lace shell); rep from * around, end as indicated.

Small Lace Shell Stitch: Sc in center-dc of next lace shell or small lace shell, *ch 1, skip 1 or 2 dc, dc in next sc, ch 1, skip 1 or 2 dc, sc in next st (center-dc of next lace or small lace shell); rep from * around, end as indicated.

Shell Stitch: Sc in center-dc of next shell, *skip 2 dc, work 5 dc in next sc, skip 2 dc, sc in next st (center-dc of next shell); rep from * around, end as indicated.

Small Shell: Sc in center-dc of next shell or small shell, *skip 1 or 2 dc, 3 dc in next dc, skip 1 or 2 dc, sc in next st (center-dc of next shell or small shell); rep from * around, end as indicated.

3-Row Shell Decrease Sequence:

ROW 1: Work small shell in sc indicated in instructions.

ROW 2: Work small shell on each side of next small shell—2 small shells.

ROW 3: Work 5 dc in sc just before first small shell, pick up loop in center-dc of each of next 2 small shells, yo hook and draw through all 3 loops for sc dec, work 5 dc in next sc after last small shell.

3-Row Lace Shell Decrease Sequence:

ROW 1: Work small lace shell in sc indicated in instructions.

ROW 2: Work small lace shell on each side of next small lace shell —2 small lace shells.

ROW 3: Work (ch 2, dc, ch 2) in sc just before first small lace shell st, pick up loop in center-dc of each of next 2 small lace shells, yo hook and draw through all 3 loops for sc dec, work (ch 2, dc, ch 2) in next sc after last small lace shell.

Bodice

With smaller hook, very loosely ch 204 (216, 228, 240, 252). Join with sl st to beg of ch, being careful not to twist sts.

ROW 1: (WS) Ch 3 (counts as dc), work another dc at base of ch-3, *skip 2 ch, sc in next ch, skip 2 ch, 5 dc in next ch; rep from * across, end last rep with 3 more dc at base of first ch-3 instead of 5 dc. Join with sl st to top of beg ch-3—34 (36, 38, 40, 42) shell sts around.

Right side-bodice

Turn, cont working one side as foll:

ROW 2: (RS) Ch 1, ++*sc in center-dc of next shell, skip 2 dc, 5 dc in next sc, skip 2 dc; rep from * until 16 (17, 18, 19, 20) shells total have been worked, ending with sc in center-dc of next shell, turn. Rem sts will be worked later for left side-bodice.

ROW 3: Sl st to center-dc of first shell, ch 1, sc in same center-dc, *skip 2 dc, 5 dc in next sc, skip 2 dc, sc in center-dc of next shell; rep from * across, ending skip rem 2 dc and sc—15 (16, 17, 18, 19) shells total, turn.

Rep Row 3, working 1 less shell each row, until 6 shells rem—12 (13, 14, 15, 16) rows total have been worked.

ROW 13 (14, 15, 16, 17): Working each armhole edge separately, turn.

Shape armhole

Sl st to center-dc of first shell, +ch 1, sc in same dc, *skip 2 dc, 5 dc in next sc, skip 2 dc, sc in center-dc of next shell; rep from * once more, skip rem sts—2 shells total. Mark this side of row to indicate which side to pick up from later, turn.

NEXT ROW: Sl st to center-dc of first shell, ch 1, sc in same center-dc, skip 2 dc, 5 dc in next sc, skip 2 dc, sc in center-dc of next shell, skip rem 2 dc and sc—1 shell total. Fasten off.+ With marked side of row facing, return to sts left unworked on Row 13 (14, 15, 16, 17), skip (2 dc, sc, 2 dc) to the left of marker for underarm, join yarn to center-dc of next shell; rep from + to + as for first armhole edge.

Left side-bodice

With RS facing, return to Row 1 sts worked for right side-bodice, skip next (2 dc, sc, 2 dc) of Row 1 for center back, join yarn to center-dc of next shell, ch 1, beg at ++ , work as for right side-bodice.

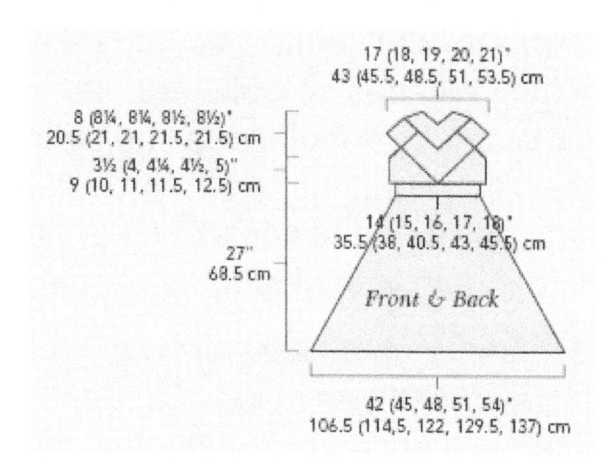

Yoke

With RS facing, join yarn to center-dc of top shell on right side-bodice, ready to work toward center back.

For sizes 34 (38, 42)":

ROW 1: Ch 3 (counts as dc), work 2 dc in same center-dc as join (for half-shell), +working down into V along side edges of rows, *skip 2 dc, sc in next sc, skip 2 dc, work 5 dc in next sc; rep from * until just before center sc at bottom of V—6 (7, 8) shells, plus a half-shell at beg; work small shell of only 3 dc in center sc at bottom of V (center back); rep from *, working up other side of V along side edges of rows, end with only 3 dc in center-dc of top shell on left side-bodice, just before armhole; ch 77 (77, 89) for sleeve+, work 3 dc in center-dc of top shell of front, ready to work into center front V; rep from + to +, join with sl st to top of beg ch-3, turn.

ROW 2: (WS) Ch 1, sc in same ch as joining sl st, +*ch 2, skip 2 ch, dc in next ch, ch 2, skip 2 ch, sc in next ch; rep from * across sleeve ch, ending with sc in top of next dc, instead of next ch—

13 (13, 15) lace shell sts for sleeve; work in shell st across V-section, dec at center V by beg Row 2 of shell dec sequence (see Stitch Guide, page 146),+ end with sc in last dc; rep from + to +, join with sl st to top of beg sc; mark center shell of each sleeve, turn.

ROW 3: Ch 3 (counts as dc), work 2 dc into same sc as join (for half-shell), +work in shell st as established, dec at center V, end with 3 dc in last sc of back; work in lace shell across sleeve as foll: *ch 2, skip ch-2, sc in next dc, ch 2, skip ch-2,+ dc in next sc; rep from *, ending with 3 dc instead of 1 in next sc (half-shell); rep from + to +, join with sl st to top of beg ch-3, turn.

ROW 4: Ch 1, sc in same ch as joining sl st, +*ch 2, skip ch-2, dc in next sc, ch 2, skip ch-2, sc in next dc; rep from * across sleeve, work in shell st across front, dec at center V,+ end with sc in last dc; rep from + to +, join with sl st to top of beg sc, turn.

Rep Rows 3 and 4 until a total of 9 rows have been completed, and *at the same time:*

Shape sleeves

Cont in established patt, working dec at center front and back, beg lace shell dec sequence (see Stitch Guide, page 146) on each sleeve at marked center shell.

NOTE: *All dec sequences are now aligned with each other.*

Cont in this manner until a total of 10 (12, 14) rows have been completed.

NEXT ROW: Change to lace shells; cont dec at sleeve centers and center of front and back. Work until 21 (21, 24) rows have been completed—32 (36, 40) lace shells around.

NEXT ROW: Change to mini shells (sc, 3 dc, sc) in place of lace shells around. Fasten off.

For sizes 36 (40)" (91.5 [101.5] cm):

ROW 1: (RS) Ch 1, sc in same center-dc as join (for half-shell), +working down into V along side edges of rows, *skip 2 dc, work 5 dc in next sc, skip 2 dc, sc in next sc; rep from * until just before center sc at bottom of V—7 (8) shells; work small shell of only 3 dc in center sc at bottom of V (center back); rep from *, working up other side of V along side edges of rows, end with sc in center-dc of top shell on left side-bodice, just before armhole, ch 71 (83) for sleeve,+ work 3 sc in center-dc of top shell of front, ready to work into center front V; rep from + to +, join to beg sc, turn.

ROW 2: (WS) Ch 5 (counts as dc, ch 2), +*skip 2 ch, sc in next ch, ch 2, skip 2 ch, dc in next ch, ch 2; rep from * across sleeve ch, end with 3 dc on top of next dc instead of next ch (for half-shell)—12 (14) lace shells for sleeve; work in shell st across V-section, dc at center V by beg Row 2 of shell dec sequence (see Stitch Guide), end with 3 dc in last sc;+ rep from + to +, ending with 2 dc in last sc, join with sl st in third ch of beg ch-5, mark center shell of each sleeve, turn.

ROW 3: Ch 1, +work in shell st as established, dec at center; work in lace shell across sleeve as foll: *ch 2, skip ch-2, dc in next sc, ch 2, skip ch-2, sc in next dc; rep from *, then rep from + for front, then rep from * for other sleeve, join with sl st to beg sc, turn.

ROW 4: Ch 5 (counts as dc, ch 2), +*skip ch-2, sc in next dc, ch 2, skip ch-2, dc in next sc, ch 2; rep from * across sleeve, work in shell st across front, dec at center V,+ end with sc in last dc; rep from + to + across back, end with 2 dc in last sc, join with sl st in third ch of beg ch-5, turn.

Rep Rows 3 and 4 until a total of 9 rows have been completed, and *at the same time:*

Shape sleeves

Cont in established patt, work dec at center front and back, beg lace shell dec sequence (see Stitch Guide, page 146) on each sleeve at marked center shell.

NOTE: *All dec sequences are now aligned.*

Cont in this manner until a total of 11 (13) rows have been completed.

NEXT ROW: Change to lace shells; cont dec at sleeve centers and center of front and back. Work until 21 (24) rows have been completed—32 (36) lace shells around.

NEXT ROW: Change to mini-shells (sc, 3 dc, sc) in place of lace shells around. Fasten off.

Skirt

With RS facing and smaller hook, join yarn at center back; ch 1, sc 168 (180, 192, 204, 216) sts evenly around lower edge of bodice, join with sl st to first sc, turn.

First diamond patt

Work as foll:

ROW 1: (WS) Ch 8 (counts as dc, ch 5), *skip next 5 sc, sc in next sc, ch 5, skip next 5 sc +, 3 dc in next sc, ch 5; rep from * around, end last rep at +, work 2 dc in lasc sc (the beg ch-8 counts as the third dc), join with sl st to third ch of beg ch-8—14 (15, 16, 17, 18) patt reps; turn.

ROW 2: (RS) Ch 3 (counts as dc), dc in base of ch, *dc in next dc, 2 dc in next dc, ch 4, skip ch-5, dc in next sc, ch 4, skip ch-5,+ 2 dc in next dc; rep from *, end last rep at +, join with sl st to top of beg ch-3, turn.

ROW 3: Ch 6 (counts as dc, ch 3), *skip ch-4, dc in next dc, ch 3, skip ch-4, 2 dc in next dc, dc in next dc, ch 1, skip next dc, dc in next dc,+ 2 dc in next dc, ch 3; rep from *, end last rep at +, dc in base of beg ch, join with sl st to third ch of beg ch-6, turn.

ROW 4: Ch 3 (counts as dc), dc in base of ch, *dc in next dc, ch 1, skip next dc, dc in ch-1, ch 1, skip next dc, dc in next dc, 2 dc in next dc, ch 2, skip ch-3, dc in next dc, ch 2, skip ch-3,+ 2 dc in next dc; rep from *, end last rep at +, join with sl st to top of beg ch-3, turn.

ROW 5: Ch 6 (counts as dc, ch 3), *skip (ch-2, dc, ch-2), 2 dc in next dc, dc in next dc, [ch 1, skip next dc, dc in next ch] 2 times, ch 1, skip next dc, dc in next dc,+ 2 dc in next dc, ch 3; rep from *, end last rep at +, dc in base of beg ch, join with sl st to third ch of beg ch-6, turn.

ROW 6: Ch 3 (counts as dc), *dc in next dc, [ch 1, skip next dc, dc in next ch] 3 times, ch 1, skip next dc, dc in each of next 2 dc, ch 3, skip ch-3,+ dc in next dc; rep from *, end last rep at +, join with sl st to top of beg ch-3, turn.

ROW 7: Ch 6 (counts as dc, ch 3), *skip ch-3, dc in each of next 2 dc, [dc in next ch, ch 1, skip next dc] 3 times, dc in next ch,+ dc in each of next 2 dc, ch 3; rep from *, end last rep at +, dc in next dc, join with sl st to third ch of beg ch-6, turn.

ROW 8: Ch 3 (counts as dc), skip first dc, *dc in next dc, dc in next ch, [ch 1, skip next dc, dc in next ch] 2 times, dc in next dc, dec next 2 dc tog, ch 2, skip next ch, dc in next ch, ch 2, skip next ch,+ dec next 2 dc tog; rep from *, end last rep at +, join with sl st to top of beg ch-3, turn.

ROW 9: Ch 5 (counts as dc, ch 2), *skip ch-2, (dc, ch 1, dc) all in next dc, ch 2, skip ch-2, dec next 2 dc tog, dc in next dc, dc in next ch, ch 1, skip next dc, dc in next ch, dc in next dc,+ dec next 2 dc tog, ch 2; rep from *, end last rep at +, skip last dc, join with sl st to third ch of beg ch-5, turn.

ROW 10: Ch 3 (counts as dc), skip first dc, *dc in next dc, dc in next ch, dc in next dc, dec next 2 dc tog, ch 2, skip (ch-2, dc), (dc, ch 1, dc, ch 1, dc) all in next ch, ch 2, skip (dc, ch-2),+ dec next 2 dc tog; rep from *, end last rep at +, join with sl st to top of beg ch-3, turn.

ROW 11: Ch 5 (counts as dc, ch 2), *skip (ch-2, dc), (dc, ch 1, dc) in next ch, ch 1, skip next dc, (dc, ch 1, dc) in next ch, ch 2, skip (dc, ch-2), dec next 2 dc tog, dc in next dc,+ dec next 2 dc tog, ch 2; rep from *, end last rep at +, skip last dc, join with sl st to third ch of beg ch-5, turn.

ROW 12: Ch 2, skip first dc, dc in next dc (do not count ch, this is equivalent of double-dec), *ch 2, skip (ch-2, dc), [(dc, ch 1, dc) in next ch, ch 1, skip next dc] 3 times, ch 2, skip (dc, ch-2),+ dec next 3 sts tog for double-dec; rep from *, end last rep at +, join with sl st to first dc, turn.

ROW 13: Ch 4 (counts as dc, ch 1), *skip (ch-2, dc), [(dc, ch 1, dc) in next ch, ch 2, skip (dc, ch-1, dc)] 2 times, (dc, ch 1, dc) in next ch, ch 1, skip (dc, ch-2),+ dc in next dc, ch 1; rep from *, end last rep at +, join with sl st to third ch of beg ch-4, turn.

ROW 14: Ch 4 (counts as dc, ch 1), *skip (ch-1, dc), [(dc, ch 1, dc) in next ch, ch 1, skip next dc, dc in next ch-2 space, ch 1, skip next dc] 2 times, (dc, ch 1, dc) in next ch, ch 1, skip (dc, ch-1),+ dc in next dc, ch 1; rep from *, end last rep at +, join with sl st to third ch of beg ch-4, turn.

ROW 15: Ch 1, *sc in next ch-1 space, ch 1, skip next dc; rep from *, join with sl st to first st—252 (270, 288, 306, 324) sts, turn.

Pineapple patt

Cont in pineapple patt as foll:

ROW 16: (RS) Ch 5 (counts as dc, ch 2), (2 dc, ch 2, 2 dc) in first ch-1 space, *ch 3, skip next 5 sts, [sc in next ch-1 space, ch 3, skip next sc] 4 times, skip next 4 sts,+ (2 dc, ch 2, 2 dc, ch 2, 2 dc) in next ch-1 space; rep from *, end last rep at +, dc at base of beg ch, join with sl st to third ch of beg ch-5, sl st into next ch-2 space, turn.

ROW 17: (WS) Ch 5 (counts as dc, ch 2), 2 dc in same ch-2 space at base of beg ch, *ch 3, skip (2 dc, ch-3, sc), [sc in next ch-3 space, ch 3, skip next sc] 3 times, skip (ch-3, 2 dc), (2 dc, ch 2, 2 dc) in next ch-2 space, ch 1,+ (2 dc, ch 2, 2 dc) in next ch-2 space; rep from *, end last rep at +, dc in same ch-2 space at base of beg ch, join with sl st to third ch of beg ch-5, sl st into next ch-2 space, turn.

ROW 18: Ch 5 (counts as dc, ch 2), 2 dc in same ch-2 space at base of beg ch, *ch 4, skip (2 dc, ch-1, 2 dc), (2 dc, ch 2, 2 dc) in next ch-2 space, ch 3, skip (2 dc, ch-3, next sc), [sc in next ch-3 space, ch 3, skip next sc] 2 times, skip (ch-3, 2 dc),+ (2 dc, ch 2, 2 dc) in next ch-2 space; rep from *, end last rep at +, dc in same ch-2 space at base of beg ch, join with sl st to third ch of beg ch-5, sl st into next ch-2 space, turn.

ROW 19: Ch 5 (counts as dc, ch 2), 2 dc in same ch-2 space at base of beg ch, *ch 3, skip (2 dc, ch-3, next sc), sc in next ch-3 space, ch 3, skip (next sc, ch-3, 2 dc), (2 dc, ch 2, 2 dc) in next ch-2 space, ch 1, skip next 2 dc, 6 dc in next ch-4 space, ch 1, skip next 2 dc,+ (2 dc, ch 2, 2 dc) in next ch-2 space; rep from *, end last rep at +, dc in same ch-2 space at base of beg ch, join with sl st to third ch of beg ch-5, sl st into next ch-2 space, turn.

ROW 20: Ch 5 (counts as dc, ch 2), 2 dc in same ch-2 space at base of beg ch, *ch 1, skip (2 dc, ch-1), [dc in next dc, ch 1] 6 times, skip (ch-1, 2 dc), (2 dc, ch 2, 2 dc) in next ch-2 space, skip (2 dc, ch-3, sc, ch-3, 2 dc),+ (2 dc, ch 2, 2 dc) in next ch-2 space; rep from *, end last rep at +, dc in same ch-2 space at base of beg ch, join with sl st to third ch of beg ch-5, sl st into next ch-2 space, turn.

ROW 21: Ch 5 (counts as dc, ch 2), *skip next 4 dc, 2 dc in next ch-2 space, ch 3, skip (2 dc, ch-1, next dc), [sc in next ch-1 space, ch 3, skip next dc] 5 times, skip (ch-1, 2 dc),+ 2 dc in next ch-2 space, ch 2; rep from *, end last rep at +, dc in same ch-2 space at base of beg ch, join with sl st to third ch of beg ch-5, sl st into next ch-2 space, turn.

ROW 22: Ch 5 (counts as dc, ch 2), 2 dc in same ch-2 space at base of beg ch, *ch 3, skip (2 dc, ch-3, next sc), [sc in next ch-3 space, ch 3, skip sc] 4 times, skip (ch-3, 2 dc),+ (2 dc, ch 2, 2 dc, ch 2, 2 dc) in next ch-2 space; rep from *, end last rep at +, (2 dc, ch 2, 1 dc) in same ch-2 space at base of beg ch, join with sl st to third ch of beg ch-5, sl st into next ch-2 space, turn.

ROW 23: Ch 5 (counts as dc, ch 2), 2 dc in same ch-2 space at base of beg ch, *ch 1, skip next 2 dc, (2 dc, ch 2, 2 dc) in next ch-2 space, ch 3, skip (2 dc, ch-3, next sc), [sc in next ch-3 space, ch 3, skip sc] 3 times, skip (ch-3, 2 dc),+ (2 dc, ch 2, 2 dc) in next ch-2 space; rep from *, end last rep at +, dc in same ch-2 space at base of beg ch, join with sl st to third ch of beg ch-5, sl st into next ch-2 space, turn.

ROW 24: Ch 5 (counts as dc, ch 2), 2 dc in same ch-2 space at base of beg ch, *ch 3, skip (2 dc, ch-3, next sc), [sc in next ch-3 space, ch 3, skip sc] 2 times, skip (ch-3, 2 dc), (2 dc, ch 2, 2 dc) in next ch-2 space, ch 4, skip (2 dc, ch-1, 2 dc),+ (2 dc, ch 2, 2 dc) in next ch-2 space; rep from *, end last rep at +, dc in same ch-2 space at base of beg ch, join with sl st to third ch of beg ch-5, sl st into next ch-2 space, turn.

ROW 25: Ch 5 (counts as dc, ch 2), 2 dc in same ch-2 space at base of beg ch, *ch 1, skip next 2 dc, 6 dc in next ch-4 space, ch 1, skip next 2 dc, (2 dc, ch 2, 2 dc) in next ch-2 space, ch 3, skip (2 dc, ch-3, next sc), sc in next ch-3 space, ch 3, skip (1 sc, ch-3, 2 dc),+ (2 dc, ch 2, 2 dc) in next ch-2 space; rep from *, end last rep at +, dc in same ch-2 space at base of beg ch, join with sl st to third ch of beg ch-5, sl st into next ch-2 space, turn.

ROW 26: Ch 5 (counts as dc, ch 2), 2 dc in same ch-2 space at base of beg ch, *skip (2 dc, ch-3, 1 sc, ch-3, 2 dc), (2 dc, ch 2, 2 dc) in next ch-2 space, ch 1, skip (2 dc, ch-1), [dc in next dc, ch 1] 6 times, skip (ch-1, 2 dc),+ (2 dc, ch 2, 2 dc) in next ch-2 space; rep from *, end last rep at +, dc in same ch-2 space at base of beg ch, join with sl st to third ch of beg ch-5, sl st into next ch-2 space, turn.

ROW 27: Ch 5 (counts as dc, ch 2), dc in same ch-2 space at base of beg ch, *ch 3, skip (2 dc, ch-1, next dc), [sc in next ch-1 space, ch 3, skip dc] 5 times, skip (ch-1, 2 dc), 2 dc in next ch-2 space, ch 2, skip 4 next dc,+ 2 dc in next ch-2 space; rep from *, end last rep at +, dc in same ch-2 space at base of beg ch, join with sl st to third ch of beg ch-5, sl st into next ch-2 space, turn.

ROW 28: Ch 1, *sc in each of next 2 ch, sc in each of next 2 dc, sc in each of next 3 ch, [sc in next sc, sc in next ch-3 space] 4 times, sc in next sc, sc in each of next 3 ch, sc in each of next 2 dc; rep from *, join with sl st to beg sc—294 (315, 336, 357, 378) sts; turn.

Second diamond patt

Cont in second diamond patt as foll:

ROW 29: (WS) Ch 6 (counts as dc, ch 3), *skip next 3 sc, dc in each of next 4 sc, ch 3, skip 2 sc, sc in next sc, ch 3, skip next 2 sc, dc in each of next 4 sc, ch 3, skip 3 next sc,+ dc in each of next 2 sc, ch 3; rep from *, end last rep at +, dc in next sc, join with sl st to third ch of beg ch-6, turn.

ROW 30: (RS) Ch 3 (counts as dc), dc in base of beg ch, *2 dc in next dc, ch 3, skip ch-3, dec next 2 dc tog, dc in next dc, 2 dc in next dc, ch 4, skip ch-3, sc in next sc, ch 4, skip ch-3, 2 dc in next dc, dc in next dc, dec next 2 dc tog, ch 3, skip ch-3,+ 2 dc in next dc; rep from *, end last rep at +, join with sl st to top of beg ch, turn.

ROW 31: Ch 6 (counts as dc, ch 3), *skip ch-3, dec next 2 dc tog, dc in next dc, 2 dc in next dc, ch 4, skip ch-4, sc in next sc, ch 4, skip ch-4, 2 dc in next dc, dc in next dc, dec next 2 dc tog, ch 3, skip ch-3, 2 dc in next dc, dc in each of next 2 dc,+ 2 dc in next dc, ch 3; rep from *, end last rep at +, dc in base of beg ch, join with sl st to third ch of beg ch-6, turn.

ROW 32: Ch 3 (counts as dc), dc in base of beg ch, *dc in each of next 4 dc, 2 dc in next dc, ch 3, skip ch-3, dec next 2 dc tog, dc in next dc, 2 dc in next dc, skip (ch-4, next sc, ch-4), 2 dc in next dc, dc in next dc, dec next 2 dc tog, ch 3, skip ch-3,+ 2 dc in next dc; rep from *, end last rep at +, join with sl st to top of beg ch, turn.

ROW 33: Ch 6 (counts as dc, ch 3), *skip next 3 sc, dec next 2 dc tog, dc in each of next 4 dc, dec next 2 dc tog, ch 3, skip ch-3, 2 dc in next dc, dc in next dc, dec next 2 dc tog, ch 11, dec next 2 dc tog, dc in next dc,+ 2 dc in next dc, ch 3; rep from *, end last rep at +, dc in base of beg ch, join with sl st to third ch of beg ch-6, turn.

ROW 34: Ch 3 (counts as dc), dc in base of beg ch, *dc in next dc, dec next 2 dc tog, ch 4, skip 5 ch, sc in next ch, ch 4, skip 5 ch, dec next 2 dc tog, dc in next dc, 2 dc in next dc, ch 3, skip ch-3, dec next 2 dc tog, dc in each of next 2 dc, dec next 2 dc tog, ch 3, skip ch-3,+ 2 dc in next dc; rep from *, end last rep at +, join with sl st to top of beg ch, turn.

ROW 35: Ch 6 (counts as dc, ch 3), *skip next 3 sc, [dec next 2 dc tog] 2 times, ch 3, skip ch-3, 2 dc in next dc, dc in next dc, dec next 2 dc tog, ch 3, skip ch-4, sc in next sc, ch 3, skip ch-4, dec next 2 dc tog, dc in next dc,+ 2 dc in next dc, ch 3; rep from *, end last rep at +, dc in base of beg ch, join with sl st to third ch of beg ch-6, turn.

ROW 36: Change to larger hook, ch 3 (counts as dc), *dc in each of next 3 dc, ch 3, skip ch-3, sc in next ch, ch 3, skip ch-3, dc in each of next 4 dc, ch 3, skip ch-3, dc in each of next 2 dc, ch 3, skip ch-3,+ dc in next dc; rep from *, end last rep at +, join with sl st to top of beg ch, sl st into next dc, turn.

ROW 37: Ch 6 (counts as dc, ch 3), *skip ch-3, 2 dc in each of next 2 dc, ch 3, skip ch-3, dec next 2 dc tog, dc in next dc, 2 dc in next dc, ch 4, skip ch-3, sc in next sc, ch 4, skip ch-3, 2 dc in next dc, dc in next dc,+ dec next 2 dc tog, ch 3; rep from *, end last rep at +, join with sl st to third ch of beg ch-6, turn.

ROW 38: Sl st into first dc, ch 3 (counts as dc), *dc in next dc, 2 dc in next dc, ch 4, skip ch-4, sc in next sc, ch 4, skip ch-4, 2 dc in next dc, dc in next dc, dec next 2 dc tog, ch 3, skip ch-3, 2 dc in next dc, dc in each of next 2 dc, 2 dc in next dc, ch 3, skip ch-3,+ dec next 2 dc tog; rep from *, end last rep at +, join with sl st to top of beg ch, sl st into next dc, turn.

ROW 39: Ch 6 (counts as dc, ch 3), *skip ch-3, 2 dc in next dc, dc in each of next 4 dc, 2 dc in next dc, ch 3, skip ch-3, dec next 2 dc tog, dc in next dc, 2 dc in next dc, skip (ch-4, next sc, ch-4),

2 dc in next dc, dc in next dc,+ dec next 2 dc tog, ch 3; rep from *, end last rep at +, join with sl st to third ch of beg ch-6, turn.

ROW 40: Sl st into first dc, ch 3 (counts as dc), *dc in each of next 4 dc, dec next 2 dc tog, ch 3, skip ch-3, 2 dc in next dc, dc in next dc, dec next 2 dc tog, ch 11, dec next 2 dc tog, dc in next dc, 2 dc in next dc, ch 3, skip ch-3,+ dec next 2 dc tog; rep from *, end last rep at +, join with sl st to top of beg ch, sl st into next dc, turn.

ROW 41: Ch 6 (counts as dc, ch 3), *skip ch-3, 2 dc in next dc, dc in next dc, dec next 2 dc tog, ch 4, skip 5 ch, sc in next ch, ch 4, skip 5 ch, dec next 2 dc tog, dc in next dc, 2 dc in next dc, ch 3, skip ch-3, dec next 2 dc tog, dc in each of next 2 dc,+ dec next 2 dc tog, ch 3; rep from *, end last rep at +, join with sl st to third ch of beg ch-6, turn.

ROW 42: Sl st into first dc, ch 3 (counts as dc), dec next 2 dc tog, *ch 3, skip ch-3, 2 dc in next dc, dc in next dc, dec next 2 dc tog, ch 3, skip ch-4, sc in next sc, ch 3, skip ch-4, dec next 2 dc tog, dc in next dc, 2 dc in next dc, ch 3, skip ch-3,+ dec next 2 dc tog; rep from *, end last rep at +, join with sl st to top of beg ch, sl st into next dc, turn.

ROW 43: Ch 6 (counts as dc, ch 3), *skip ch-3, dc in each of next 4 dc, ch 3, skip ch-3, sc in next ch, ch 3, skip ch-3, dc in each of next 4 dc, ch 3, skip ch-3, dc in next dc,+ dc in next dc, ch 3; rep from *, end last rep at +, join with sl st to 3rd ch of beg ch-6, turn.

ROW 44: Ch 1, sc in base of ch, *sc in next dc, sc in each of next 3 ch, sc in each of next 4 dc, sc in each of next 3 ch, 2 sc in next sc, sc in each of next 3 ch, sc in each of next 4 dc, sc in each of next 3 ch, sc in next dc; rep from *, join with sl st to first sc—336 (360, 384, 408, 432) sts, turn.

Scallops patt

Cont in scallops patt as follows:

ROW 45: (WS) Ch 7 (counts as dc, ch 4), *skip 4 sc, dc in next sc,+ dc in next sc, ch 4; rep from *, end last rep at +, join with sl st to third ch of beg ch-7, turn.

ROW 46: (RS) Ch 1, *skip dc, (sc, hdc, dc, ch 2, dc, hdc, sc) all in next ch-4 space, skip dc; rep from *, join with sl st to beg sc, turn.

ROW 47: Sl st into next (sc, hdc, dc and ch-1 space), ch 8 (counts as dc, ch 5), *skip (dc, hdc, sc, hdc and dc), dc in next ch-1 space, ch 5; rep from *, join with sl st to third ch of beg ch-7; sl st into next ch, turn.

ROW 48: Ch 1, sc in same ch at base of ch 1, *sc in next dc, sc in each of next 5 ch; rep from *, end last rep with sc in each of last 4 ch, join with sl st to beg sc—336 (360, 384, 408, 432) sts; turn.

ROW 49: Ch 4 (counts as dc, ch 1), dc in base of ch, *ch 1, skip next 3 sc, dc in each of next 9 sc, ch 1, skip next 3 sc, (dc, ch 1, dc) in next sc, ch 1, skip next 3 sc, (2 dc, ch 1, 2 dc) in next sc, ch 1, skip next 3 sc,+ (dc, ch 1, dc) in next sc; rep from *, end last rep at +, join with sl st to third ch of beg ch-4, sl st into next ch-1 space, turn.

ROW 50: Ch 4 (counts as dc, ch 1), dc in same ch-1 space at base of ch, *ch 1, skip (next dc, ch-1, 2 dc), (2 dc, ch 1, 2 dc) in next ch-1 space, ch 1, skip (2 dc, ch-1, dc), (dc, ch 1, dc) in next ch-1 space, ch 1, skip (next dc, ch-1), dc in each of next 9 dc, ch 1, skip (ch-1, dc),+ (dc, ch 1, dc) in next ch-1 space; rep from *, end last rep at +, join with sl st to third ch of beg ch-4, sl st into next ch-1 space, turn.

ROW 51: Ch 4 (counts as dc, ch 1), 2 dc in same ch-1 space at base of ch, *ch 1, skip next (dc, ch-1, dc), dc in each of next 7 dc, ch 1, skip next (dc, ch-1, dc), (2 dc, ch 1, 2 dc) in next ch-1 space, ch 1, skip next (dc, ch-1, 2 dc), (2 dc, ch 1, 2 dc) in next ch-1 space, ch 1, skip (2 dc, ch-1, next dc),+ (2 dc, ch 1, 2 dc) in next ch-1 space; rep from *, end last rep at +, dc in same ch-1 space at base of ch, join with sl st to third ch of beg ch-4, sl st into next ch-1 space, turn.

ROW 52: Ch 4 (counts as dc, ch 1), 2 dc in same ch-1 space at base of ch, *[ch 1, skip (2 dc, ch-1, 2 dc), (2 dc, ch 1, 2 dc) in next ch-1 space] 2 times, ch 1, skip (2 dc, ch-1), dc in each of next 7 dc, ch 1, skip (ch-1, 2 dc),+ (2 dc, ch 1, 2 dc) in next ch-1 space; rep from *, end last rep at +, dc in same ch-1 space at base of ch, join with sl st to third ch of beg ch-4, sl st into next ch-1 space, turn.

ROW 53: Ch 4 (counts as dc, ch 1), 2 dc in same ch-1 space at base of ch, *ch 2, skip (2 dc, ch-1), dc in each of next 7 dc, ch 2, skip (ch-1, 2 dc), [(2 dc, ch 1, 2 dc) in next ch-1 space, ch 1, skip (2 dc, ch-1, 2 dc)] 2 times,+ (2 dc, ch 1, 2 dc) in next ch-1 space; rep from *, end last rep at +, dc in same ch-1 space at base of ch, join with sl st to third ch of beg ch-4, sl st into next ch-1 space, turn.

ROW 54: Ch 4 (counts as dc, ch 1), 2 dc in same ch-1 space at base of ch, *[ch 1, skip (2 dc, ch-1, 2 dc), (2 dc, ch 1, 2 dc) in next ch-1 space] 2 times, ch 3, skip (2 dc, ch-2, next dc), dc in each of next 5 dc, ch 3, skip next (dc, ch-2, 2 dc),+ (2 dc, ch 1, 2 dc) in next ch-1 space; rep from *, end last rep at +, dc in same ch-1 space at base of ch, join with sl st to third ch of beg ch-4, sl st into next ch-1 space, turn.

ROW 55: Ch 4 (counts as dc, ch 1), 2 dc in same ch-1 space at base of ch, *ch 3, skip (2 dc, ch-3), dc in each of next 5 dc, ch 3, skip (ch-3, 2 dc), [(2 dc, ch 1, 2 dc) in next ch-1 space, ch 1, skip (2 dc, ch-1, 2 dc)] 2 times,+ (2 dc, ch 1, 2 dc) in next ch-1 space; rep from *, end last rep at +, dc in same ch-1 space at base of ch, join with sl st to third ch of beg ch-4, sl st into next ch-1 space, turn.

ROW 56: Ch 4 (counts as dc, ch 1), 2 dc in same ch-1 space at base of ch, *[ch 1, skip (2 dc, ch-1, 2 dc), (2 dc, ch 1, 2 dc) in next ch-1 space] 2 times, ch 4, skip (2 dc, ch-3), dc in each of next 5 dc, ch 4, skip (ch-3, 2 dc),+ (2 dc, ch 1, 2 dc) in next ch-1 space; rep from *, end last rep at +, dc in same ch-1 space at base of ch, join with sl st to third ch of beg ch-4, sl st into next ch-1 space, turn.

ROW 57: Ch 4 (counts as dc, ch 1), 2 dc in same ch-1 space at base of ch, *ch 4, skip (2 dc, ch-4, next dc), dc in each of next 3 dc, ch 4, skip next (dc, ch-4, 2 dc), [(2 dc, ch 1, 2 dc) in next ch-1 space, ch 2, skip (2 dc, ch-1, 2 dc)] 2 times,+ (2 dc, ch 1, 2 dc) in next ch-1 space; rep from *, end last rep at +, dc in same ch-1 space at base of ch, join with sl st to third ch of beg ch-4, sl st into next ch-1 space, turn.

ROW 58: Ch 4 (counts as dc, ch 1), 2 dc in same ch-1 space at base of ch, *[ch 2, skip (2 dc, ch-2, 2 dc), (2 dc, ch 1, 2 dc) in next ch-1 space] 2 times, ch 4, skip (2 dc, ch-4), dc in each of next 3 dc, ch 4, skip (ch-4, 2 dc),+ (2 dc, ch 1, 2 dc) in next ch-1 space; rep from *, end last rep at +, dc in same ch-1 space at base of ch, join with sl st to third ch of beg ch-4, sl st into next ch-1 space, turn.

ROW 59: Ch 4 (counts as dc, ch 1), 2 dc in same ch-1 space at base of ch, *ch 5, skip (2 dc, ch-4), dc in each of next 3 dc, ch 5, skip (ch-4, 2 dc), [(2 dc, ch 1, 2 dc) in next ch-1 space, ch 2, skip (2 dc, ch-2, 2 dc)] 2 times,+ (2 dc, ch 1, 2 dc) in next ch-1 space; rep from *, end last rep at +, dc in same ch-1 space at base of ch, join with sl st to third ch of beg ch-4, sl st into next ch-1 space, turn.

ROW 60: Ch 4 (counts as dc, ch 1), 2 dc in same ch-1 space at base of ch, *[ch 2, skip (2 dc, ch-2, 2 dc), (2 dc, ch 1, 2 dc) in next ch-1 space] 2 times, ch 2, skip (2 dc, 2 ch), (dc, ch 1, dc) in next ch, ch 2, skip (ch-2, next dc), (dc, ch 1, dc) in next dc, ch 2, skip next (dc, ch-2), (dc, ch 1, dc) in next ch, ch 2, skip (ch-2, 2 dc),+ (2 dc, ch 1, 2 dc) in next ch-1 space; rep from *, end last rep at +, dc in same ch-1 space at base of ch, join with sl st to third ch of beg ch-4, sl st into next ch-1 space, turn.

ROW 61: Ch 4 (counts as dc, ch 1), 2 dc in same ch-1 space at base of ch, *ch 2, skip (2 dc, ch-2, next dc), [(dc, ch 1, dc) in next ch-1 space, ch 2, skip next (dc, ch-2, next dc)] 3 times, skip 1 more dc, [(2 dc, ch 1, 2 dc) in next ch-1 space, ch 2, skip next (2 dc, ch-2, 2 dc)] 2 times,+ (2 dc, ch 1, 2 dc) in next ch-1 space; rep from *, end last rep at +, dc in same ch-1 space at base of ch, join with sl st to third ch of beg ch-4, sl st into next ch-1 space, turn.

ROW 62: Ch 4 (counts as dc, ch 1), 2 dc in same ch-1 space at base of ch, *[ch 2, skip (2 dc, ch-2, 2 dc), (2 dc, ch 1, 2 dc) in next ch-1 space] 2 times, ch 2, skip (2 dc, ch-2, next dc), (2 dc, ch 1, 2 dc) in next ch-1 space, ch 2, skip next (dc, ch-2, dc), (dc, ch 1, dc) in next ch-1 space, ch 2, skip next (dc, ch-2, dc), (2 dc, ch 1, 2 dc) in next ch-1 space, ch 2, skip next (dc, ch-2, 2 dc),+ (2 dc, ch 1, 2 dc) in next ch-1 space; rep from *, end last rep at +, dc in same ch-1 space at base of ch, join with sl st to third ch of beg ch-4, sl st into next ch-1 space, turn.

ROW 63: Ch 4 [counts as dc, ch 1], 2 dc in same ch-1 space at base of ch, *ch 2, skip (2 dc, ch-2, 2 dc), (2 dc, ch 1, 2 dc) in next ch-1 space, ch 2, skip (2 dc, ch-2, next dc), (dc, ch 1, dc) in next ch-1 space, ch 2, skip next (dc, ch-2, 2 dc), [(2 dc, ch 1, 2 dc) in next ch-1 space, ch 2, skip (2 dc, ch-2, 2 dc)] 3 times,+ (2 dc, ch 1, 2 dc) in next ch-1 space; rep from *, end last rep at +, dc in same ch-1 space at base of ch, join with sl st to third ch of beg ch-4, sl st into next ch-1 space, turn.

ROW 64: Ch 4 (counts as dc, ch 1), 2 dc in same ch-1 space at base of ch, *[ch 2, skip (2 dc, ch-2, 2 dc), (2 dc, ch 1, 2 dc) in next ch-1 space] 3 times, ch 2, skip (2 dc, ch-2, next dc), (2 dc, ch 1, 2 dc) in next ch-1 space, ch 2, skip next (dc, ch-2, 2 dc), (2 dc, ch 1, 2 dc]) in next ch-1 space, ch 2, skip next (2 dc, ch-2, 2 dc),+ (2 dc, ch 1, 2 dc) in next ch-1 space; rep from *, end last rep at +, dc in same ch-1 space at base of ch, join with sl st to third ch of beg ch-4, sl st into next ch-1 space, turn.

ROW 65: Ch 4 (counts as dc, ch 1), 2 dc in same ch-1 space at base of ch, *ch 2, skip (2 dc, ch-2, 2 dc), (2 dc, ch 1, 2 dc) in next ch-1 space; rep from *, end with dc in same ch-1 space at base of ch, join with sl st to third ch of beg ch-4—588 (630, 672, 714, 756) sts total; 84 (90, 96, 102, 108) scallops separated by ch-2. Fasten off.

Finishing

Weave in loose ends. Block to measurement.

Lily M. Chin, the world's fastest crocheter, is author of her own crochet book and is always seeking new ways to invent in crochet. Find her online at lilychinsignaturecollection.com.

Abbreviations

beg	begin(s); beginning
bet	between
blo	back loop only
CC	contrasting color
ch	chain
cm	centimeter(s)
cont	continue(s); continuing
dc	double crochet
dtr	double treble crochet
dec(s) ('d)	decrease(s); decreasing; decreased
est	established
fdc	foundation double crochet
flo	front loop only
foll	follows; following
fsc	foundation single crochet
g	gram(s)
hdc	half double crochet
inc(s) ('d)	increase(s); increasing; increased
k	knit
lp(s)	loop(s)
MC	main color
m	marker
mm	millimeter(s)
patt(s)	pattern(s)

pm	place marker
p	purl
rem	remain(s); remaining
rep	repeat; repeating
rev sc	reverse single crochet
rnd(s)	round(s)
RS	right side
sc	single crochet
sk	skip
sl	slip
sl st	slip(ped) stitch
sp(s)	space(es)
st(s)	stitch(es)
tch	turning chain
tog	together
tr	treble crochet
WS	wrong side
yd	yard
yo	yarn over hook
*	repeat starting point
( )	alternate measurements and/or instructions
[ ]	work bracketed instructions a specified number of times

Standard Yarn Weight System

YARN: Fingering, 10-count crochet thread
GAUGE*: 33–40 sts
HOOK (METRIC): 1.5–2.25 mm
HOOK (U.S.): 000 to 1

YARN: Sock, Fingering, Baby
GAUGE*: 21–32 sts
HOOK (metric): 2.25–3.5 mm
HOOK (U.S.): B-1 to E-4

YARN: Sport, Baby
GAUGE: 16–20 sts
HOOK (metric): 3.5–4.5 mm
HOOK (U.S.): E-4 to G-7

YARN: DK, Light Worsted
GAUGE: 12–17 sts
HOOK (metric): 3.5–4.5 mm
HOOK (U.S.): G-7 to I-9

YARN: Worsted, Afghan, Aran
GAUGE: 11–14 sts
HOOK (metric): 5.5–6.5 mm
HOOK (U.S.): I-9 to K-10½

YARN: Chunky, Craft, Rug
GAUGE: 8–11 sts
HOOK (metric): 6.5–9 mm
HOOK (U.S.): K-10½ to M-13

YARN: Bulky, Roving
GAUGE: 5–9 sts
HOOK (metric): 9 mm and larger
HOOK (U.S.): M-13 and larger

Crochet Gauge

To check gauge, chain 30 to 40 stitches using recommended hook size. Work in pattern stitch until piece measures at least 4" (10 cm) from foundation chain. Lay swatch on flat surface. Place a ruler over swatch and count number of stitches across and number of rows down (including fractions of stitches and rows) in 4" (10 cm). Repeat two or three times on different areas of swatch to confirm measurements. If you have more stitches and rows than called for in instructions, use a larger hook; if you have fewer, use a smaller hook. Repeat until gauge is correct.

Wraps Per Inch

If you substitute or spin a yarn for a project, you can compare the weight of the yarn to the project yarn by comparing wraps per inch. To do this, wrap your yarn around a ruler for one inch and count the number of wraps. If you have more wraps per inch, your yarn is too thin; fewer wraps per inch, your yarn is too thick.

The Craft Yarn Council of America has set up guidelines to bring uniformity to yarn labels and published patterns.

Yarn Weight: The yarn weight symbols that appear in pattern instructions are based on the system outlined above. We have consulted the yarn label, the manufacturer's website, and other resources, to classify these yarns as accurately as possible.

*Guidelines only: The above reflect the most commonly used gauges and needle or hook sizes for specific yarn categories.

Glossary

Parts of a Stitch

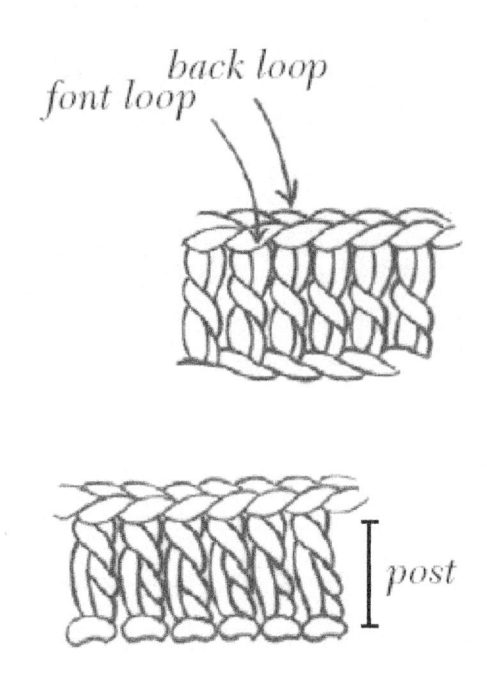

font loop *back loop*

post

Chain *(ch)*

Make a slipknot on hook, *yarn over and draw through loop of slipknot; repeat from * drawing yarn through last loop formed.

Single Crochet *(sc)*

*Insert hook in stitch, yarn over and pull up loop (Figure 1), yarn over and draw through both loops on hook (Figure 2); repeat from *.

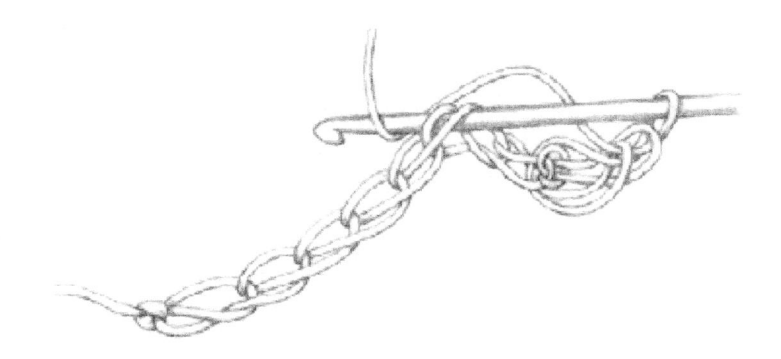

Figure 1

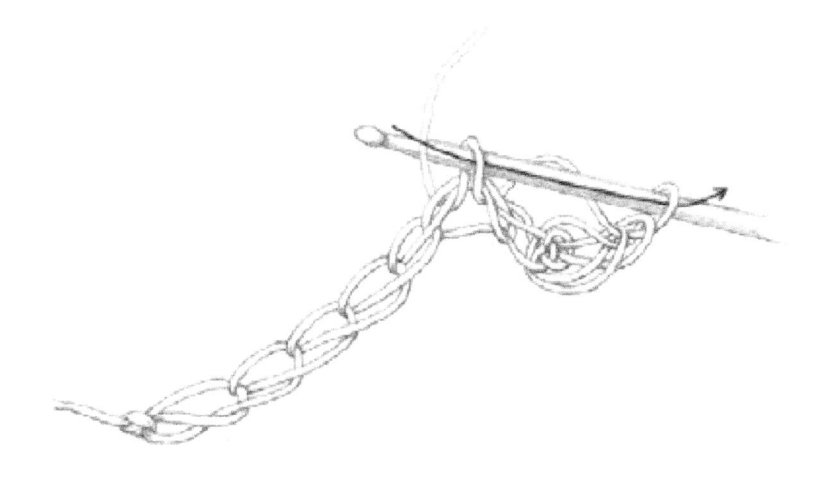

Figure 2

Single Crochet Two Together *(sc2tog)*

Insert hook in next stitch, yarn over and pull up loop (2 loops on hook, Figure 1), insert hook in next stitch, yarn over and pull up loop (3 loops on hook), yarn over and draw through all 3 loops on hook (Figure 2)—1 stitch decreased (Figure 3).

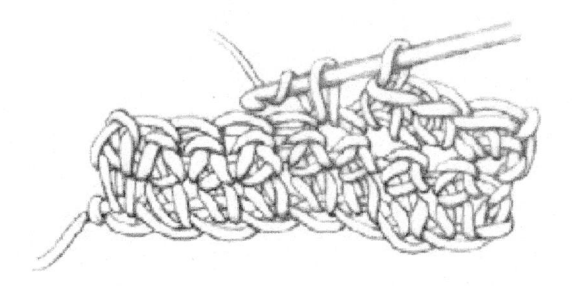

Figure 1

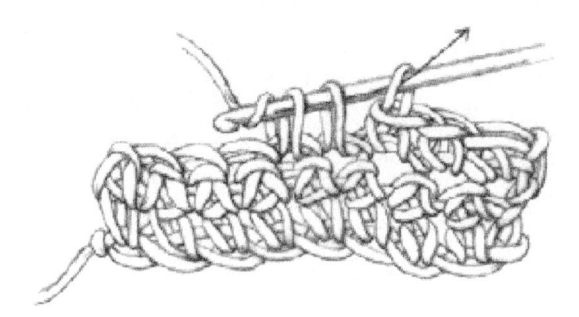

Figure 2

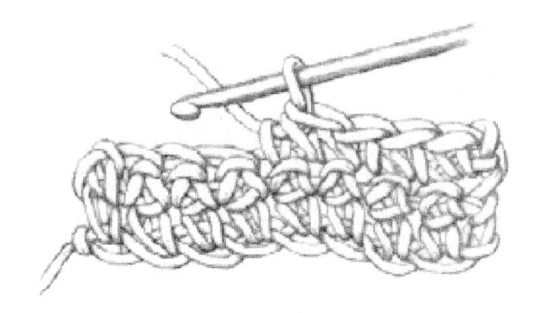

Figure 3

Single Crochet Three Together *(sc3tog)*

[Insert hook in next stitch, yarn over, pull loop through stitch] 3 times (4 loops on hook). Yarn over and draw yarn through all 4 loops on hook. Completed sc3tog—2 stitches decreased.

Extended Single Crochet *(esc)*

Insert hook in next stitch or chain, yarn over and pull up loop (2 loops on hook), yarn over and draw through 1 loop (1 chain made), yarn over and pull through 2 loops—1 esc completed.

Foundation Single Crochet *(fsc)*

Ch 2, insert hook in 2nd ch from hook, yarn over hook and draw up a loop (2 loops on hook), yarn over hook, draw yarn through first loop on hook, yarn over hook and draw through 2 loops on hook—1 fsc made.

*Insert hook under 2 loops of ch made at base of previous stitch, yarn over hook and draw up a loop (2 loops on hook), yarn over hook and draw through first loop on hook, yarn over hook and draw through 2 loops on hook. Rep from * for length of foundation.

Reverse Single Crochet *(rev sc)*

Working from left to right, insert crochet hook in an edge stitch and pull up loop, yarn over and draw this loop through the first one to join, *insert hook in next stitch to right (Figure 1), pull up a loop, yarn over (Figure 2), and draw through both loops on hook (Figure 3); repeat from *.

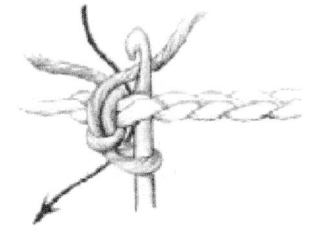

Figure 1

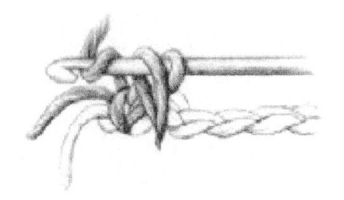

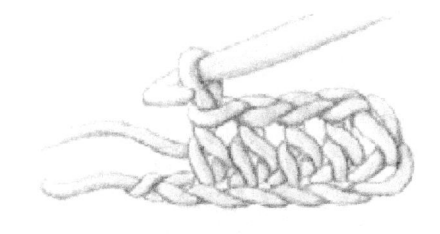

Figure 2

Figure 3

Half Double Crochet *(hdc)*

*Yarn over, insert hook in stitch, yarn over and pull up loop (3 loops on hook), yarn over (Figure 1) and draw through all loops on hook (Figure 2); repeat from *.

Figure 1

Figure 2

Half Double Crochet Two Together *(hdc2tog)*

[Yarn over, insert hook in next stitch, yarn over and pull up loop] 2 times, yarn over and draw through all loops on hook—1 stitch decreased.

Double Crochet *(dc)*

*Yarn over, insert hook in stitch, yarn over and pull up loop (3 loops on hook; Figure 1), yarn over and draw through 2 loops (Figure 2), yarn over and draw through remaining 2 loops (Figure 3); repeat from *.

Figure 1

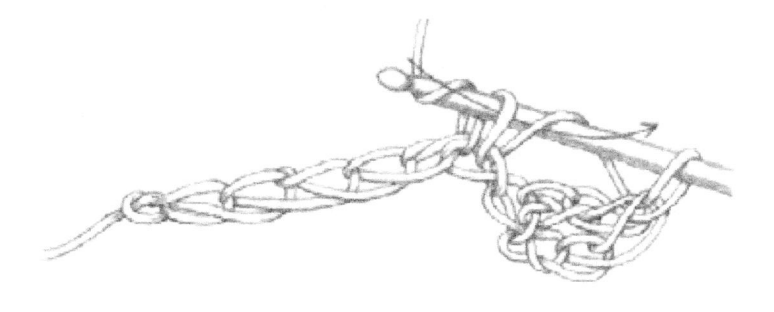

Figure 2

Figure 3

Double Crochet Two Together *(dc2tog)*

[Yarn over, insert hook in next stitch, yarn over and pull up loop, yarn over, draw through 2 loops] 2 times, yarn over, draw through all loops on hook—1 stitch decreased.

Treble Crochet *(tr)*

*Yarn over 2 times, insert hook in stitch, yarn over and pull up loop (4 loops on hook; Figure 1), yarn over and draw through 2 loops (Figure 2), yarn over and draw through 2 loops, yarn over and draw through remaining 2 loops (Figure 3); repeat from *.

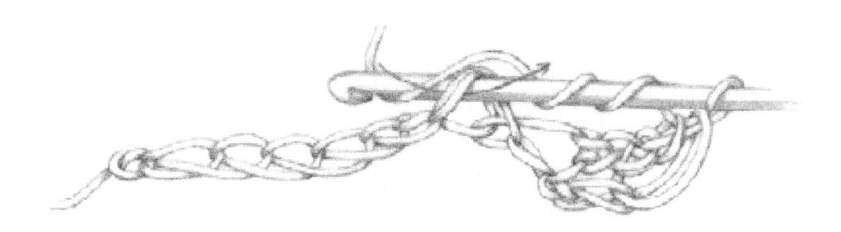

Figure 1

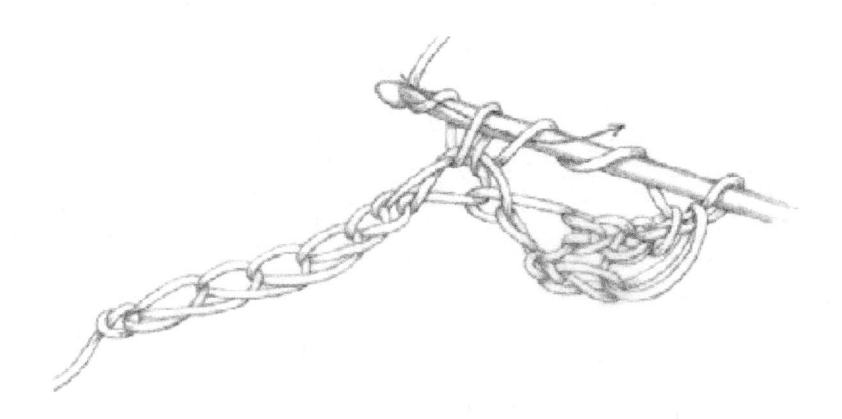

Figure 2

Figure 3

Slip Stitch *(sl st)*

*Insert hook in stitch, yarn over and draw loop through stitch and loop on hook; repeat from *.

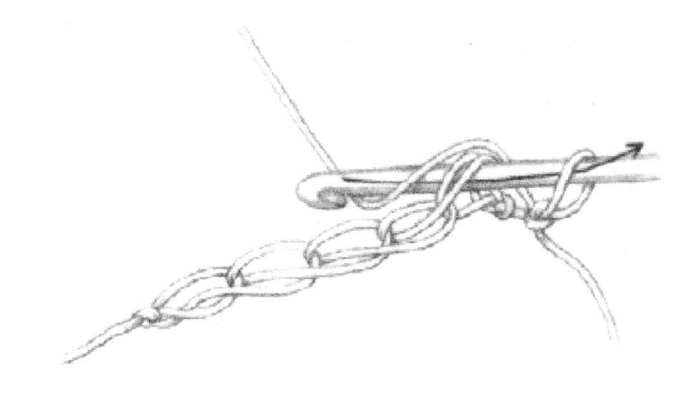

Solomon's Knot

Draw loop on hook to ¼"–½", yo and draw through loop on hook (long ch made; Figures 1–2), sc in chain just made by inserting hook between thread found at back and 2 loops at front of chain to complete stitch (Figures 3–5).

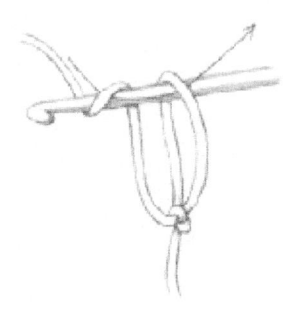

Figure 1

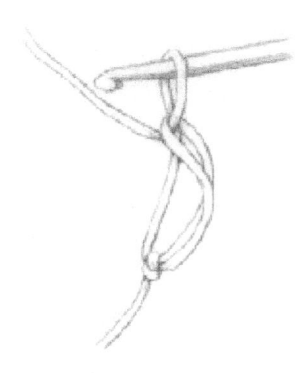

Figure 2

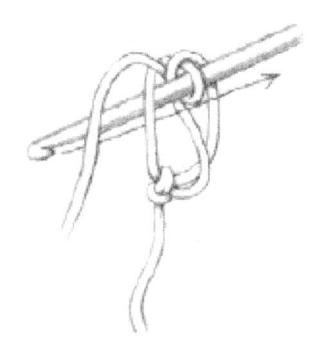

Figure 3

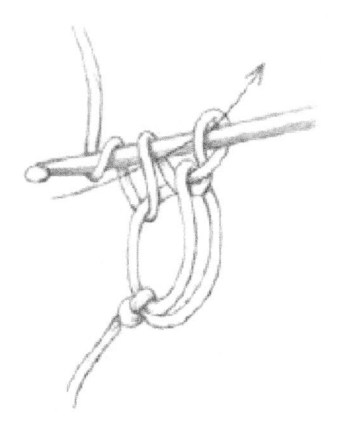

Figure 4

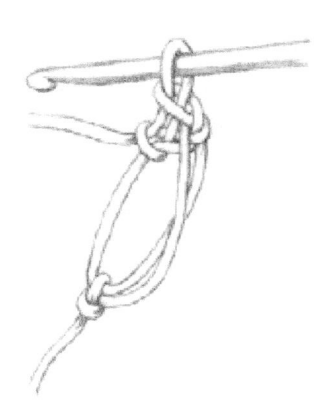

Figure 5

Tunisian Bind-off

*Insert hook behind front vertical bar, yarn over and pull up loop, yarn over and draw through both loops on hook; repeat from * across.

Mattress Stitch

With Right Side facing, use threaded needle to *bring the needle through the center of the first stitch or post on one piece, then through the center of the corresponding stitch or post of the other piece; repeat from * to end of seam.

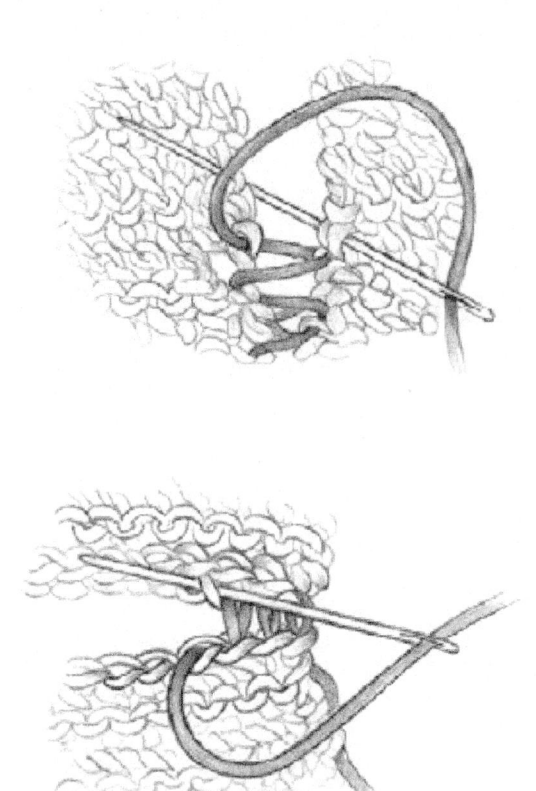

Printed in Great Britain
by Amazon